William Dickson

Letters on Slavery

William Dickson

Letters on Slavery

ISBN/EAN: 9783337816544

Printed in Europe, USA, Canada, Australia, Japan

Cover: Foto ©Thomas Meinert / pixelio.de

More available books at **www.hansebooks.com**

LETTERS

ON

SLAVERY,

BY

WILLIAM DICKSON,

FORMERLY PRIVATE SECRETARY TO THE LATE
HON. EDWARD HAY, GOVERNOR OF BARBADOES.

TO WHICH ARE ADDED,

ADDRESSES TO THE WHITES, AND TO THE FREE
NEGROES OF BARBADOES; AND ACCOUNTS
OF SOME NEGROES EMINENT FOR THEIR VIRTUES
AND ABILITIES.

"Behold and see if there be any sorrow like unto *our* sorrow."
                              JEREM. LAMENTS.

"Pollenti stabilit, manu (Deus almus eandem
"Omnigenis animam, nil prohibente dedit)
"Ipsa coloris egens virtus, prudentia; honesto
"Nullus inest animo, nullus in arte color."
                      F. WILLIAMS, a Negro Poet

LONDON:

PRINTED AND SOLD BY J. PHILLIPS, GEORGE-YARD, LOMBARD-
STREET; AND SOLD BY J. JOHNSON, ST. PAUL'S CHURCH-
YARD, AND ELLIOT AND KAY, OPPOSITE SOMERSET-
PLACE, STRAND.——M.DCC.LXXXIX.

1789

INTRODUCTION.

MY original design, was to lay before the Public a free and impartial sketch of negro slavery as it now exists in the island of *Barbadoes*; to show how it would be affected by the abolition of the slave-trade; and to prove by arguments, founded on *facts*, the natural equality of the natives of the immense continent of Africa to the rest of mankind.—I am conscious, I have not wilfully misstated or exaggerated any one circumstance; and I have written with the caution of a man who expects to meet with the most pertinacious contradiction. ——To give as agreeable an air, as I could, to a subject in itself dull and disgusting, I have preferred the looser form of letters to the formality of a regular treatise.— The sketch I have given of the state of slavery in *Jamaica* was no part of my plan, but was drawn after that plan was compleated. This I hope will apologize for some repetitions in the latter part of my book.

The name and authority of an author have perhaps greater weight with some readers than his arguments. Such persons regard a proposition as true, not so much because a celebrated man has demonstrated it, as because he has affirmed it. Those undoubtedly are bad arguments which require foreign aid; but knowing that, on account of the obscurity of an author, even good arguments do not always operate with their whole intrinsic force, I have had frequent recourse to works of acknowledged merit, quotations from which, I am sensible, form the best part of my book.—Yet, as a citizen of the *free* republic of letters, I reserve, in the fullest extent, the right of private judgment, which will not surely be denied me while endeavouring to vindicate rights more valuable

a

valuable for an injured race of men. Of this right I am the more tenacious, as it is well known that some, otherwise great and benevolent, philosophers, in their attempts to gain certain ends, have gravely reasoned on phænomena which never were ascertained or which never existed, and have perplexed the world with systems useless and incongruous in themselves, contradictory to one another, derogatory to the glory of the Creator, and in their consequences, subversive of the dearest interests of mankind. By the authority of those writers, or indeed of any description of writers, I do not think myself bound to be governed, except in so far as they appear to me to have been governed by unbiassed reason and philosophy. But, scepticism apart, which has misled them into theories inconsistent with the sober parts of their works, the writers alluded to, like all the other great writers of Europe, universally favour the cause which I think it my duty, as far as I am able, to support.

Of the quick succession of praise and blame the reader of these sheets will observe several instances which, if justice be done to the writer, will not be attributed to him but to his subject. In treating such a subject, *Impartiality* will assume sometimes the smile of Panegyric, and sometimes the frown of Satire. To me it seems impracticable to treat impartially of the severe usage of human creatures in language which shall not appear more or less severe; and altogether impossible faithfully to describe shocking abuses, in a way that shall be perfectly agreeable to those who may be inclined to palliate or conceal them.

On the other hand, I have laboured to guard the reader against an impression which, it must be owned, all faithful representations of the West Indian slavery are but too apt to make on inattentive minds. I scruple not to reprobate slavery, both in its consummately absurd principle,* and in its too general practice; but God forbid my book should lead to the supposition, that there are not

---

* That any man, whatsoever, is competent to hold, in the person of another man the same absolute property which he holds in a horse, a dog, or even in any inanimate piece of goods. See Blackstone's Comm. b. 1. ch. 14. and Montesquieu's Sp. of Laws, b. 15.

persons

portions of worth and humanity in the West Indies. Barbadoes, in particular, is adorned with many such characters; and has even produced eminent advocates for the Africans. Not to mention private letters and an able anonymous writer, who signs himself *A West Indian*, I have understood that a Mr. ALLEYNE (a name justly distinguished in Barbadoes for humanity and good sense) did himself and that, his native, island much credit by exerting his eloquence and learning in behalf of the negro *Somerset*. To the honour of that island too, I ought to mention that it gave birth to that able and respectable advocate for humanity DEAN NICKOLLS, and to a certain other clergyman, of great worth and learning, who hath favoured the same cause with an extract from his private journal which I have subjoined in the appendix. The reader will determine whether the characters of JOSEPH RACHELL and JOHN do most honour to Barbadoes where they practised their virtues, to the *insulted and injured* NEGROES, or to human nature.

But the character of the whites (and I will add of the blacks) in Barbadoes, depends not on that of a few individuals, however distinguished for virtue and talents. Every period of it's annals (I have reasons for wishing the fact to be particularly noticed) hath been marked with *loyalty* and an attachment to England which, I humbly think, ought to recommend that ancient colony to the special attention of Government. About the close of the last century, a single estate in Barbadoes equipped a company of soldiers to be sent against Guadaloupe. In the war before the last, that colony raised both men and money to assist in the reduction of the French islands: and their conduct, on a similar occasion, during the late war, ought to be remembered to their praise.* Yet every real friend of the colony laments, with me, the neglect of a militia, which, in proportion to the size of the island, might easily be rendered the most respectable in the West

---

* On very mature recollection the author cannot be altogether certain whether the provisions mentioned p. 95, were actually shipped or not for St. Lucia; for he then lived in the country; and the alacrity of all ranks to provide live stock and corn for so patriotic a purpose would make the same impression on the author whether the supplies were or were not accepted. It is sufficient for the honour of the island that they were provided, voted and offered.

Indies,

Indies, and which, could *all* the negroes be prudently relied on, would be irresistible.

I have represented the slavery of Jamaica exactly as I found it in their own papers, which, independently of any thing I have written, demonstrate the horrid abuses practised in that island. But far be it from me to favour a supposition that there are not characters in that island, both public and private, who deserve well of mankind. Jamaica, it appears, may justly boast of a GRAY, an EDWARDS, and no doubt of other distinguished advocates for humanity. On those gentlemen in particular, and on the legislature of Jamaica in general, the late unanimity of that numerous and respectable body, in endeavouring to meliorate the condition of the slaves, reflects much honour. Nor is this the only instance of their conduct which merits praise. 'For the purchase of wine,' says DOCTOR HUNTER, 'ample provision was made by 'the island; and it ought to be mentioned that the GE-'NERAL ASSEMBLY OF JAMAICA, both in this and in 'every thing else, appertaining to the accommodation of 'the troops, shewed, at all times, a most laudable dispo-'sition to make the greatest exertions.'*—The spirit good sense and humanity of the printers† of the Jamaica newspapers ought not to be forgotten: for they have shewn themselves superior alike to the taunts of the 'pro-'fligate' and the malevolence of the 'unmerciful;'‡ discouragements which all good men must expect to meet with in the discharge of their duty. Were I to give a similar account of the Barbadoes printers and their *worthy* correspondents, it would be said I courted their applause. Let the humane enquirer into this subject compare the Barbadoes Gazette and Mercury with the other West Indian prints, and judge for himself.

To a certain other sugar colony, the excellent essays, of which the following is an extract, would have done more credit, had not *The Council* of that colony sent for

---

* Obs. on the Diseases of the Army in Jam. printed 1788—p. 324.
† I am sorry to except the printer of the Sav. la Mar. Gaz. see p. 332.
‡ See p. 141.—The printers of the Jam. Gaz. have inserted the D. of MIDDLEHAM's valuable letter, at full length, in their paper of March 1, 1788.

the printer and commanded him not to presume to insert any more such improper stuff in his paper—an interference which the Council of Barbadoes would have despised. The worthy and respectable author has dared, in the midst of enemies, to own the obnoxious essays; and I think it not improbable that they may come regularly before the public. 'We next behold,' says he, 'our African conducted to the estate of the proprietor, where, for a short
'time, his wants are well supplied; and he is treated
'with some attention and indulgence. Happy would it
'be for him, and much to his owner's *true interest,* if
'this indulgence were founded on the pure motives of
'justice and humanity; and if it were part of a system
'of rewards and punishments to govern him in propor-
'tion to his deserts. But sorry we are to discover, that
'it is *an indulgence merely to beguile him into the preserva-*
'*tion of his existence*—to train him on to that labour of
'which he must soon take an equal share with the rest;
'and, when he is thus broken to the yoke, is to cease.
'It is indeed an indulgence cruel in its consequences and
'absurd in its operation; for instead of being continued
'and increased, in proportion to service and good con-
'duct, it is customary to withdraw it at the time he be-
'comes useful—to leave him, in the vulgar phrase 'to
'shift for himself,'—to consign him over to a system, the
'only characteristic features of which are coercion and
'punishment. Here then looking up in vain for that
'notice and favour which he may be inclined to deserve,
'and expecting nothing more for his best exertions than
'the negative advantage of an exemption from correction,
'he enters upon the train of his miseries and his toils.
'He is often spoken to reproachfully*—always with in-
'difference, his little wants and his interests are too fre-
'quently passed over with contemptuous neglect; nay
'sometimes his supplications for some trifling boon ex-

* 'Curses (if I may use a vulgar expression, which for aught I know may not be peculiar to the West Indies) Curses do not make holes in the 'skin,' though, in some cases, they are peculiarly brutal, not to say *hurtful* (see p. 12.). I have therefore taken but little notice of the abusive language of drivers, &c. &c. to slaves. To me, when I first arrived in the West Indies, the indecent language, oaths and imprecations I too often heard, not to mention other things which were *wholly new* to me, were, to the last degree, shocking and intolerable; but custom diminishes the force of such impressions.

pose

'pose him to abuse and punishment. No kind no sooth-
' ing words, that precious balm which benevolence pours
' into the wounds of suffering and of sorrow, are ever
' applied to him; but unbeloved and unbefriended—the
' butt of ill humour and of passion—the spectacle of over-
' weening authority to look down upon and despise—he
' continues to beat the same toilsome and wearisome
' round, till death issues that summons, which he is not
' unwilling to obey, and with the happy superstition of
' his untutored mind, he anticipates his return to that
' state'

"Where *slaves* once more their native land behold,"
No FIENDS *torment*, no CHRISTIANS *thirst for gold.**

The narrow limits of my work oblige me to omit some collateral matter I had collected, including an account of the state of society in Africa, extracted from the best modern authors, and particularly from a work published by authority, at Paris, 1776, intitled ' Histoire de Lo-
' ango, &c. ' The History of Loango, Kakongo and
' other kingdoms in Africa, &c. dedicated to MONSIEUR'
(the king's brother) ' by the *Abbé Proyart*.' This re-
spectable work, indeed, deserves a better reception in this country, than to be published in mutilated fragments; for I will venture to say, that a good translation of it would compleatly overthrow the orang outang system, and effectually quash that silly scepticism, respecting the moral and intellectual faculties of the African which, of late, hath wofully perplexed certain men of scrupulous consciences, who in such cases can have no rest till they publish their doubts, for the *benefit* of mankind.—Among other instances which the present controversy affords of the strong support a cause may receive from the confes-
sions of adversaries, I mention with pleasure Lieutenant Matthews's voyage to Sierra Leone. This author is a-
gainst the abolition of the slave trade; but his account of the country and the inhabitants appears to be just and candid, and it does so much credit both to the heads and to the hearts of the Africans that I cannot but recommend it to the attention of my readers; especially as the book contains not a single argument for the toleration of

* Pope.

the

the slave trade which can work conviction in minds accustomed to reasoning of any sort. All such arguments vanish before those of Mr. Clarkson† like ghosts before the rising sun.

I believe most conscientious inquirers into this subject are convinced that *evils of the very worst kind* attend the slave trade and the West Indian slavery. Such persons will not wonder at some warm language which has dropped from my pen. But the conviction of enlarged minds is not the conviction of the crowd who are seldom strongly affected with remote objects. Hence, perhaps, a coolness, respecting the *slave-trade*, in some who are professed friends to its abolition: nor, can it be expected that the whips and chains and tortures of *slavery* will operate with their full force on men who have never witnessed their deplorable effects. For my own part, I am convinced, *particularly* by the Jamaica papers, that the irresistible eloquence of a Chatham, the emphatic language of a Shakespeare—nay the divine fervour of an Isaiah could not have done more than justice to this subject.

Still I shall not be at all surprised if *certain readers*, unable to explain away facts (not to mention arguments) should affect to represent these letters as the mere effusions of a heated imagination, and the writer as an intemperate zealot, perhaps as a rank republican—just as if an abhorrence of slavery implied a love of anarchy. The fatal effects these extremes have ever had on the happiness of mankind should teach Britons to revere and to support the constitution of their country as the noblest that human wisdom ever devised, or an indulgent Providence ever favoured.—But the author treats not of any kind of lawful *government* which is the very bond of society, but of *tyranny* which dissolves it; not of *subjects* or *citizens*, but of *slaves*; and not of *political* but of PERSONAL SLAVERY—a state which is the very negation of law and morality, a state which, as he has proved it to involve every crime, can have no lawful existence among men; and which, as the worst of all possible social evils, all civilized nations and all wise statesmen, should, by a general combination,

† See Essay on the *Impolicy*, &c.

and

and gradual measures, labour to root out from the face of the earth. Such are the sentiments of Montesquieu* and of Neckar, and such, we humbly trust, are the sentiments of a great majority of the Legislature of these kingdoms, and, particularly, of a Statesman to whose virtue and abilities the credit and the constitution of his country owe still more than those of the rival state do to a NECKAR. —" Would it be a chimerical project," says this last great man, " to propose *a general compact* by which all " the European nations should unanimously agree to a- " bandon the African slave-trade ?"†

*** The author has aimed at perspicuity, but he pretends not to strict technical propriety, of stile, which can be expected only from professional men. In this respect he may have failed; but more perhaps in appearance than in reality. The imperfection of the remarks he has made on the slave-laws may induce some humane and able gentleman of the law, *who resides or has resided in the West Indies,* (and such he could name) to review the negro codes, and to point out their numerous defects and their general inefficiency.

* For the sentiments of Montesquieu and Raynal, see p. 99, note.
† NECKAR on Finance, v. 1. p. 330.

TO SIR JAMES JOHNSTONE OF ELPHINSTONE AND WESTERHALL, BART. MEMBER OF PARLIAMENT FOR THE BURGH OF DUMFRIES, ETC.

SIR,

I AM persuaded the best apology I can offer for the liberty I take in addressing the following Letters to you is, that they are intended to promote the cause of humanity; and, being the work of an obscure individual, they will derive weight and importance from being addressed to a British Senator, who is possessed of a large property in the West Indies.

Truth affects not the pompous language of panegyric. The part you take, in the ensuing parliamentary discussion of the Slave Trade, will publish to the world what language best suits your character. The opposition of interest, real or apparent, to principle, constitutes an ordeal, which nothing short of the most pure and disinterested virtue can endure. I will venture to say, that the friends of humanity have no reason to be anxious about the issue: for, to such men, and to such senators, as Sir JAMES JOHNSTONE, and many such I trust there are, they may safely commit the cause of the injured Africans.

With the respect due, not only to an honest man, and to a virtuous Senator, but to a *humane, disinterested Planter*, I have the honour to be,

Sir, your most obedient, humble Servant,

WILL^{M.} DICKSON.

LETTER II.

*——— Quid me, alta silentia cogit
Rumpere?* VIRG.

SIR, *Febr.* 15. 1788.

OF all the prejudices that ever blinded mankind, that which leads our African Traders and our West Indian Colonists to imagine that they ought to be the sovereign arbiters of the liberties and the lives of the enslaved Negroes, is one of the most monstrous and absurd— a prejudice peculiarly repugnant, if not in some degree dangerous, to the constitution of this free country.

Such usurped powers, it was easy to foresee, would be supported with a perseverance proportioned to their *seeming* importance, and to the degree in which they appear to affect the interests of the slave merchants, and of that useful, and, on several accounts, respectable class of men, the West Indian Planters. When the interests of men are engaged, their passions will not long remain neuter. Hence it is altogether impossible to write against the African trade, or the West Indian bondage, without inducing censure or provoking resentment, if not persecution. I confess, therefore, that I should scarcely have taken upon me to communicate to you, and, through you, to the public, the little knowledge of this disagreeable subject of which I am possessed, had not I, in common with every man who has resided in the West Indies, been publicly and earnestly requested by the friends of humanity, and, urged, by the apologists, especially by the *anonymous* apologists, for slavery, to publish what I know of the treatment of the slaves in that part of the world.

In support of a bad cause, bold and adventurous assertion will often supply the place of fact, particular truths will be magnified into universal propositions, and plausible sophistry will assume the gait, and usurp the throne of reason. I should have continued to view such artifices with secret indignation, had not a writer, who has assumed the signature of *Civis*, in the Morning Chronicle of the 5th, been so insufferably peremptory in his language, that I
resolved,

resolved, at all events, that he should not pass unnoticed. This writer appears to me to possess, and if he be the person I suspect, I may say, I know, he possesses, talents worthy of better employment than writing in a newspaper in favour of slavery. I am ready to allow the person I allude to a great degree of personal worth in every other particular, and am willing to make ample allowance for his prejudices. It would give me great pain, if any *unnecessary* expression should drop from my pen, which might *personally* hurt him or any of his friends. But, after all, I am perhaps mistaken in my conjectures. All I know, with certainty, is, that the language of *Civis* is indecent, and such as *if* directed to, or obliquely aimed at me, I would in no situation bear. I must observe too, that the present letters are not intended as a formal answer to his piece, which may be said to be the *occasion*, rather than the *cause* of their appearance; and that, whoever he be, I shall take no farther notice of him, unless he should choose, *in propria persona*, to controvert any of the *facts* which I shall mention, *as having fallen within my own immediate observation.*

Another writer, in the above useful and well conducted paper, who signs himself *A Friend to Mankind*, had asserted, that he knew an instance of a Negro having been stabbed to death by a white man, in one of the principal towns in a certain island; and that the perpetrator of the deed escaped with impunity. This, if I rightly remember, is the purport of that writer's assertion. It corresponds so very exactly with *one* deed which was committed, while I resided in the island of Barbadoes, that, calling to mind the freedom with which, while there, I have often treated the subject of slavery, and that, though I had it in my power, I never did enslave, or contribute to enslave, a fellow-creature, I have reason to think, that some of my Barbadian friends will suspect me to be the person who signs himself *A Friend to Mankind*. For their satisfaction, and to free myself from the odium of having officiously meddled in this business, I think proper to declare, that I am, neither directly or indirectly, concerned in the piece which bears that signature. If I had written such a piece, I should certainly have made choice of some fact which fell more immediately within my own knowledge,

knowledge, and where would have been the impropriety of such a step? But, since *Civis* calls so very loudly for *names*, I will tell him, that, some years ago, one *Bentham Jones* ran a negro through the body with a bayonet, in *Speights-town, Barbadoes*. The negro was the property of the deceased *Joseph Harris*, Esq. of the same town. Whether Jones was convicted or not, and *fined* for the deed, I do not at present recollect. Certain it is, he died in his bed; and yet, for aught I know, the law *, as it now stands, might have been satisfied.

As I did not see this deed perpetrated, I must rest it on the general, uncontradicted report of the town where it happened. Since, by having been, in some measure, compelled to publish it, I have been dragged into a controversy, which, but for the rooted prejudices and the appa-

---

* ' If any negro or other slave, under punishment, by his master or his order, for running away, or any other crime or misdemeanors towards his said master, unfortunately shall suffer in *life* or member (which seldom happens) *no person whatsoever shall be liable to any fine therefor*. But, if any man shall of wantonness, or only of bloody mindedness, or cruel intention, *wilfully kill* a negro, or other slave, of *his own*, he shall pay into the *publick treasury fifteen pounds* Sterling; but if he shall so *kill another man's*, he shall pay to the owner of the negro *double the value*, and into the *publick treasury twenty-five pounds* Sterling; and he shall farther, by the next justice of the peace, be bound to his good behaviour, during the pleasure of the Governor and Council, and not be liable to any other punishment or forfeiture for the same. Neither is he that *kills* another man's negro, or other slave, *by accident*, liable to any other penalty, but the owner's *action at law*. But, if any *poor small freeholder*, or other person, *kill* a negro or other slave by night, out of the road or common path, and stealing or attempting to steal his provision, swine, or other goods, he shall *not be accountable* for it; any law, statute, or ordinance to the contrary notwithstanding.' Laws of Barbadoes, No. 82. ch. 19. Hall's edit. 1764. This law was passed in the memorable year *One thousand six hundred and* EIGHTY-EIGHT !—To annul the crime of murder, to set a pecuniary value on the lives of men, and to cast the *price of blood* into a *public treasury*—there exists not upon the earth a legislature competent to enact such a law !! It has been reprobated, in severe terms, by several excellent writers. But the present inhabitants of Barbadoes ought not to be reproached for the barbarous acts of their ancestors, any more than the present English ought to be reproached for the equally barbarous laws of villainage, whence those acts appear to have been copied, or the Scotch, because the feudal tyranny had some operation, in a corner of their country, within the present century. The Barbadians, however, it must be owned, will be very blameable, to use a mild term, if they suffer themselves to be governed any longer, either by the letter or the spirit of this law, if they do not tear it from their statute-book, and consign it to that utter and everlasting oblivion, to which, in this enlightened age, under the auspices of a merciful king, every barbarous usage, within the happy pale of the British empire, is evidently hastening.

rent

rent interests of men, could never have been a controversy at all, I shall proceed to delineate the present state of slavery in Barbadoes, with freedom, but with impartiality. I shall afterwards relate some facts, similar to that above mentioned, interspersing and adding such reasonings, as the subject on which a great deal yet remains to be said, may appear to suggest, or which a contracted plan will allow.

In prosecuting this subject, I shall most carefully avoid all personal allusions, which can possibly be avoided; and shall decline mentioning such names as may tend to hurt the feelings of the meanest innocent inhabitant of an island, for which, as an ancient, valuable and loyal British colony, I cannot but express my regard. I might justly be charged with ingratitude, if I did not acknowledge, that I have been treated by many worthy and respectable individuals, in that hospitable island, with the greatest kindness; and, by some, with marks of friendship and esteem. But the soldier does not fight with less ardour, because he has friends in the enemy's camp. No *private* attachment can vacate or supersede man's *public* duty—his duty to his king and country, for example, or to hundreds of thousands of his oppressed fellow-creatures, or to the inhabitants of a whole quarter of the globe. The man who can raise his views to such objects will disregard all attempts to misinterpret his motives, or to impeach his conduct—he will pity the poor, narrow-minded authors of such attempts, and will rise superior to them. But, I am sure, those persons in Barbadoes, whose good opinion I value, do not expect me, or any man, to make a base, hypocritical profession of approving a domination, which (if one may judge by their humane conduct) *they are conscious,* reason condemns, and the heart detests. Could I suppose them capable of forming an expectation so ungenerous, I would say to them, ' Amicus Plato, amicus ' Socrates, sed major amica *humanitas.*'

I have the honour to be, &c.

LETTER III.

SIR,

ALthough slavery, properly speaking, admit of no distinctions of rank, yet some slaves live and are treated so very differently from others, that a superficial observer would take it for granted, they belong to classes of men, who hold distinct ranks in society, so to speak, by tenures essentially different.

The porters, boatmen, and fishermen in the towns, and on the coast; the black drivers, boilers, watchmen, and other black officers on estates; the mechanics; and above all, the numerous and useless *domestics*, both in town and country: All of these, *comparatively*, and many of them, *really*, live in ease and plenty; nor can they be said to feel any of the hardships of slavery, but such as arise from the caprices of their owners, which, however, are, sometimes, intolerable enough. To these I may add, most of the slaves who *work out*, as it is called; that is, find employment for themselves, and make their owners a weekly return out of their earnings; also many, or, perhaps most of the slaves belonging to the small settlers, called *ten-acre-men*, who raise provisions on little possessions called *places*; for in general, it will hold good, That the happiness of the slave, *cæteris paribus*, is in the inverse ratio of the size of the estate.

On the other hand, truth obliges me to say, that the great body of the slaves, the field-people, on sugar-plantations, are generally treated more like beasts of burden, than like human creatures; since they cultivate the land, with *no assistance* from cattle, and suffer every hardship which can be supposed to attend oppressive toil, coarse and scanty fare, bad lodging, want of covering in the wet season, and a degree of severity which frequently borders on, and too often amounts to, inhumanity.

In order, Sir, to form any thing like a just idea of the condition of slaves, it is absolutely necessary to attend to the distinctions

tinctions.† Another circumstance must not be overlooked: The field-negroes divide their year into the *crop-time* and the *hard time*. During the former, though they labour almost incessantly, the nutritious effects of that noble balsamic plant, the sugar cane, are very visible on them. But, should the dry weather continue long, after the crop is over, as is often the case, the poor creatures, having then nothing but their bare allowance to subsist on, soon begin to prove, by their famished looks, the total insufficiency of that allowance for their support. Before the end of the drought, they are often quite emaciated. When the rains set in, they are succeeded by a quickness and luxuriance of vegetation, of which we have no example in this country. The field-negroes too soon begin to devour the crude fruits, and the produce of their little spots of ground, which co-operate with change of weather, bad lodging, and other causes, in inducing fluxes, and a disease resembling the dropsy. I even remember particular negroes, who were regularly plump, or in good case, and emaciated or swelled, every year. No man, who does not reside constantly in the West-Indies, and who does not see the plantation slaves, for a series of years, and at all times of the year, can possibly know much of their condition, upon the whole.

Such, Sir, are the general rules; but, like all other general rules, they admit of many exceptions. Those, who wish for full information on this subject, must consult An Essay on the Treatment, &c. by that sensible, spirited, and praise-worthy writer, the Rev. J. Ramsay. That performance, some local circumstances excepted, will apply very well to the Island of Barbadoes.

It is equally my duty and my wish, to do all the justice in my power, both to the owner and to the slave. I therefore beg leave to mention such, of those local differences, as appear to me, materially, to affect the condition of the latter. This will lead me to be a little more particular than I intended on their treatment, which depends so intirely on the various dispositions and circumstances of

---

† Such is the difference between the treatment of house and field-negroes, that *to turn a house negro into the field*, is universally considered as a *punishment*; and, on some plantations, it is a very severe punishment. If a house-negro ever choose, or seem to choose, to go into the field, it is to flee from unsupportable domestic tyranny.

their owners and managers, that it is altogether impossible to write, on the subject, with that degree of certainty which will effectually preclude the contradiction of *those who are disposed and resolved to cavil*. It is evident, that where the owner's will is the law, no rule can be laid down, which will universally apply to upwards of four hundred sugar plantations, besides a great number of cotton places, and other small possessions, into which, before the late hurricane, Barbadoes was divided. Of the uncertainty we are speaking of, abundant advantage hath been taken. Engaging descriptions have been drawn of the comparatively happy state of the slaves, on particular estates, and attempts have been made to make the public believe, that those descriptions are applicable to *all*.

But, Sir, is it not altogether astonishing, that men will insist that the slaves, in the West-Indian Islands, are, upon the whole, well treated; while, with the same breath, they demand annual supplies of people from Africa, to fill up the places of vast numbers, who sink into the grave under this good treatment? Is not this an excellent example of the Hudibrastic mode of reasoning? ' Hoc *fateor*; sed *contra* sic argumentor.' For, did the sun ever shine upon that *happy people*, who, far from increasing and multiplying, *could not keep up their numbers by propagation*? What *happy* country, except some modern *European Colonies*, was ever known incessantly to swallow up its inhabitants?

But to proceed: The division and kinds of labour, as well as the number of hours the negroes are employed in it, are much the same in Barbadoes as Mr. Ramsay represents them in St. Kitt's. His assertion, That the plantation-bell rings about four o'clock, has been flatly contradicted; but this shall not deter me from stating what I know of this particular. I pretend not to fix the precise minute; but I ever did hear it reckoned at or about four o'clock. I lodged for some years, within hearing both of a church and a plantation-bell. The former rang at five o'clock, the latter a considerable time before it. I always rose early, often at five o'clock, for the benefit of air, exercise and sea-bathing; and, when I wished to be up earlier than usual, I desired to be called when the plantation-bell rang. It may be considered as a *warning-bell* to rouse the negroes from their slumbers, and to prepare them for *turning out*. To my knowledge many of

them

them are *in the field at dawn*. If *necessary*, I could corroborate these assertions with two other circumstances, which I perfectly recollect; but *at present*, I decline mentioning them, especially as one of them would be generally disagreeable, and the other involves a personal allusion. This rule I shall observe in other instances.

As in St. Kitt's, so in Barbadoes, the *picking* of grass is a great hardship. Some circumstances, however, render it easier in the latter, than Mr. Ramsay represents it in the former island. The negroes certainly do not go so far to seek it in Barbadoes, which contains far less variety of surface and exposure than St. Kitt's, and no eminences which deserve the name of mountains. It would therefore less avail the Barbadian negroes to wander very far from home, and to trespass on other estates, which in respect of vegetation, are more equally circumstanced than the lands can be in St. Kitt's. Little Indian or Guinea corn were planted in St. Kitt's when Mr. Ramsay wrote. In Barbadoes, large fields of both are cultivated; and Indian corn is very often planted among the young canes. The blades of this last are excellent provender or *horse meat*, as it is called; and the Guinea corn, perhaps still more nutritive, is repeatedly cut down with *knives for that use*, before it is allowed to shoot. It is broke in about Christmas; its blades, while green, having still afforded some provender. About the same time, they begin to cut the canes, the tops of which, affording, however, but poor nourishment, maintain the cattle for the greater part of the crop-time; but when, towards the end of that period, they become withered, they are but of little use as provender. There is, in Barbadoes, no substitute for hay;* so that during the rest of the dry season, when ' Earth clad in russet, scorns the ' lively green,'† the cattle, and indeed the negroes, as we have seen, experience all the poverty of winter, without its resources. Indeed, notwithstanding the exertions of the latter, I have, in some years, been surprised that the former were kept alive; since the natural grass, weeds,

---

* In Jamaica, they convert into hay Guinea grass, the blades of Indian and Guinea corn, and even the wire grass, and sour grass, which, while green, no cattle will taste. See Long's History of Jamaica, vol. I. p. 455.
† Churchill.

and

and vines, picked chiefly in the gullies and other broken land, must be allowed to be very inadequate to their support. The natural grass in the West Indies does not so completely cover the soil as in Europe; so that the picking of it is a very slow operation, and cannot but be distressing to the negroes; and it is more or less so to the great gang, in proportion as the small gang, generally employed in weeding and picking grass, is more or less numerous. I have often seen the negroes serving the cattle in the middle of the day, and in the evening; and I have, at times, met on the roads, gangs of slaves going to *throw grass* by moon-light. The small patches of those excel a species of grass called Guinea grass, Scotch grass, &c. also the vines of the sweet potatoe, plantain leaves, &c. scarcely appear to me to deserve a place in a general account.—In St. Kitt's, it seems *the law* subjects trespassing grass-pickers to a very harsh punishment, *twenty lashes* with a *long cart-whip*. In Barbadoes such a law exists, but I do not think it is very rigidly executed.

The mode of tying and feeding the black cattle in Barbadoes (for there are but few mules on that island) on unsheltered dung-heaps, called *penns*, is perhaps, without a single exception, as wasteful and absurd in Barbadoes as it can be in St. Kitt's. For this, and the cause just mentioned, the Barbadian cattle, in general, are emaciated and weak; so weak indeed, that I have often seen fourteen, sometimes sixteen of them faintly drawling along with a cart, containing two hogsheads of sugar. A slave, when entrusted with absolute power, will be as apt to abuse it, as a free man. The black carters not only beat the poor animals without mercy, but drive the butt-ends of their whips violently against their sides, which, in their emaciated state, very often occasions large wind-galls or ruptures. Nor do the creatures get leave to exert, with advantage, the little strength they possess; for by this absurd and cruel mode of driving, they often take a serpentine direction, and thus counteract the efforts of one another. In the *present* method of tilling the land, *intirely* by manual labour, it would be difficult, if not impossible, to shelter and feed the cattle after the English mode. As the dung is carried out, or distributed over the lands intirely by the slaves, it must be made on the field for which it is allotted and the penn or penns must be carefully proportioned

tioned to the size of that field. Hence a proper shelter would require frequent removal, to say nothing of the expence. That cattle, especially working cattle, ought to be protected alike from the oppressive heats and the wasting rains, in that sultry climate, is certain; and that the planters are convinced of this truth, appears from their generally furnishing sheep-penns with sheds. I hope to be excused for thus glancing at the treatment of brutes, while my subject is that of men. 'A merciful ' man,' says Solomon, ' is merciful to his beast;' but, in the West-Indies, and, I suppose, in every country of slavery, the whole animal ' creation groans, being bur-' dened.'†

In St. Kitt's, according to Mr. Ramsay, the plantation work, on some estates, is but little interrupted by Sunday. In Barbadoes, no plantation-business is done on that day, except throwing grass to the cattle, and perhaps digging a few roots, for the allowance of the slaves. In *crop-time*, however, the earlyhours of Sunday morning, like those of every other morning, are too often infringed upon. *Sunday is a day of rest to the cattle, but I cannot, with any propriety, affirm it to be a day of rest to the slaves.* During that day, the field negroes in Barbadoes are, almost universally, employed either in cultivating their little spots of ground (which have been dignified with the illusive name of *gardens*) in order to eke out their scanty allowance of food; or in travelling, many of them, for several miles, to market, with a few roots, or fruits, or canes, sometimes a fowl or a kid, or a pig. The masons, carpenters, &c. do little jobbs on their own account.

Mr. Ramsay tells us, that in St Kitt's, some planters trust to their own skill, or to quack medicines in treating the sick; but I may venture to affirm, that there is not a single estate in Barbadoes that does not pay a doctor, at the rate of five shillings currency, or about three and nine-pence sterling, annually for each negroe, sick or well. The doctors either attend themselves, or send their journeymen, at least once a week, at all times. I have always understood too, that the sick, in general, are well treated; but, except in one (town) instance, I cannot affirm this, from my own knowledge.

† St. Paul.

Of the treatment of pregnant women, and of their babes on estates, while the former are lying in, I know almost nothing; but, before they are delivered, and while the latter are at the breast, their treatment is generally, I do not say universally, such as Mr. Ramsay describes. When I first went to Barbadoes, I was particularly astonished to see some women far gone in their pregnancy, toiling in the field; and others, whose naked infants lay exposed to the weather, sprawling on a goat-skin, or in a wooden tray. I have heard, with indignation, drivers curse both them and their squalling brats, when they were suckling them.

On the estates of one or two eminently worthy and humane gentlemen, I have always understood that the breeding wenches are treated remarkably well; and particularly that they are allowed proper clothes for their infants; and, when they come out, a new suit, better than common, for themselves, and a small matter in money; but this is not the ordinary practice. The children of domestic slaves, and of such as belong to the middling and the lower ranks of people, are treated, in all respects, as well as white children, and, if any thing, thrive better.

After the children on estates are weaned, and are able to run about, they are often put under the management of a careful old woman, and are employed in picking vines, insects, &c. for the small and feathered stock. Hence they are called the *hog-meat-gang*, or the *pot-gang*, from their being fed with dressed victuals. Although an old woman, who has many to attend to, cannot be expected to supply the place of the mother; yet I have seen numerous gangs of such urchins, all in the best possible health and spirits. From the hog-meat gang, they are translated into what is called the *little gang*, which is employed in weeding, collecting grafs, and other light work, till the individuals who compose it are able to take their station in the *great gang*, a transition which compleats the hardship and misery of a field negro. Till now he had been employed, as young people might be, and indeed, sometimes, are employed, without injury, in this and other countries. Now he must till the ground, carry out the dung, and, in short, must go through *all* the drudgery of husbandry, which cattle perform in every civilized country under heaven, except the West-Indian Islands.*

---

* ' How can a country be said to be *civilized*, in which *domestic slavery* still exists ?' Coxe's Travels into Poland, &c. vol. 3. p. 174.

The

The weekly allowance of a field negro, in Barbadoes, varies, like every other circumstance of his treatment. But I am of opinion, it may, in general, be safely reckoned from six to nine pints of Guinea corn*, an excellent species of grain, or from nine to twelve pints of Indian corn †, which is less nutritive; with three or four herrings, or from one pound and a half to two pounds and a half of salted cod-fish, often of a bad quality. Formerly, they had shads from America. More grain and less fish is given in Barbadoes, than, according to Mr. Ramsay, is allowed in St. Kitt's; an advantage which may be owing to much greater attention being paid to the raising of provisions, in the former island than in the latter. Flour, and that worst of all species of food, horse-beans, form but a small part of the diet of the slaves, in Barbadoes; but they frequently have eddoes ‡, and sweet potatoes ∥, and sometimes yams § and plantanes **, all of them excellent vegetables; the allowance of which, as well as of the *small* quantities of salted beef and pork, which are served out to them (on holidays especially) I do not recollect. When they hole land, they have each about a gill of rum and molasses, at noon. All the provisions produced in Barbadoes are excellent in their kind. Indian corn is less nutritive, if not less wholesome, when too long kept, than European grain; but I take it no grain (wheat excepted) is more wholesome or nutritive than Guinea corn. I forgot to mention, as a part of their food, *pigeon peas* ††, so called from their having been formerly given to pigeons, and other feathered stock; but which are now discovered to be very good food for men; and, by many white people, are preferred to any kind of European peas. In shape and size they resemble vetches, and grow on a wooded shrub, about the size of tall broom. Ockras, ‡‡ and several other excellent vegetables, enter more or less into their diet.—It must be owned, that, when in health, the field-negroes never do taste, at least they are not allowed, butchers meat, milk, butter, or any kind of *fresh animal* substance (flying-fish ∥∥ *sometimes* excepted) which,

when

---

* The Holcus Sorghum of Linnæus.   † Zea, Mays.
‡ Arum esculentum.   ∥ Convolvulus Batatas.   § Dioscorea Alata, Bulbifera, Sativa.   ** Musa paradisaica.
†† Cytisus Cajan.   ‡‡ Hibiscus esculentus.
∥∥ Exocœtus volitans.—The catching of flying-fish is, I believe, peculiar to *Barbadoes* They are caught, chiefly during the crop, and add to
the

when cheap, those who are near enough to the towns, occasionally buy with the money they receive, at nights, for horse-meat and other stolen articles. On the other hand, no fault, I think, can reasonably be found with the quality of the *vegetable* part of their diet; especially since the Indian corn from America has been, in a great measure, exchanged for grain, produced in their native soil, to which the former is not only naturally inferior; but it was sometimes musty, and too often damaged. The quality of their diet, in the gross, salt-fish, &c. included, is, perhaps, not nearly so objectionable as its quantity; which, in general, is far from being proportioned to the toil they undergo. The grinding and sifting of their corn, after the labour of the day is over, may be regarded as a hardship, though not as a great hardship. Most plantations are furnished with hand-mills for this purpose; but a few have wind-mills with mill-stones. Many negroes grind their corn, in their houses, between two stones.—Artificers, when working at their trades, have a *bit*, or near 6d. ster. *per* day, a very sufficient allowance. Some domestics are wholly, and others partly, fed from the family-table. Sometimes victuals are separately dressed for them. When they have no victuals, they receive 3 bits each *per* week, a most ample allowance for people who cannot be said to work, in the English sense of the word.

In St. Kitt's, according to Mr. Ramsay, they punish with a *cart-whip*. The instrument of correction commonly used in Barbadoes, is called a *cow-skin*, without which a negro driver would no more think of going into the field, than a coachman in England would think of setting out on a journey without his whip. It is composed of leathern thongs, platted in the common way, and tapers from the end of the handle (within which is a short bit of wood) to the point, which is furnished with a lash of silk-grass †, hard platted and knotted, like that of a horse-whip, but thicker. Its form gives it some degree of elasticity towards the handle; and, when used with *severity*

---

the plenty of that season. They are of a very equal size, being about as big as middling herrings. Like the herring too, the flying-fish, in some seasons, affords much relief to the poor. I have seen them at all prices, from 6 to 60 for a bit, or 6d. ster.

† Agave Americana.

(which

(which is far from being always the case) it tears the flesh, and brings blood at every stroke. The law has limited the number of lashes to forty*, or rather, forty save one, which, if inflicted by an unfeeling hand, is a very severe punishment; more severe, perhaps, though less tedious, than two hundred from the cat-o-nine-tails used in the army. Nine and thirty lashes are very seldom, I may say never, ordered by magistrates, unless for crimes which *really* do deserve such rigour, and which in this country would often be punished with the gallows; or, for flagrant insults to white men, which seldom escape either publick punishment, or private revenge. Owners very seldom go so far, in a regular way. But, Sir, punishment is not always regular. *Fits of passion*, to which even good owners are subject, disdain the restraints of law, of humanity, and of interest. *Intoxication, ill-nature,* and *revenge,* declare open war against humanity. In such cases, no trouble is taken to count the stripes; but they are laid on, furiously and indiscriminately, over all the body, the face, and the naked breasts of the women sometimes not excepted. Then it is, that tyranny rages, without controul. Then it is, that the law should wrest the instrument of oppression from a hand which is no longer capable of using it with moderation. The law should do more, Sir: it should make the tyrant tremble, it should make him *suffer,* for daring to debase a man *far beneath* the condition of a brute!!

Suppuration is always, and, in wet weather especially, convulsions are sometimes the consequence of a *severe flogging;* and the cicatrices of the wounds form large wheales, which the wretches carry to their graves. The backs and posteriors of many of the slaves, of both sexes, which are often covered with such wheales, are melancholy proofs of the severity of their owners and managers. I have seen both men and women, at their field labour, lacerated with the recent or suppurating wounds of the cow-skin. Some few work with a chain fastened round both ancles, which, from its length, they are obliged to tuck up, to enable them to walk; others have a chain locked, or an iron collar, with projecting prongs, riveted round the neck; others a *boot,* or ring of broad bar-iron

* See Deut. ch. xxv. ver. 3.

hammered

hammered round one ancle; and those whose labour is nearly stationary, are chained to a 56 lb. weight, or a log of wood *. These last, with whipping, confinement in the dungeon, fetters or stocks, are the common punishments inflicted on runaways. But, on several plantations, they are not often incurred or inflicted.

Mutilation, except by watchmen, or by the sugar-mills, is very far indeed from being common in Barbadoes; and, as in St. Kitt's, when it happens, is mentioned, by the better sort of people, with consummate detestation. It is to be lamented, however, that this is the *only* punishment which owners suffer for atrocious acts of cruelty (for mutilation never fell within my immediate knowledge) to their own slaves. An arrest and damages are the consequences of striking, without provocation, the slave of another, *when the fact can be proved*. I may affirm too, that *dropping with burning sealing-wax, or hot syrup*, with other infernal tortures, are now very rare indeed in Barbadoes.† An instance of such torture never fell within my observation; and I recollect only a few facts of this kind which forced themselves on my belief, and which I shall afterwards relate. Still the common punishments are openly and avowedly inflicted, *too often with a degree of severity, which no* INDIVIDUAL *of the human race ought to be suffered to exercise on a fellow-creature*—a severity which, in too many instances, contributes to shorten life, and which no absurd claim of property, in the persons of men, can possibly authorize.

Regular punishments, in consequence of the sentence of a magistrate, are inflicted by a constable. Owners in the towns, when they punish regularly, employ a fellow called a *Jumper*, and who is generally a constable. Besides his cow-skin, the jumper carries in his pocket a rope, with which he ties up refractory slaves by the hands,

* 'If any person shall take off any *pot-hook, ring,* or *collar,* from a slave's neck or leg, he shall forfeit 10l to such slave's owner, to be recovered as servants wages; and, if the offender is a slave, he shall receive 40 lashes, by order of any Justice." Laws of Barbadoes, No. 116. d. 7. Hall's Abridgment, p. 62.

† A Barbadian gentleman, now in England, on my reading the above passage to him, mentioned an instance of this horrid species of cruelty, which, he is well informed, was inflicted about 20 years ago. But, though he is not disposed to palliate such deeds, he thinks with me that they are extremely infrequent.

till

to a cleat,* till he inflict the number of lashes ordered. Some few people pay the jumper by the year; others send for him occasionally, and many (perhaps too many, as things now stand,) seldom or never send for him at all. The worthless pampered domesticks in Bridge-town, often really deserve to be visited by the jumper, and sometimes by a more severe executioner.—When I lived in Bridge-town, my servant, who was left entirely to my management, and who, like very many of the slaves in that place, was an incorrigible gambler, was seen at his sport by a certain magistrate. The fellow not only stood his ground, after his companions had dispersed, but used some very improper language. I carried him to the magistrate he had offended, who politely left the punishment to me. As the fellow had never been before a magistrate, I requested that he would name the punishment, and pronounce sentence with all due solemnity; when the punishment he ordered was—six lashes. I regretted that the matter had not been regularly tried, before another magistrate; but, *of my own sovereign will and pleasure*, I ordered double the number of lashes, which were inflicted before the magistrate's door.—My gambler's next offence was of a more heinous nature: It was receiving stolen goods to the amount of about *three pounds sterling* (which might have been proved by the evidence of the honest man to whom he offered them, for a trifle) besides other valuable goods, in the theft of which, I really believe, he was concerned. The fellow was sentenced to receive twelve lashes. Here again I interposed *my authority*, and ordered eighteen; but, in neither instance, did I allow the skin to be cut. I must own, nothing but shame prevented me from having the full lash of the law inflicted for an offence, for which, in this country, the culprit must inevitably have died. Such lenity is certainly praise-worthy, when thefts are committed by poor half-starved field-negroes, whose cases are most humanely considered by magistrates, in Barbadoes; but it is evidently misplaced on the town profligates, who, almost universally, are well fed, and not worked at all. The two worthy and humane persons above alluded to, must excuse me, if I say, that they acted very right as men and as gentlemen, but certainly very wrong as magistrates.

* Not off the ground; but merely to confine the offender to the spot.

Severe as the treatment of the field-negroes in Barbadoes may appear, I have reason to think that it is much milder than in most of the other, especially the *new* islands; having repeatedly heard persons, from those islands, *ridicule* the lenity of the Barbadian discipline; and, indeed, the laxity of the police of Bridge-town deserves to be ridiculed. I have heard a person, from one of those islands, make a kind of boast of their staking negroes down to the ground, and placing a driver on each side, like men threshing corn. In Barbadoes, regular punishment is never inflicted in this manner. The culprit always stands, or, when refractory, is tied up by the wrists. Even this mode, to the female sex, at least, one would think sufficiently harsh. *A woman imploring mercy!* with her petticoats or rags tucked up, or holding them up with her own hands (and both I have too often seen) to have the whip applied by an unfeeling jumper or driver, and at the will of an owner or manager, perhaps yet more unfeeling, and on a part which decency ought to veil, is one of those sights at which uncorrupted nature revolts.—But suffice it to glance at scenes which cannot but affect the feelings of my amiable countrywomen, 'tremblingly alive,' as they are known to be, to every sentiment allied to humanity. Should any of them honour these sheets with a perusal, I know that, at this passage, plain as it is, they will drop a tear. In Barbadoes, tears flowing from the eyes of ladies often mitigate the rigour of punishment. The mothers and the daughters of a brave nation will not be less compassionate. They will exert their irresistible influence, in favour of unprotected, insulted, outraged *women*. With their native dignity, they will generously step between the violators of the rights of the sex, in Africa, and the innocent victims of their brutality.

The punishments of capital crimes of negroes against whites, in Barbadoes, are dreadful and excruciating, to a degree far beyond any idea I could have formed of the duration and poignancy of human suffering, had I not been an unhappy eye-witness of one of those scenes of horror. In the year 1774, an overseer, on a cotton-place, was murdered by the negroes, who were said to have been driven to that act of violence, by oppression and hunger.

hunger.* It was the practice, on that place, to give the slaves no allowance of food, during the plentiful season of the crop, but to leave them to subsist, as they could, by committing nightly depredations on the neighbouring sugar estates, or by corresponding with the thievish negroes on such estates; at the same time, that nothing was abated from their usual labour.—For this murder, five negro men were *gibbeted alive*, and a negro woman, whose guilt was not fully proved, was chained to the gallows, to be a spectator of their prolonged tortures. On the afternoon of the third or fourth day of their agony, I went to see them; but, in no instance, did I ever so heartily repent of my curiosity. 'Animus meminisse horret, luctuque refugit.' By that time, two of them had expired, and were dragged into the sea; and the surviving three exhibited a spectacle of woe, which, at this moment, I shudder to call to mind, and which no language can describe. The under jaw of one of those wretches had slipped through the collar of the irons. These were too long, but the collar was too small to let his head through, and had torn open his mouth, and dragged up his upper lip, nose, and cheeks, over his eye-brows, leaving his upper jaw bare; so that he was, in a manner, suspended by the head. Yet he still breathed, and his groans were truly piercing. The two others still spoke, in a hoarse, faultering voice; but so that most of what they said might, with attention, be understood; and one of them, more than once, called upon God to witness his innocence and his sufferings, and to receive his soul. Their affecting petitions for a little water were answered only by the worse than brutal, by the savage, insults of the constables and other poor whites, collected around the gallows, who told them that they would get no water in hell, whither they were hastening; for that they might be assured, God would have no mercy on their souls, since they had no mercy on the worthy man they had murdered. Indeed, so much did those fellows (one of whose order the negroes had killed) seem to enjoy the scene, that a man

---

* 'But in regard there are some masters and owners of negroes, and other slaves, who do not make *sufficient conscience of providing what is necessary for their negroes, or other slaves, and allowing them time to plant and provide for themselves, for which cause such negroes and other slaves are necessitated*, &c.' Hall's Laws of Barbadoes, No. 82, cl. 16.

would certainly have been infulted, who had dared, in their hearing, to commiferate fufferings fo fhocking to human nature. To fome gentlemen, unacquainted with the baleful influence of flavery in hardening the heart, this laft circumftance may feem incredible. I cannot help it; but I have the comfort to be confcious that I am relating the truth. The horrible, hideous, diftorted features, the wild, ftaring eyes, the piercing groans, and the agonizing throes of thofe wretches, whofe whole frames were convulfed with inconceivable tortures, fo compleatly 'harrowed up my foul,' that it was long ere this fcene of horror ceafed to haunt my imagination; and, while I breathe, I fhall never forget it.

A few years ago, a moft fhocking murder was committed, by the negroes, on a medical gentleman of acknowledged worth and humanity, and whofe unhappy fate was greatly and juftly lamented by all ranks of people. Various were the conjectures on the motives which could inftigate the negroes to commit this horrid affaffination. For my own part, I had, and ftill have, my doubts, refpecting that mysterious affair—mysterious, I fay; for, befides fome other curious circumftances, it appeared extraordinary that the Doctor though murdered, was not robbed. Four negro men were *burnt alive* for this deed in Bridge-town; but though I lived there, at the time, yet my curiofity had been fo thoroughly fatiated with the gibbeting, that I did not go to fee the execution.

A favourite young wench, who had the care of her mafter's child, difliked the employment fo much, that fhe poifoned the infant, with laudanum. This was not the firft child of her mafter's whom fhe was fufpected to have thus deftroyed; and the laft fact was fully proved. At the requeft of her humane miftrefs, fhe was hanged.

Some years before I arrived in Barbadoes, a white perfon was murdered by a negro, for which his fuppofed murderer was gibbeted alive at Orange-fort. After he had been fufpended, I think, for eight and forty hours, the real criminal furrendered himfelf to juftice, declaring, That an innocent man was then fuffering for a crime which he had committed; that, if the man died, he fhould be guilty of two murders, and that he rather chofe to expire, by that dreadful, lingering torture, than to drag on a miferable life, and, at laft, pine to death, under the un-
fupportable

supportable consciousness of such guilt. The innocent man was accordingly taken down, and the criminal put up in his place, where he survived six or seven days. While the life of the former was in suspence, as it was for many days, the gentleman, whose negro carpenters had constructed the gallows, was thrown into such agony of mind, by the guilt which, with an amiable weakness, he supposed, he had incurred, by having had even this small concern in the business, that his faculties became manifestly deranged. He was seen to kneel down in the street, and most pathetically implore the Almighty, not to lay innocent blood to his charge. Nor is this to be wondered at; for the horrible nature of this punishment is sufficient to throw even the most unconcerned spectator into a deep melancholy. I was afterwards well acquainted with this most worthy and intelligent person, and often had a wish to know his opinion of the justice and expediency of such punishment; but I never could ask him the question. No doubt his opinion was the same with those of a few other worthy persons, his friends, with whom also I had the honour and the happiness to be acquainted.

The three first mentioned murders are the only deeds of the kind, which, so far as I can recollect, were perpetrated by negroes, while I lived in Barbadoes, which was for upwards of thirteen years. Though, for some years, I have been but ill able to defend myself, I have rode and walked, for many miles, unarmed, and at all hours of the night, and never was once molested by a negro in word or deed. A gentleman who resided, for a much longer period, in one of the Leeward Islands, assures me, that he remembers not a single instance of any white person having been robbed, murdered, or even materially hurt by a negro, except that one of those wretches was accused of *striking* a sailor, for which he *lost his right hand*. Sailors, it must be owned, are, sometimes, apt to treat the negroes very ill. In both islands, there cannot be so few as 120,000 negroes and people of colour, many of whom, it is well known, are daily receiving the most intolerable provocation, are daily treated with the most consummate injustice. I cannot *positively* assert that the above are all the instances of whites murdered by negroes which occurred during my residence in Barbadoes. But let the number be doubled; and then let the criminal calendar calendars, of almost any country in Europe, be consulted for such an example of the infrequency of murder. Where, then, is the *necessity*, where is the expediency, of such horrible tortures? Why, in the name of humanity, in the name of Christianity, in the name even of that frigid principle, *policy*, are negroes to be *gibbeted* and *burnt alive*, for the murder of white men, and the latter, *at the worst*, only *fined* and *imprisoned* for murdering them?

The happiest of men should I think myself—I should indeed think that I had not lived in vain, if, even at the risk of my own (temporal) ruin, by the cruel and insidious machinations of interested malice, this publication should, in any degree, contribute to prevent the repetition of such execrable tortures. I fear, I have more to answer for than the gentleman above alluded to, had, for having concealed, but for a day, such shocking scenes from the public.

I have the honour to be, &c.

LETTER IV.

' *L'agriculture ne pourra jamais prospérer là où l'agri-*
' *culteur ne possede rien en propre.*'

Cath. II. Imp. de Russ. Inst. pour le nouv. code de loix. p. 83.

SIR,

BY way of supplement or postscript to my last long, and, I fear, tedious, letter, I now beg leave very briefly to describe the mode of cultivating a cane-field, or of *holing* land, and *turning* or carrying out dung, which I have always considered as the most laborious tasks of the negroes. The first circumstance that struck me, on viewing this *manual* species of cultivation, was, that weak slaves are unavoidably oppressed by it.

I have seen land lined off into square spaces, four feet each way, which, I believe, is the general rule in Barbadoes. The *holes*, therefore, may be about three feet square, and seven or eight inches deep, with a space or
distance

diſtance between each, and another ſpace or *bank*, at right angles to the diſtance, to receive the mould.* The holes are dug, with hoes, by the ſlaves, in a row, with the driver at one end, to preſerve the line. They begin and finiſh a row of theſe holes as nearly, at the ſame inſtants, as poſſible ; ſo that this *equal* taſk muſt be performed, in *the ſame time*, by a number of people who, it is *next to impoſſible*, ſhould all be *equally ſtrong* and dexterous ; eſ-pecially as few or no field negroes, who can wield a hoe, are exempted from it. Thus the weak muſt be oppreſſed. The driver is often obliged to ſet ſuch negroes, as can-not keep up with the reſt, to work, in a ſeparate corner, by themſelves; but, I am ſorry to ſay, he too often firſt tries the effect of flogging, which is alſo ſometimes the puniſhment for not digging the holes deep enough.

In turning dung, a taſk equally as laborious, and, per-haps, more haraſſing than holing, each negro carries, on his head, a baſketful of it. The gang muſt walk over a ſurface, now rendered very uneven by the holes, the driver bringing up the rear, and often ſmacking his whip, and, I wiſh I could ſay, I never ſaw him apply it to the backs of the ſlaves, to increaſe their ſpeed. But, I am ſorry to add, I have more than once ſeen this ; and, on one large plantation, in particular, I remember to have obſerved, with indignation, a white driver uſing his whip, on a gang turning dung, in a manner altogether ſhameful. Whether the driver or the owner, who I think then reſid-ed on the eſtate, was to blame for this, I cannot ſay. Here, Sir, is another *equal* taſk, to be performed in an *equal* time, by people of *unequal* ſtrength. In turning dung, therefore, as in holing, the weak, under ſtrict drivers, at leaſt, are unavoidably oppreſſed. Both of them are very laborious taſks, conſidering the climate, the ſcanty fare of the negroes, and the number of hours they work ; eſpecially, as thoſe taſks are often performed rather in a hurry, as when advantage is to be taken of a heavy rain ; or when the plantation-work, from various cauſes, happens to be backward, or has not kept pace with the

---

* The origin of holing I take to have been, the impoſſibility of uſing any other inſtruments, than the hoe or the ſpade, among the roots of the trees when the iſlands were firſt cleared. Barbadoes is ſaid to have been covered with wood of uncommon hardneſs. No other mode of culture has, ſince, been ſeriouſly perſevered in.

advancement

advancement of the season—circumstances these, which, in my humble opinion, would render the *limited* tasks proposed by Mr. Ramsay, impracticable, except in so far as various tasks might be suited to the various strength of the slaves.

In this work, the negroes have *no help at all* from cattle or implements of husbandry, the *hoe* and the *basket*, only excepted. This circumstance alone may serve to convince the public of the state of debasement to which the negroes are reduced. For what, Sir, would be the condition of the people even in this *temperate* climate, if the land, instead of being ploughed, were, universally, dug with the spade or the hoe, and the dung not only spread, but carried out and distributed over the fields, by human creatures, drudging under the scourge of overseers?

Several objections are made to the use of the plough, in Barbadoes.—Some of the land, it is said, is too full of stones. Much land is ploughed in the northern parts, at least, of this kingdom, which is much more stoney and gravelly than by far the greater part of the soil in Barbadoes; and ley-land, is, besides, often bound up with the roots of heath, furze, or broom; but, in the land of that island, there are no roots, whatever, that can impede the hoe, still less the plough.—But other parts of the land are too steep.—What an objection would this be to the use of the plough in some countries? I have frequently seen land ploughed, and so, I suppose, have most men who have visited the mountainous parts of Britain, so steep that a furrow could only be taken in coming down hill, and steeper than any arable land in Barbadoes, except in those parts of the island called Scotland and St. Joseph's, which, though far from being the highest, is the most precipitous surface I ever saw.—But the soil of steep land is apt to be washed away by the torrents of rain, and would be too much loosened by the plough.—Very steep land might be holed, and, if the declivity be not excessive, might be ploughed across, and not up and down, leaving spaces like the present banks.—But there is not sufficient provender for the cattle.—The preceding objections have a partial, this a very general application. It might, however, in a very great measure, be removed, by cultivating grasses, of which there are several excellent species; and, perhaps, by sowing, rather than planting, Guinea corn,

corn. Of these, several crops might be produced in a year; and it would be difficult to shew, why they might not be converted into hay, as in Jamaica. Oats and beans might be had from this country. Ships, which go out in ballast, might carry even hay. The truth is, that, hitherto, little attention has been paid to the raising of provender, just as, before the late war, too little attention was paid to the raising of ground-provisions. The cattle, at present, are too generally fed, or rather, for part of the year at least, more than half starved, on picked grass and weeds, the collection of which, as we have observed, is a great hardship to the slaves.

I have not affirmed that the plough would answer in *all* situations, for planting *canes*; but this I can affirm, that a certain gentleman assured me, that he and, a neighbour of his, an eminently worthy and humane clergyman, found the plough to succeed perfectly in planting and digging provisions; and he added, that the negroes were unspeakably eased by it; but, I think, they were obliged to lay it aside for want of provender. For the sake of the former worthy person too, as well as the cause of humanity, I regretted that he was rather in straitened circumstances; and, it is well known, that improvements of every kind, are attended with more or less expence. It is, indeed, impossible to object to the plough in planting and digging provisions, which would be a great point gained. I have seen the land so bound up with drought, that a negro, who might have dug 80, or even 100 caneholes, in a day, in soft land, could not make out more than 50 or 60. The plough would, therefore, be of great use in breaking up cane-land, when so hardened. The holes might, afterwards, be formed with the hoe—if, indeed, there must be holes; but I do not see why the dung might not be carted out to the land, then spread by the negroes, and the canes planted with the plough, as the potatoe is in Britain—a root which, it must be observed, is *not indigenous* in this country. But this, as well as such of the foregoing agricultural observations as do not depend on fact, I must submit to the consideration of the candid and humane *Barbadoes* planter.

The following quotation contains the opinions of two of the greatest writers of Europe, on the abridgment of labour:—' Such trades (those of manufacturers) were at
'Athens

'Athens and Rome, all occupied by the slaves' (*white slaves*, like those at Algiers!) 'of the rich, who exercised them, for the benefit of their masters, whose wealth, power and protection, made it almost impossible for a poor free man to find a market for his work, when it came into competition with that of the slaves of the rich.* Slaves, however, are *very seldom inventive*; and all the most important improvements, either in machinery, or in the arrangement or distribution of work, which facilitate and abridge labour, have been the discoveries of freemen. Should a slave propose any improvement of this kind, his master would be very apt to consider the proposal as the suggestion of laziness, and a desire to save his own labour, at the master's expence. The poor slave, instead of reward, would probably meet with much abuse, perhaps with some punishment. In the manufactures carried on by *slaves*, therefore, *more labour* must generally have been employed to execute the same quantity of work, than in those carried on by *freemen*. The work of the former must, upon that account, generally have been *dearer* than that of the latter. The Hungarian mines, it is remarked by Mr. Montesquieu, *though not richer*, have always been wrought *with less expence*, and, therefore, *with more profit*, than the Turkish mines in their neighbourhood. The Turkish mines are wrought *by slaves*; and *the* ARMS *of those slaves* are the ONLY MACHINES the Turks have ever thought of employing. The Hungarian mines are wrought by *freemen*, who employ *a great deal of machinery*, by which they facilitate and abridge their own labour.' †

To a little genius, every new phœnomenon is a new mystery; because he has no general principles to refer it to. The views of great men are extensive, and their reasonings and observations are of general and easy application. Accordingly one would suppose Mr. Montesquieu and Dr. Smith, had the West-Indian slavery particularly in their eye, when they made the above obser-

---

* This is most notoriously the case in Barbadoes. So many blacks are now bred to all kinds of trades, that the poor white artificers often find it difficult to get bread.

† *Wealth of Nations*, v. 3. p. 37. See also v. 2. p. 87, et seq.

vations.

vations. The whole of the above excellent passage is true of our present subject; the latter portion of it particularly applies to that part of it we are now treating. For *Hungarian* read *Cochin Chinese*, for *Turkish* read *West Indian*, for *in* read *of*, for *neighbourhood* read ANTIPODES, and for *Mines* read *Plantations*, and the application is compleat.

But while the Turks can procure slaves from the distant provinces of their empire *, and so long as the West Indians can import them from Africa, there is reason to fear that no other instruments than *the arms of those slaves* will ever be found to succeed, or, indeed, will ever be, *earnestly*, persevered in, in working the mines of the one or the plantations of the other. By the way, Sir, should it be objected to the few observations I have ventured to make, on the use of implements of husbandry, That I am no planter, I would answer, That Dr. Smith certainly never was in ancient Rome or Athens, and probably never in any country of slavery; that I question whether Mr. Montesquieu ever examined the Turkish and the Hungarian mines, and yet that these great men reason most admirably and conclusively on slavery; that, on the other hand, I (if it be not a species of egotism to mention myself, in the same sentence, with two such names) have seen the West Indian husbandry for years together; that, though I always disliked it, I was for some time, occasionally employed in it; and that I never saw any thing mysterious in the planting of canes and the making of sugar.

But I, by no means, wish the reader to rest on my *dictum* respecting the use of the plough. According to Mr. Long, it was tried successfully in Jamaica, and more land was turned up in a day, by a single plough, and more effectually (for the hoe does not turn up the soil, especially the deep soil, properly) than could have been effected, in the same time, by 100 men. Land, which was ploughed before it was holed, produced three hhds. of sugar per acre, and by the common mode of culture, it yielded only two. 'The *plough itself* might be used, in some situations, per-

---

* ' Egypt, according to Monf. Maillet sends continual colonies of
' *black* slaves to the other parts of the Turkish empire, and receives, an-
' nually, an equal number of WHITES, the one brought from the in-
' land parts of Africa, the other from Mingrelia, Circassia and Tartary.'
Hume's Essay on the Populousness of Ancient Nations.

' haps,

'haps, to advantage, or *saving of labour*.' Letters to a Young Planter, p. 3. I must remark that this is the opinion of a person, who, afterwards, wrote an *Apology* for negro slavery; and that he there speaks of Grenada, an island incomparably more mountainous than Barbadoes. I know not whether I ought to mention the planting of canes, with the plough, in Cochin China, since I cannot procure Mr. Le Poivre's book. It appears, however, from a certain author who has quoted him, that the vast empire of China, supposed, by some, to contain as many inhabitants as all Europe, is chiefly supplied, from Cochin China, with sugar raised by freemen, with the plough; that the annual export of that commodity is equal to 500,000 hhds. each 1600 lb. which considerably exceeds the quantity made in the West Indies, by all the European colonies put together; and that the brown sugar is sold at 3s. 4d. sterling per hundred pound, white at 6s. 8d. and candied at 8s. ' In the British ' islands, the common price of sugar, in time of peace, is ' generally found to be 25s. sterling per Cwt. In the ' East Indies, as I am credibly informed, it is no more ' than 2s. 6d. And what is the reason of this? Why, ' In the West Indies, sugar is raised and manufactured by ' *slaves*, in the East Indies, by *freemen* only?' *

The laconic answer, as I before intimated, to the few hints I have ventured to offer, on the use of the plough, will probably be, ' Ne sutor ultra crepidam.' But let no gentleman ridicule those hints, till he can conscientiously affirm, that he has rationally and earnestly endeavoured to reduce to practice, and has actually found impracticable, what Mr. Long has written on it's use, as the result of his own experience and observation, in the 443 and 12 following pages, of the first vol. of his excellent History of Jamaica—a work which no planter should be without. Let him also consult the political Essays on the present state of the British empire. ' Why, therefore,' the author of this last ingenious work, asks, p. 279, 'Why, therefore, will the ' West Indians not make trial of the plough? That in-
' dolence, and idea of walking in beaten tracts, which is
' so prevalent in all concerned in the culture of the earth,

* Dispute between Great Britain and Ireland, by the able Dean of Gloucester.

' indeed,

'indeed, *peculiarly so*, are the only circumstances to which
'we can refer for an answer.'

I have the honour to be, &c.

LETTER V.

SIR,

I MUST now proceed to the most mortifying part of a mortifying subject, that of recounting some particular instances of cruelty and murder.

When I first arrived in the West Indies, every thing I heard and saw, concerning a state of mankind so new to me as slavery then was, made a deep impression, and some things were indelibly stamped, on my mind. Indeed I could have given a better account of the treatment of the negroes, after I had been six months in Barbadoes, than I can at this moment.

Among many other negroes, who bore more or less the marks of ill treatment, one of the first objects who presented himself to my view, on my landing in Barbadoes, was a negro man, whose whole body, his *face* not wholly excepted, was covered with scars, most of them old, but some of them recent. One of his legs was loaded with an iron ring or *boot*, at least half an inch thick, and upwards of two inches broad, for I never afterwards saw a larger. I eagerly enquired into the cause of what I saw, and was told that the man had been thus treated by his owner, a noted gambler, whom I, afterwards, knew to be a barbarous wretch. I asked by what authority his owner thus treated him, and was answered, that he was his *owner's property, who had a right to treat him as he pleased*. From that moment, I suspected that there was 'something *rotten* in the state of Denmark.' Farther observation verified my suspicion. I had read and heard general descriptions of slavery; but never conceived that the power of the owner was so very absolute and unlimited, as I found it to be.—Could such a wretch be publicly exhibited, in this country, he would make more
converts

converts to the side of humanity, than all that has been written on the subject.—At the bar of either house, a negro loaded with chains, and covered with scars and stripes would effectually plead the cause of his much injured countrymen.

In the year 1773, some months after my arrival in Barbadoes, I, one morning, saw the body of a negro man, who had been run through, the foregoing night, it was said, with a spit. It lay in the dry channel of a watercourse, near a fence within which the fact was committed.—The neighbours covered it with loose gravel; but, a succeeding flood having washed off this slight covering, the naked, putrid corse was again exposed to view, and removed to a little distance. This slave was probably killed in the act of theft, to which slaves are often prompt by their own bad dispositions, but more frequently, perhaps, impelled by the irresistible calls of hunger; which had been apparently the case with this wretch, whose body was much reduced. This deed was never, that I heard of, so much as inquired into; and the deep impression it made on my mind, at the time, is my only reason for mentioning it. To speak the truth, I wish it may make a similar impression on the mind of my reader. If it do, he will detest slavery, as long as he lives. The naked body of a murdered man lying neglected, or treated, in all respects, like a dead dog, must needs be a new and a shocking spectacle to any European youth, especially to a country youth from Britain, on his *first arrival*, in a land of slavery.

Some time after this, I saw a fine, tall, young man, whose limbs, especially his forearms, had been cut and mangled in a most shocking manner. It was said, and I had every reason to believe, this was done by a watchman. His vitals were not wounded; so that he still had some slight appearances of life; but it seemed to me, impossible that he should recover.

A person, justly detested for his cruelty, tied the hands of his negro man behind his back; then, hoisting him up by them, with the dislocation of both his shoulders, whipped him, while thus suspended, very unmercifully. I did not see this punishment inflicted; but the poor wretch entirely lost the use of one arm, which was attributed, by the neighbours, to the cruel treatment just described.

scribed. His master, though a tyrant, was a well informed man, and probably had a mind to imitate the Russian *knoute*; for I never heard of another instance of of the same mode of punishment. The fellow either naturally was, or this treatment rendered him, desperately wicked; and was afterwards hanged, for attempting a rape on a white woman. That he might have been extremely rude to the woman, I did not doubt; but that a fellow, disabled as he was, should make such an attempt, appeared to me rather improbable. This might have been the reason why his punishment was so mild. The punishment inflicted on negroes for this crime (an instance of which happened many years before I went to Barbadoes) is too shocking for description.

In one of the towns, I, one evening, heard the report of a musket. Suspecting mischief, I immediately repaired to the street from whence the sound seemed to have proceeded; and there beheld one negro man lying dead, and another dangerously wounded in the neck. The piece had been loaded with small shot; and hence, I believe, was fired, not with an intention to kill, but only, by *peppering*, as it is there called, to disperse a noisy crowd of negroes. To pepper negroes, with small shot, is not common; but salt or Guinea-corn, which smart, but do not materially hurt them, are sometimes used for that purpose.—At the instance of the owner of both the slaves, an inquiry was made into this affair; but, though it happened in a populous street, yet as no *white* person was present, nothing was, or, according to the present laws, *could be* proved.

I once heard the jumper * of one the towns boast of ' a deed without a name.' He boasted that he killed a negro (who, he said, was an out-law, and had insulted his brother) that he took out his heart, and cut his body, to use his own words, ' into pound-pieces.' From the well-known barbarity of this savage, I readily believed him. An affair which he afterwards transacted I was compelled to believe. An old lady, who had lost a sum of money, sent for this fellow, to try, by torturing her own slaves, to discover the thief. The mode of torture he used was this. He tied together, at one end, five sticks, each

* See page 16.

seven or eight inches in length. Each of the slave's four fingers were put between two of the sticks; so that, when the opposite ends of the two outside sticks were squeezed, they acted as a system of levers, of which the fingers were the fulcra. Let any gentleman try the effect of a pair of nut-crackers, or other instrument, referable to the lever, on one of his fingers, and then imagine the pain to be multiplied fourfold, and he will get some faint idea of this most exquisite torture. On a subsequent examination of black witnesses, before a certain sensible and humane magistrate, it appeared that this shocking and *singular* torture was inflicted in the open hall of the owner's house, which is situated in a public street, and that it was seen by a gentleman passing, whose evidence of the torture nullified that of the tortured wench concerning the theft. If this gentleman's affidavit did not nullify the testimonies of the rest of the old woman's negroes, it, at least, spread such a thick cloud of uncertainty on the whole affair, that no capital punishment followed. To interfere between owner and slave, except in the way of interception for a runaway, which is often made, is looked upon as being very impertinent. He incurred the old lady's highest displeasure for what she called his officiousness in looking in at her door; but, when it, afterwards, turned out, that the money was stolen by a white man, who was intimate with one of her wenches, she came to his house and very cordially thanked him, for having saved the life of the innocent negro who was suspected. Neither the owner nor the tormentor suffered, or, indeed, could, legally, suffer, any punishment whatever, for thus torturing innocent people. As I am particularly acquainted with the above gentleman, I dare mention this as a fact, which I can depend upon, as much, if possible, as if I myself had seen it; and, to the best of my recollection, he related it exactly as above.—I overheard the same adept in those hellish mysteries, very near whom I lived for a few years, describe a mode of torture which he called *cat-harping*. This is suspending a negro, by the thumbs and the great toes, in some unnatural posture, of which he did not give a very clear idea, and then whipping him, while thus suspended. I do not recollect whether he said he himself had inflicted this torture, or that he had seen it inflicted, but one or

the

the other he did say. On occasion of this description, a gentleman, who heard it, told me there was an instance of it's having been inflicted, about five and thirty years ago, by a person, now alive, who possesses a large estate; but who was then a manager. The shocking particulars I shall not relate, because I heard them mentioned only as matter of report.

Should it be asked why I hint at a deed which I do not undertake to support, I would answer, that this species of torture *has an appropriated name* (though I never, but once, heard it) that I heard that name explained; and that the infliction and the inflictor of this torture (who cannot possibly be discovered by my faint allusion) were mentioned, by a person of veracity, as matter of current report, in the neighbourhood of the manager, who had, moreover, the character of being cruel. These circumstances, taken together, convince me that this horrid torture *has been* used, though, I firmly believe, it *has now* no existence, in Barbadoes.—It is nevertheless proper and necessary that such deeds should be *hinted at*; because what has been *may be again*; for I know of nothing to hinder owners from torturing their slaves, in any manner they chuse. The law takes no cognizance of such crimes.

X, a man of property, cut off both the ears of Z's negro-man. Z, unable, no doubt, to prove the deed, and to recover damages, took his revenge by beating X, till, as was said, the poor mutilated wretch interposed, to prevent his owner from committing murder. Having recovered of the blows, X indicted Z, at the sessions, for an assault. The case of assault was tried, at least I saw both the parties appear, in the public Court-house, in Bridge-town. I do not recollect how the matter terminated: but it would be doing extreme injustice to the better and the middling classes of people, not to add that, by them, X was universally hissed and despised.—I have no acquaintance with this man; but, for the sake of his connections, I am very sorry that truth and humanity oblige me to mention this notorious instance of cruelty and meanness —meanness, I say, not in having had recourse to the law, but in mutilating a helpless slave.

I sincerely lament that, to the above instances of cruelty and murder, truth and humanity constrain me to add

C a fact

a fact which affects the community; or, at least, demonstrates the total inefficiency of the laws, of Barbadoes—a fact, which has never, that I know of, appeared in print, and which, though notorious as the meridian sun, will, I dare say, be disputed, with the utmost virulence and obstinacy.—In Barbadoes, Sir, I am sorry to say, there are some owners, who, when their slaves become incapable of labour, from age, ill usage, or disease, especially *leprosy*; inhumanly expose them to every extreme of wretchedness, by turning them out to shift for themselves. The poor creatures generally crawl to Bridge-town, for the advantage of begging in that populous place; and they are often to be seen in the streets, in the very last stage of human misery, naked, famished, diseased and forlorn; to the great annoyance of the humane part of the inhabitants, many of whom I have heard complain of this disgraceful nuisance. While able, they wander about; and, when their strength fails, generally fix in some corner or thoroughfare, and depend on the casual charity of the passengers.

Besides several worn out and leprous negroes, who frequented the more public parts of the town, especially the market and both the bridges, I particularly remember an exposed and worn out negro-woman, who was free from external disease, and who was, for a long time, about Mr. Jackson's gate, over the bay; also a most miserable leprous woman, who lay, for a considerable time, in the alley parallel to, and between, Broadstreet and Jew-street. Of the fate of those wretches, I am ignorant; but those who were stationary cannot but be remembered by many people. Whether they may be disposed to confirm or to contradict my testimony, is quite a different question.—One evening, on passing the ruins of a house which, about three years before, had been thrown down by the hurricane, I was alarmed by deep human groans. Following the sound, which was my only guide, I perceived they proceeded from a negro who lay, on the lee-side of a wall, struggling in the agonies of death. Next morning, at dawn, I repaired to the place, and beheld the naked and extenuated corpse of a negro woman, surrounded with ordure and vermin. She appeared to me to have been a worn out slave, and to have died of a flux; for I saw no marks of cutaneous disease.—Would to God, Sir,

Sir, every man, who may be disposed to think, to write or to speak favourably of slavery, had seen this melancholy spectacle!

The only shadow, and it is but a shadow, of extenuation, which can be offered for this criminal practice, is, that negroes who are very lazy, or very miserably oppressed, have been sometimes known, by certain applications, of a corrosive or irritating nature, to induce and keep open, sores upon their legs and feet, to prevent them from working; just as a most excellent negro-cooper in Bridge-town whom I heard mentioned, cut off one of his hands with his adze, upon an unreasonable daily task being imposed on him.—One fellow, who was strongly suspected of the above practice, and of pretending to be lunatic; but who was, otherwise, in good health, used to beg all day, for, in every thing that concerned his subsistence, he shewed no signs of lunacy, and lodged, at night, in an old kitchen-chimney near me; but he was so noisy and so profane, that I was forced to take methods to dislodge him, which I, at last, effected, by rendering his dormitory untenable.

Medical people are the best judges of the extent of such practices among the negroes, which, indeed, I do not think are very common. Yet I can mention two well authenticated instances. A certain Doctor found that a patient of his, who was a very worthless, drunken fellow, had removed his dressings, and applied some irritating vegetable to an ulcerated toe. This so exasperated the Doctor, that he immediately amputated the toe, which effectually cured the fellow. Another, whom he had under his care, was suspected of a similar practice; and he, at last, detected him scraping the edges of his sores with an old knife, and about to apply some stuff of his own. Upon this, the Doctor washed the sores, of which he had several, with a most tormenting mixture, I think it was sea-salt and rum. The sores, after this, healed apace; and his patient was never more troubled with them.

It is also said, that some negroes innoculate themselves for leprosy; but I never could believe this; for great must be the laziness of that slave, and horrid, indeed, must be the tyranny under which he groans, which could force him to induce a disease, the most pitiable, perhaps, which afflicts the human species.—But, granting these facts, if the latter be a fact, their full weight, they never can extenuate the brutal practice of abandoning such wretches; much less *worn out*, *aged* and *innocent* people, who labour under no infectious disease, or who have no disease at all. —That even leprous negroes are not universally abandoned by their owners, I can give *one* instance. A handsome, negro girl was seized with, and died of, this frightful distemper; but her humane owner not only provided for her, at home; but, by some means or other, her clothes, which were of the best kind, were kept clean and neat to the last. I could mention some instances of white lepers being attended with equal care; and I never heard that their attendants suffered by this, their humane conduct.

I do not, at present, *perfectly* recollect any other acts of murder and shocking barbarity, which fell within my own observation, or which I deem *sufficiently* authenticated; but, to say the truth, the murder of slaves is an occurrence which but too often happens in Barbadoes; and unless it has been attended with circumstances of uncommon barbarity, is seldom heard of, beyond the little district where it happens. No coroner's inquest sits on the body of a slave; nor is any legal inquiry made into his murder, unless at the instance of his owner; but even this does not always take place; for the proof of such deeds is *peculiarly difficult*.

As I shall not swell this catalogue with deeds for which I have no better evidence than general report; or indistinct recollection; so neither shall I attempt the impracticable task of enumerating the endless instances, not of *actual*, perhaps, but of *virtual*, murder, by hunger, severity and oppression, which spread a caliginous shade on the annals of slavery, in the island of Barbadoes. This last species of murder is *very far* from being peculiar to that island; but, in all ages and nations, ever has been, and ever will be, the necessary consequence of human creatures being reduced to the condition of brutes, by holding all that is dear to them on the base and accursed tenure of unqualified personal bondage.

It may be said, there are *laws* for the punishment of such enormities, as we have been describing. That laws may have been enacted in Barbadoes, for preventing

venting or limiting the abuse of the owner's *exorbitant* power, I do not mean to deny; but, I affirm that they lie, in a great measure, dormant;* and are very far from being generally and rigorously inforced. Men are sometimes punished, in this country, for cruelty to brutes; but I am sorry to say I know of no instance of an owner having been even prosecuted for abusing his slave. But no laws can reach the nameless and endless injuries which the blacks very often suffer from miscreant white men, against whom *their evidence is not, in any shape, admitted*. Many of the numerous, poor whites, in Barbadoes, whom we shall, hereafter, describe, are totally ignorant and regardless of all laws human and divine. ' Misera est ser-
' vitus, ubi jus est incertum, incognitum aut iniquum.'

It has been affirmed that an owner's regard to his interest, independent of the law, will effectually prevent him from abusing his slave; and so it might, were there no other principle of action in man. But a *regard to interest* must be a very strong principle in *both* parties, or their *angry passions* must be very weak, if the effect ascribed to the former be always produced. If interest restrain the owner from severity, it will *more* powerfully restrain the slave from inducing that severity; since, to sleep in a sound skin, is still more the interest of the latter than of the former. Whence, then, the complaints of the slaves provocations? Post-horses and sand-asses, though, they have no passions which ought to provoke men, are often worn out by oppression: Yet it is their owner's interest to preserve their lives, as forming a very great proportion of his property. If a regard to interest prevent not the gamester, the drunkard or the sensualist from ruining their fortunes, why is it expected to work such wonders in defence of the slave, who, sometimes, may fall into the hands of a man who unites all these characters; for, in every country, such men are to be found? These arguments will prove to others the futility of this principle. From long observation, I am convinced that the owner's regard to his interest is, *by no means*, a *sufficient* barrier against his tyranny, especially when provoked.

* ' *If slaves were treated with more humanity than they* GENERALLY *are*,
' and the *laws* of this island, for the ordering and governing of them,
' were duly put in execution, they might be rendered very useful as well as
' valuable.' Hall's Laws of Barbadoes, *note* at the end of No. 82.

But

But I do not affirm that it is no check, or that, on some owners, it may not be an effectual check.—Those who are called *life negroes* sometimes experience the melancholy consequences of their present possessor not being much interested in their welfare. A bad man, who is to hold a set of negroes, for example, only during the life of an infirm wife, may be suspected of not being very anxious for their preservation.† The miserable lot of such slaves is universally considered as the very worst condition in which they can be situated. But for the *laws* and *customs* of their country, *British apprentices* would too often be as ill used as life-negroes; for human nature is every where, nearly the same.

I have the honour to be, &c.

LETTER VI.

SIR,

I Shall, now, with all possible candour and impartiality, give a *general sketch* of the character of the whites in Barbadoes; with respect to humanity and its contrary.

The *ladies*, as will naturally be supposed, deserve the first place on the side of humanity—a virtue which many of them carry to an excess, which is not only troublesome to their husbands, but really injurious to their slaves. To the humanizing influence of the softer sex, who are proportionably far more numerous in Barbadoes than in any other British colony, the negroes are undoubtedly indebted, in a great measure, for the superior lenity they experience in that island. But humanity is not the only amiable trait in the character of the Barbadian ladies. Their œconomy, sobriety, fidelity and attachment to their husbands deserve much praise. They would suspect me

† ' Tenants for life, or dower wilfully destroying or disabling such negroes, to pay *treble* their value to the party In reversion.' Laws of Barbadoes, No. 117, cl. 18. But slaves may be harrassed a thousand ways without *immediately* disabling or destroying them; and when they are so disabled or destroyed, *the perpetrator remains to be convicted!!*

of flattery, were I to exempt them from the common failings of their sex—affectation—a preference of frivolous men and frivolous accomplishments, and a little indulgence in scandal, that bane of every small community.—Gentlemen of the learned professions, in point of humanity, are scarcely inferior to the ladies.—The inhabitants of the towns may, in general, be said to be humane. Many of them, indeed, treat their domestics with a degree of indulgence, which, in their present uncultivated state (for the foppish dress of the black beaux and belles does not constitute cultivation) they are in general but ill able to bear, and which they very often abuse. Hence, the fiddling, dancing, drinking, gambling, and the consequent quarrels, thefts and burglaries, which, every night, more or less, disturb the peace, and prey on the property of the inhabitants of Bridge-town.—Many of the independent owners of plantations justly deserve places, and some of them eminent places, on the side of humanity. I said *independent*; since, without independence, an owner's humanity is likely to be little felt by his slaves. The quantity, quality and price of the provisions which a planter, who is indebted to his town-agent, can procure, depend almost solely on the will and good pleasure of the latter. Should the poor planter complain, the levying of an execution, or the foreclosing of a mortgage, are arguments powerful to silence him. I need not add, that, besides their inability to provide properly for their slaves, owners, whose affairs are involved, are under strong temptations to over-work them, in order to get out of debt.

The proportion of humane country people who are not, like the town's people, subjected, in a body, to the view, it is impossible to ascertain. Some managers are of the middling and the better sorts of people, others of a class which we shall presently sketch; and a few gentlemen of good education and in easy circumstances, exercise that profession. These last may naturally be supposed to be the most distinguished for humanity; especially as they can live independent of their employment, as managers. But where a man's bread depends solely on that employment, he must, of course, accommodate his conduct, towards the slaves, more to the will of his employer than to his own; and where his continuance in place depends, as it too often does, on that first of all objects, large crops, the

slave

slave will suffer hardship from a hand which reluctantly imposes it.

With respect to white inhabitants, Barbadoes is *peculiarly* circumstanced. The lands in that island were originally cleared and cultivated by bond-servants of that description. This circumstance accounts for Barbadoes having even at this day, a far greater proportion of whites than any other European settlement in the West Indies. In 1676, it contained about 50,000 whites,* a great part of whom have since emigrated; but, before the great hurricane in 1780, the whites were still computed at 22,000,† a population, *of itself,* proportionably greater than that of Britain in the ratio of 97 to 90.‡ To this number of whites, the business of the plantations, now cultivated by negroes, cannot give employment; there being no departments for them to fill, except those of manager, book-keeper, distiller and driver. As every plantation however, must send, or ought to send, its proportion of whites into the militia, many of them are still retained on the estates, where they obtain a very scanty subsistence by cultivating, *with their own hands,* little odd skirts of land which they hold as *tenants,* by this kind of

---

* See the History of the European Settlements in America, vol. 2. p. 87.

† One of the causes of depopulation assigned by Dr. Franklin, is *The Introduction of Slaves.* ‘The negroes brought into the English sugar ‘ islands, have greatly diminished the whites there. The poor are by this ‘ means, deprived of employment, while a few families acquire vast ‘ estates, which they spend on foreign luxuries; and educating their ‘ children in the habit of those luxuries, the same income is needed for ‘ the support of one, that might have maintained one hundred. The ‘ whites who have slaves, not labouring, are enfeebled, and therefore ‘ not so generally prolific; the *slaves,* being *worked too hard, and ill fed,* ‘ *their constitutions are broken, and the deaths among them are more than the* ‘ *births; so that a continual supply is needed from Africa.* The northern ‘ colonies having few slaves, increase in whites. Slaves also pejorate ‘ the families that use them; the white children become proud, dis- ‘ gusted with labour, and being educated in idleness, are rendered unfit ‘ to get a living by industry.' Thoughts on the Peopling of Countries.

‡ The area of Barbadoes, according to Guthrie, or rather Templeman, is 140 square miles, equal to that of the Isle of Wight; but Mayo, in his map, makes it, I think, 106,000 acres, or 165 5-8ths square miles, which I adopt, as being, probably, more accurate. Great Britain, on an area of about 77,200 square miles, is computed to contain about 9,000,000 of people. I have just seen a map of Europe, which makes the area of Great Britain nearly 100,000 square miles; but from what authority I cannot tell.

military

military tenure. *That all the lands in Barbadoes originally were, and that parts of them still are, cultivated by* WHITES, are circumstances the more worthy of attention, as it has been boldly asserted, that white men cannot stand field-labour in the West-Indies. In the sequel, it will appear, that, in case of the abolition of the slave-trade, there will be no necessity whatever to substitute white hands for black ones, in planting the sugar-cane; yet, did such necessity exist, I do not see why temperate, seasoned white men might not perform that labour, in the *open fields*, which, in Barbadoes, they often do perform among bushes in the sides of gullies and other rough ground where they are exposed to the scorching sun, without having much refreshment from the cooling breeze.— Why cannot white field-labourers stand the climate, as well as sailors, house, mill and ship-carpenters, plumbers, copper-smiths, black-smiths, brick-layers, and masons of that colour? The fact is, that, in Barbadoes many whites *of both sexes*, till the ground, without any assistance from negroes, and poor white-women often walk many miles loaded with the produce of their little spots, which they exchange in the towns for such European goods as they can afford to purchase.—The rest of the poor whites subsist by fishing, by the mechanic employments just mentioned, or by keeping little retail-shops; and some of these last make a practice of buying stolen goods from the negroes, whom they encourage to plunder their owners, of every thing that is portable.

Many of the poor whites are disposed to take, and too many of them do take, every advantage over the negroes which the laws* leave in their power. Some of them too much depend, for a subsistence, on robbing the slaves of, or, at least, taking, at their own prices, the trifling commodities the poor things may be carrying to market, or, by seizing and *illegally* converting to their own use, articles of greater value which the slaves may have purloined from their owners. Should a slave struggle, as he often will, to retain the disputed article, a beating is, sometimes, added to the *robbery*, as it is justly called, by the better sort of people. For such usage the party injured has no redress, for he often dares not complain to his

* See Hall's Laws of Barbadoes, No. 264. cl. 3.

owner, and, when he does, the fact remains *to be proved*. Thus a poor field-negro, after having travelled eight or ten miles, on Sunday, is frequently robbed, by some town-plunderer, within a short distance of his (or her) market, and returns home, fatigued by the journey, and chagrined from having lost a precious day's labour, and, perhaps, the fruits of his address, on the foregoing night. To me it has often been matter of astonishment, that white men are so seldom knocked on the head, in consequence of injuries so intolerable. I have heard both owners and managers regret that slaves are so much in the power of ill-disposed whites, in this very respect, and humanely consider the theft of a few canes, a *bottom* of sugar, &c. as a venial kind of trespass, which they were often to expect; adding, that even when the article stolen was more considerable, as a *pot* of sugar, a jar of rum or melasses, &c. they much rather wished that the slave should have the use of it, than a worthless white man. I am inclined to think that this is almost the only evil which the slaves in Barbadoes suffer in a greater degree, than those in the other islands, owing to the greater number of poor whites with which that island abounds: nor do I see how on the present system of things, this sore grievance can be remedied.

In consequence of this redundancy of white men, in Barbadoes, their wages, as servants on plantations (and, indeed, as clerks in the towns) are pitifully low; and are, sometimes, paid in indifferent produce, charged to them at a price which their creditors cannot allow, when they take such produce in payment for the coarse clothes, which the poor fellows may have taken up, at a price, proportioned to the distance and uncertainty of the payment. Their diet, in general, is both coarse and scanty, so scanty, indeed, that, in order to get victuals, they are, sometimes obliged to connive at the villainies of the principal negroes on the estates. Hence some of the book-keepers, distillers and drivers become worthless and abandoned; and, in truth, as unworthy of trust as the negroes themselves.

It cannot be expected that men thus treated should, in general, be distinguished for humanity; but their want of that virtue is the less felt by the slaves, as the former are always under the immediate controul of the owners or managers.

managers.—When such men become managers, which they sometimes do, we may easily guess what use they will make of the exorbitant, or, at least, the very ample powers annexed to that station. Indeed they, sometimes, lose their employment, merely on account of their severity. It is also true, that the negroes, if they dislike a manager, though, perhaps, without any good reason, sometimes teize and harrass him, till they provoke him to treat them with severity; and then they run with complaints to the attorney or the owner, who, perhaps, is more to blame than either, by putting it out of the manager's power to feed the people well, and to work them moderately.

Thus, Sir, in some instances, the ill treatment of the slave is owing to the inhumanity or ill temper of the manager; or, in some degree, to those of the driver; in others to the inhumanity, parsimony or straitened circumstances of the owner; in others, again, to the perverseness of the slave himself, who, it must be remembered, is *not paid* for the labour which he is *compelled by stripes* to undergo. When all these causes are combined, which, from the nature of the thing, cannot but, sometimes, happen, the slave must be completely wretched, and every person concerned in his treatment, unhappy.

From the preceding facts and observations, we may draw this general conclusion, which may, afterwards, be useful to us in our reasonings: *That all possible cases of ill treatment result, either mediately or immediately, from the* REPUGNANCY *(for it cannot properly be called a relation) which necessarily subsists between those natural enemies* OWNER *and* SLAVE. 'This, (says Locke,*) is the perfect con-
' dition of *slavery*, which is nothing else but *the state of*
' *war continued*, between a lawful conqueror and a cap-
' tive.'

On the other hand, it is perhaps equally certain, That, in countries where the greatest part of the inhabitants are in a state of absolute, unconditional slavery, the little protection and happiness which the slaves enjoy, must be owing more to the lenity, good sense and spirit of particular owners than to any protecting laws which can be devised to bind such communities. Laws framed by *owners* (espe-

---

* On Government, b. 2. ch. 4.

cially

cially by owners who are greatly out-numbered by their slaves) must, at best, be easily eluded, partial if not oppressive in their nature, and feeble in their operation. All history bears witness to these truths, at the same time, that they are, with demonstrative evidence, deducible from the constitution of the human mind. 'According to an-'cient practice,' says Hume, '*all checks* were on the *in-*'*ferior*, to restrain him to the duty of *submission: none* 'on the *superior*, to restrain him to the *reciprocal* duties 'of gentleness and *humanity*.'* He might have extended this observation to the colonies of some modern European states, of the slave-laws, of which, we may truly say,

——— Humana *malignas*
Cura dedit leges.   Ovid.

We have seen how the white servants and the slaves, in general, are treated in Barbadoes. There are no *bond-servants* now in that island. The last, I believe, who were sold there, were a few of the deluded people, whose lives were justly forfeited, to the laws of their country, in 1745. One of them still survives; and it will not be foreign to my subject to mention what I heard of his history.—His master having understood that the highlanders could not properly be called freemen, in their own country, took it for granted, that they were slaves, in the same sense with the negroes in Barbadoes; for it is probable that he could not distinguish between an oppressive and usurped domination, and a patriarchal kind of dominion which though, like all other species of arbitrary power, it was often abused, and therefore was deservedly abolished, was yet founded on ancient custom, and, on the whole, was agreeable, if not, perhaps, flattering, to the prejudices of the people. He, accordingly, treated the man with great severity; and, at last, proceeded to such excesses, that the blood of the highlander was roused, and he proceeded to equal excesses, in his turn. His master, finding his servitude altogether unprofitable, and that he was not to be reformed by stripes and chains, gave him his freedom. How he afterwards subsisted, I know not; but he has for some years lodged in the poor-house in Bridge-town, totally blind and superannuated. He is at no loss for food in that hospitable place; but people are

* Essay on the Populousness of Ancient Nations.

too apt to give him money and strong drink, with which, I imagine, he was always accustomed to besot himself. His countrymen are at no other expence with him than giving him his dinner, on the anniversary of their tutelar Saint.* His companions, I heard, were very well treated, and probably deserved good treatment better than he did; for I have reason to think his temper was always obstinate, and, like the temper of most Britons, peculiarly unadapted for a state of slavery.

Kenneth Morrison, a poor, but unoffending, highlander, was reduced to the hard necessity of indenting himself to the master of a West Indian ship, who sold him, as a bond-servant, in Barbadoes, many years ago. He was treated with great cruelty, and, in particular, was let down into an old well, as a place of confinement. Luckily he was able to prove this fact; and sued for and obtained his freedom. Having been a good scholar and a sober man, he commenced teacher; and, in that capacity, was so fortunate as to attract the notice of the Governor (I think, Governor Grenville) who discovered his merit, sent him home for holy orders, and gave him a parish. Having arrived at a respectable station, he did not forget that excellent maxim, 'Non ignarus mali, miseris succurrere disco.' 'He had suffered persecution, and had learned mercy.'† Obtaining a place in the commission of the peace, he distinguished himself by a spirited, inflexible adherence to justice, and 'respected not persons in judgment;' a conduct which, in most countries, will be more applauded by the *poor* than by the *rich*. Mr. Morrison was many years rector of St. James's parish; and died, eight or nine years ago, much regretted, especially by the indigent and the unprotected.

I have the honour to be, &c.

* The English, Scotch, and Irish have societies for the relief of their poor countrymen, which were particularly useful to many distressed seafaring men during the late war. The writer of these letters had the honour to be box-keeper or treasurer to one of those societies, when he left Barbadoes—a circumstance which he does not mention out of vanity; but he thinks the public ought to know that the person who now addresses them was deemed worthy of confidence, in that, as well as in a department of greater importance.

† Sterne.

LETTER

LETTER VII.

SIR,

HAVING given a free, but a candid and impartial, sketch of the general condition of the slaves, and of the character of the whites, so far as it is concerned in the present subject, I should now proceed to a more pleasing task, that of paying my little tribute of just applause to the virtues of some worthy individuals. But *unnecessary* personal allusions of any kind may justly be considered as entirely foreign to a subject of this public nature, not to mention the tendency they have to awaken detraction*; to which, however, the characters I now have chiefly in view may bid defiance. Suffice it, therefore to say, that there are gentlemen residing chiefly or entirely in Barbadoes, who study to make their slaves happy—as happy as is compatible with their present *debased state*—a state, however, from which one or two worthy persons are endeavouring to raise them; and, I have been told, with a promising degree of success. A few gentlemen of Barbadoes, who reside constantly in England, and whom universal fame allows to possess the most consummate good-

---

* All small communities are, more or less, infested with slanderers. In Barbadoes, such persons do not always content themselves with *whispering* defamation; but I have known the two presses teem, for months together, not with political, only, but with indecent and virulent, personal invective. This assertion and several others I have advanced, I could support, *if necessary*, by extracts from a collection of Barbadoes papers, now in my hands. I have no personal cause to complain of the anonymous writers of Barbadoes, having never been once so much as alluded to by them. But I always detested the practice of scribbling in newspapers, on any other, at least, than general subjects. In no newspaper, did I ever make even the remotest personal allusion, except, in a piece signed *Octavius*, in the Barbadoes Mercury, of November 13th 1784. That piece was intended to place in the proper point of view the character of a respectable gentleman of the Island who possesses good qualities, which he in vain endeavours to conceal, and who had been rather lightly indeed, than injuriously treated, by one of those scribblers. ——*Octavius* never was answered.——

Magna est VERITAS *et* PRÆVALEBIT!!

ness

ness of heart, take care that their estates be supplied with proper stores of all kinds. I have always understood that the managers of those gentlemen have it in their power, and are *strictly ordered* to treat the slaves humanely.

But, Sir, there is some reason to think, that many worthy Planters who reside in this country, do not know every thing that passes on their estates, in the West Indies; but this I know, that an apprentice to one of the eminently humane gentlemen I allude to, was almost killed with downright drudgery; and was so much pinched in his food, that his father, who was well able to maintain him, and who lived at the distance of three miles, was obliged to send daily supplies of dressed victuals for him and his fellow-'prentice, a youth from this country. For this ill treatment, I am confident, the manager *alone* was blameable; for, during the first years of his apprenticeship, the lad made no complaints, having, at that time, had no reason to find fault with his treatment. The plantation was then superintended by a gentleman, who never had it in his nature to treat any human being ill. I have since heard the young man say, that he was then treated with a fatherly attention; and particularly that he often dined at the gentleman's table. This worthy person gave up the management, I think, on account of his advanced age; and was succeeded by a young tyrant, who not only harrassed and starved, but often *horse-whipt* the youth, (for it is unlawful to beat a white apprentice with a *cow-skin*) after he had attained his eighteenth or nineteenth year, was near six feet tall, and knew his business well. When decent, well educated, white apprentices were thus treated, it is easy to guess what the negroes suffered. Indeed I have heard, and I believe, that he ruled them with a rod of iron; and, particularly that, while a batchelor, he, sometimes, treated some of the young wenches ill, for no other reason, but because they refused to submit to his lust.

Vice serves as a foil to illustrate virtue. By way of compensation to the inhabitants of Barbadoes, for having stigmatized an individual of their number, I must beg leave, Sir, to deviate a little farther from my plan, while I commemorate the virtues of the most respectable, I may well say *venerable*, West Indian gentleman, I ever had

the

the honour of knowing. The person I allude to, was the late HENRY BISHOP, Esq. who was generally known by the name of *the old Gentleman* in Speights.—The excellent education he gave his children bear witness to his parental care. As a guardian, I have repeatedly heard his praises celebrated. As an *owner*, he was indulgent, even to a fault; for a fault there certainly is, in excessive indulgence to *slaves*. On their complaining of the severity of any of his managers, I have heard him speak to his man of business to this effect, 'Write to that fellow to take care what he does; for 'I will not suffer him, or any man, to abuse my people.' When any barbarous deed was mentioned in his hearing, Mr. B. would openly exclaim, 'The scoundrel ought to 'be hanged!!' Such, I remember, was his indignant language, on seeing three wretches carried past his door, who were chained together, and had been most barbarously whipt, and brutally treated by their owner, who, by his cruelty, has since rapidly reduced himself to beggary. It is not wonderful that such a man should be hated by all, and both hated and feared by most, of those whose praise would be dishonour. Some cowardly miscreant, whom, no doubt, Mr. B's. freedom had offended, one night, fired a musket loaded with ball, into the apartment, where he slept. Though Mr. B. had, in the earlier part of his life, carried on a very great trade with the Americans, he was a declared enemy to their cause; and, from principle and conviction, was most firmly and conscientiously attached to his Sovereign and to this country—a sentiment, indeed, in which Mr. B. was, by no means, singular. I well remember, his sending (by a person who had lived with him about five and thirty years) to the commanders in chief of the fleet and army in America, each a hogshead of his best old rum, to drink success to the British arms.—These few loose anecdotes, which I know to be true, will give a juster idea than a laboured, fulsome panegyric, of the character of a man who did honour to the island of Barbadoes, and who would have done honour to any country. Such, Sir, are the very terms in which I have, more than once, heard Mr. B. mentioned by a certain honourable and worthy person, now deceased,—an honest man and a faithful, well informed servant and Representative of his

Sovereign,

Sovereign; whose praise was, on every account, estimable; and, it is well known, that he never descended to the meanness of flattery.—Mr. B. died, much regretted, by every good man, who had the honour of his acquaintance, in the year 1781, aged 83.

His funeral sermon, preached by a certain learned, diligent and worthy clergyman, who, in the discharge of his duty, never gave 'flattering titles unto man,' was one of the very few discourses of the kind to which I have listened with satisfaction.

Some account of the late Joseph Callender, a humane, sensible, placid and facetious old Quaker, ought to follow that of Mr. B. whose constant companion he was, for a series of years; and who did himself infinite credit by the choice of such a friend. But I have already too much receded from my plan. I must observe, however, that J. C. has often told me, that though he had spent a long life in Barbadoes, he never was molested, in any manner, by a negro!

I dare appeal, Sir, to every good man in the island of Barbadoes, whether, in these instances, I have aimed at deceiving the living, out of respect for the dead.

I have the honour to be, &c.

LETTER VIII.

SIR,

I NEED not inform you—that more of our words and phrases than men generally suppose are loose, unmeaning, and indefinite; and—that education engrafts on the human mind *prejudices* which the most acute philosophers have not always been able to distinguish from original *principles* in our nature. In this subject, we have examples of, as well as exceptions from, these positions.

Of loose indefinite words and phrases we have but too many examples; for most of the controversies which in all ages have perplexed and tormented mankind, are founded on them. Thus when we say, A Spaniard, or any other subject of an absolute monarchy, is a slave, and, A negro, in the West Indies, is a slave, we make two very different affirmations, arising from the very different senses of the word *slave*. The master of a servant or apprentice differs so entirely from the master of a slave, that, knowing how apt men are to be misled by loose, popular terms, we choose, in these letters, to write OWNER and *slave* * rather than *master and slave* †. Again, mercy to a horse differs from mercy to a man; and I sincerely wish, there was not a similar difference between humanity to a slave, in a country of slavery, and humanity to a freeman in a free country. Those punishments would be accounted cruel, in this kingdom (at least if *arbitrarily* inflicted) which pass, in the West Indies, for nothing more than ordinary discipline.

The advocates for a bad cause, in order to make ' the ' worse appear the better reason,' are often forced to avail themselves of the imperfection of language we are speaking of. Thus, when the apologists for slavery assert, that the negro-slaves in the West Indies are not in a worse condition than the poor in England, they plainly can mean, by the word *slave*, nothing more than what is commonly meant by the word *drudge*, or a person who toils hard, and lives on a poor diet. The great Locke, who was well accustomed to resolve complex into their component simple ideas did not confound those terms. 'I con-' fess,' says he, ' we find among the Jews, as well as ' other nations, that men did sell themselves; but, it is ' plain, this was only to *drudgery*, not to *slavery*‡.' Nor has that able and accurate reasoner, Dr. A. Smith, confounded them. ' The Blacks, says he, ' who make the

---

* OWNER and *slave*, expressing the property the former absurdly claims in the person of the latter. For the derivation of the word *slave*, see the History of the Decline and Fall of the Roman Empire, vol. 5, p. 543.

† ' The *odious* names of *master* and *slave*, the most *mortifying* and *depres-* ' *sing* of all distinctions to human nature, were abolished.' History of Charles V. vol. 1. p. 49. The benign spirit of Christianity effected this great change. For an excellent account of the manner in which our religion operated on the manners, the opinions and the civil rights of the Europeans, see vol. 1. p. 321. of the same admirable work. Consult also the Spirit of Laws, b. 24. ch. 3, 4, &c.

‡ On Government, B. 2. ch. 4.

greater

" greater part of the inhabitants both of the southern
" colonies upon the continent, and of the West India
" islands, *as they are in a state of slavery*, are, no doubt,
" in a *worse condition* than the *poorest people either in Scot-*
" *land or Ireland.* We must not, however, upon that
" account, imagine that they are *worse fed.*'† But, by
the way, Sir, had Dr. A. Smith ever seen the treatment of
the slaves, he would have said, That, in proportion to
their labour at least, they are often much worse fed than
any set of people in these kingdoms.

The labouring poor in England, it hath been said, are
slaves to *necessity*. If this be the blind metaphysical quid-
dity which hath caused so much wrangling in the schools,
then our adversaries mistake their men, for (some) English
philosophers, not English peasants, are enslaved by it. If
that necessity be meant, which binds man to his social
duties, then, I apprehend, the monarch on the throne is
as much subjected to it as the peasant at the plough-tail.
If by necessity be understood, that law which said, ' In
' the sweat of thy face, shalt thou eat bread,' then the
English peasant has the comfort to know that this merciful doom is not confined to him alone, but extends to
every husbandman and manufacturer in the world.—The
British poor, like the poor in all countries, certainly do
suffer hardships, some of which are *unavoidable*, and others
the effects of their *own vices*; but both must be carefully
distinguished from those more galling miseries which proceed from the *usurped and abused power of tyrants.* In
common, too, with all their species, from the prince to
the beggar, they feel ' the heart-ach, and the thousand na-
' tural shocks that flesh is heir to.' Whips and chains and
tortures are *arbitarily* superadded to compleat the wretchedness of the slave. And, Sir, is it nothing to be exemp-
ed from those whips and chains and tortures ? Is it nothing to have property, person and life effectually protected ?

But let us, for a moment, allow, That the condition
of the *English* poor is *not better* than that of negro-slaves;
will it not follow, *a fortiori*, that the condition of the
Scotch and the *Irish* poor is *worse* ? Whence comes it,
then, that miserable Scotland and miserable Ireland, far

† Wealth of Nations, p. 450.

from requiring or receiving any foreign supplies of people, send abroad so many supernumerary inhabitants, and furnish so many thousands and tens of thousands of brave and hardy soldiers and sailors, to stand or fall by the side of the English, in fighting the battles of their country? Thus, on the supposition, that the condition of the West Indian slaves is *as good* as that of the English poor, it must be *better* than that of the poor of the sister kingdoms; and, consequently, supplies of negroes from Africa are so very far from being necessary, that a vast surplus of the blacks might be sent to people some uncultivated region.

But this parallel, though execrable, is interesting. Let us therefore examine it a little more closely. Had it been fairly drawn, house-negroes in the West Indies, would have been compared to domestic servants, in this country; artificers to artificers; and field-negroes to peasants. With respect to food and clothes, I readily allow that the first classes are as nearly on a level, as they can be, in countries so different; and, from a house-negro, not a fourth part of the easy business of a family is exacted, that an English servant performs. But can an English servant be flogged, or hampered in irons, at the pleasure of his master? Can he be turned out to be loaded with dung, or to dig in the field, with a cow-skin smacking behind him? I do not say, that house negroes, in general, experience such vicissitudes; for very many of them never dug a cane hole, or received a severe stripe, in their lives; but such vicissitudes, *all* of them are liable to experience. —The condition of the black artificers approaches, in a general way, to that of white ones in this country, allowing, as before, for the effects of caprice and tyranny. Here the artificer, though he works, incomparably harder, has greatly the advantage of the house-negro; for he is very often let out, and those who hire artificers do not punish them, unless they be very worthless, and then, they do it by the owner's authority.—Between the field-negro and the British peasant, God forbid the comparison should hold good. Say, the latter works harder if you will, and lives as poorly as the former; still, thank Heaven! he suffers not half the miseries of slavery.—The peasant can chuse or change his employer; the negro is enslaved for life.—The peasant *rests*; the slave *labours* on Sundays.—

Bad

Bad weather and the long winter evenings give the peasant some respite from the hardest parts of his toil; the negro drudges almost incessantly.—The peasant's family cannot be separated from him; that of the negro, alas! is often scattered to the four winds.—The peasant may defend his person against any aggressor; at the negro's peril, does he lift his hand against the meanest white man, who may chuse, in the absence of whites, to attack him.—The persons and the chastity of the peasant's wife and daughter are most effectually guarded from violence. —Before the negroe's face, whenever his owner or manager thinks fit, his wife or daughter may be exposed naked and scourged by the ruthless hand of a driver: and will it be affirmed that their chastity is never violated with absolute impunity?—The peasant's evidence is good, and the laws protect his life, as well as that of the first nobleman in the kingdom; the evidence of the negro is not admitted against a white man, and, for this reason *alone*, were there no other, the laws do not, cannot protect him.—In two *significant* words, the peasant is a FREEMAN; the negro is a SLAVE.—In sickness, or old age, I own, and the many anxious cares attendant on a provision for them, the case of the former is often more pitiable than that of the latter, under a humane and independent owner; but we have seen that all owners are not independent, and have lamented that, to aged and infirm slaves, they are not, always, humane.

Let no man say, I attempt to explain away the miseries of the poor in this country. I have only proved that, on the whole, their condition is far more eligible than that of West Indian slaves, in general, is. *In general*, I say; for, unless the parallel will hold generally, I see no end it can answer, but to mislead the public; if, indeed, any man of common sense can be made to believe so incredible an assertion.

To what purpose have the valiant British nations steadily persevered, for centuries together, in vindicating their invaluable rights—the sacred rights of men?—to what purpose have they nobly fought and bled, and several times hardily wrested the iron rod out of the fell grasp of grim tyrants?—with what propriety, can they be said to have obtained and to enjoy advantages above every nation

tion under Heaven; if, after all their heroic exertions, their condition be not preferable to that of *negro slaves* ?

Such arguments as the foregoing, I have, sometimes, used in the West Indies; but I little expected ever to feel myself called upon to repel this most daring, most insufferable insult to my country and to her *laws*, in the center of the city of London.

But, in my eagerness to prove what, one might suppose, would need no proof, that the condition of poor, but *free*, peasants, in Britain, is vastly more eligible than that of West Indian *slaves*, I have lost sight of the second position, at the beginning of this letter, That the prejudices arising from education are, sometimes so strong as to be mistaken for principles impressed by the hand of nature. From that position, it would seem to follow that an education in a land of slavery, and the domination which, from their infancy, the West Indians are accustomed to exercise over their slaves, will totally eradicate the tender feelings of the heart, and render them *peculiarly* tyrannical and cruel. This inference, like several other plausible inferences, in our subject, is, by no means, just. Not to mention, that the higher ranks of the Barbadians are generally educated in England, it is not true, that, *from their infancy*, they are accustomed to domineer over the negroes. Even the meanest Barbadians are brought up with very high ideas of the superiority and prerogatives of white men; but the children (of the better sort especially) are not allowed to shew them by any acts of cruelty; at least, I never heard of, nor observed, any instance of this kind, worthy of notice; and I had the best opportunities for making the observation. Europeans, of whom, it is true, there is but a small proportion in Barbadoes, always appeared to me to be fully as severe owners as West Indians. These last are very far from being more severe, than any other men would be, if invested with the same unlimited power. The slave, perhaps, has been born on the same estate, or even under the same roof, with his West Indian owner; has, probably, been fed with the remnants of the same board; or may have been the humble companion or the faithful attendant of his childhood and youth; and, above all, the West Indian has been familiarized with the perverseness, thievishness and negligence of *slaves*. On the humanity

of

of the European the wretch cannot plead such claims; and he who, in his own country, was accustomed, either to command with gentleness, or to obey with alacrity, is not prepared to bear the perpetual provocations of *slaves* with the patience of a stoic.

But, Sir, absolute power ever has been, and ever will be abused. It is well known that *apprentices*, though the power of their masters is very far from being absolute, but is limited by the impending terrors of the law, are often ill-treated in every great town in Britain; and, particularly, that the *climbing-boys*, among the chimney-sweeps are very cruelly treated, *even in this metropolis*, an evil which, it is said, will shortly engage the attention of the legislature. If *apprentices* are ill treated *in London*, are we to wonder that *negro slaves* are ill treated, *in the West Indies?* Farther, free negroes are generally more severe, because less enlightened, owners, than white people; black drivers are known to be more rigorous than white ones; negro children often suffer severely under the lash of their mothers; dogs under that of watchmen; and draught cattle under that of black carters. Mareschal Saxe observed, that, in the quarrels which took place between his baggage-waggoners and their horses, the two-legged animals were always in the wrong. But be it remembered, that the negroes are not passive *brutes*, but *men*, endowed with reason which condemns, and with unconquerable passions which rebel against, servitude; and that those passions are often kept in an unceasing ferment by unrewarded toil and ill usage, and, sometimes roused, even to desperation, by acts of injustice and cruelty. If such be frequently their treatment, is it surprising that slaves should be indocile, stubborn, averse from labour, and regardless of their owner's interest? Such passions are infectious: they fly from the bosom of one slave to those of his fellows; and, as may be expected, by every man who has the least knowledge of human nature, the behaviour of the slaves is often such, that their owners and managers must be more or less than men, to bear their provocation. Hence a frequent conflict between the angry passions of the owner and those of the slave, a conflict in which the former often loses sight of his *interest*, and the latter of his safety.

The cause of the conduct both of owner and slave, which we have been describing, is, by no means, to be looked for in the dispositions of either party as men; but in their repugnancy (for, if it be a relation, it is the relation of the devil and the damned) or in the opposition of their interests and passions, as *owner* and *slave*—a position to which I before referred *all* the ill treatment of the slave; and which, till I see it's fallacy demonstrated, I shall hold to be as certain, as any one principle in moral philosophy.

Thus, Sir, we have no reason to suppose that the white natives of the West Indies are more rigorous owners than Europeans; or that either of them are more rigorous than any other men would be, in the like circumstances.

On the other hand, many, I may say, most, of the Africans, when they first arrive in the West Indies, are as simple and innocent as any country-people in Britain. Most of them learn their villainy, or rather are driven to it, in the West Indies. For, if oppression ' will make ' even a *wise* man mad,' what will be it's effect on the *uncultivated* mind of a negro? Hence we may account, in some measure, for the common and perhaps, partly, just, opinion, that African negroes are more bloody-minded than Creoles; because the spirit of the former has not been so entirely bowed down and crushed under the yoke of slavery, as that of the latter. For what we call *bravery* in an European, our shameful prejudices have no other name than *ferocity* † in an African.—For the other *failings* of the slaves—for unless they, themselves, are wholly blameable for them, they cannot be called *vices*—for their other failings, I say, it is easy to account. They have no *character to support, and are pinched in their food*, therefore they are *thievish*; they are *compelled* to work *without pay*, therefore they are *stubborn*; their *genius and inclination are not consulted*, therefore they are *stupid*; they have *no interest in their own labour*, therefore the are *careless* of its success; *no person consults their ease*, therefore they

---

* ' Forasmuch as the negroes, *and other* SLAVES, brought unto the ' people of this Island, are of *barbarous, wild and savage nature* !! &c.— Laws of Barbadoes, No. 82.

consult

consult it themselves, and are *lazy*. I ask, where is that virtuous people who, if thus treated, would not become thievish, stubborn, stupid, careless and lazy *? By the way, Sir, if the negroes be so much lazier than all other men, as has been pretended, what must be the nature of those punishments which force such beings to work?

But, although I am clearly of opinion, that West Indians are not more rigorous owners than Europeans are, nor Africans more worthless slaves, than Europeans would be; yet I am very far from affirming, that the being bred in a land of slavery has not an irresistible tendency to fix monstrous *prejudices* (I say nothing here of *vices*) in the minds of the mere, ignorant vulgar. The poor whites in Barbadoes have no idea that the blacks are, any way, intitled to the same treatment as white men.—Once, I heard a poor white man affirming that a person, (I think a Moravian) ought to be hanged, for preaching to the negroes. I asked him, if he did not read, in his Bible, that the gospel was to be preached to all mankind? He readily confessed his ignorance of the gospel; but still strenuously insisted, that the man ought to be hanged—for preaching to the negroes. A person (who, I thought, might have known better things) asserted, in conversation with me, that the negroes were a base race, and inferior to the whites—because, forsooth, they had not souls to be saved †; a reason near of kin to that which was urged in

---

* For half his virtues Jove conveys away,
Whom once he dooms to see the *servile* day.
POPE's Hom. Odyss.

† ' *A negro has a soul*, an' please your Honour, said the Corporal
' (doubtingly)—I am not much versed, Corporal, quoth my Uncle Toby,
' in things of that kind; but, I suppose, God would not leave him
' without one, any more than thee or me.—It would be putting one
' sadly over the head of another, quoth the Corporal.—It would so, said
' my Uncle Toby—Why then, an' please your honour, is a *black* wench
' to be *used worse* than a *white* one?—I can give no reason said my Uncle
' Toby—Only, cried the Corporal, shaking his head, because she has no
' one to stand up for her—'Tis that very thing, Trim, quoth my Uncle
' Toby, which recommends her to protection and her brethren with her;
' 'Tis the fortune of war which has put the whip into our hands *now*;
' *where it may be, hereafter, Heaven knows*—but, be it where it will, the
' *brave, Trim, will not use it unkindly*—God forbid, said the Corporal——
' Amen! responded my Uncle Toby, laying his hand upon his heart.—
STERNE.

the fifteenth century, for enslaving them, namely, 'That they had the colour of the damned.' In short, the vulgar, in Barbadoes, are as much convinced that negroes are naturally inferior to men of their own colour, as the vulgar in all countries are, that the sun moves, and that the earth is at rest. Many such vulgar errors, the first principles of the illiterate, might be mentioned; arguments against which may puzzle them, but cannot shake their belief.

The extreme ignorance of many of the poor Barbadian whites, cannot justly be attributed to the want of opportunities of instruction; for there are schools, in every parish, which, I believe, are well attended to; at least, I knew two parochial schools where this was the case; but the poor creatures cannot always spare their children from home, after they become capable of giving them the least assistance in their field-labour. Nor are the clergy blameable for that ignorance. There are, in Barbadoes, eleven beneficed clergymen, some curates, and several more in orders, who are not provided for. In general, they are far from being deficient either in point of learning or exemplary conduct; and they regularly perform divine service in all the eleven churches, besides two or three chapels of ease. Most of the churches are well attended, by the better and middling sort of people, especially by the ladies. The large and elegant church of St. Michael, in Bridgetown (the inside dimensions of which, including chancel and spire, are 136 feet by 60) is better attended, I am sorry to observe, than a great number of *both* the established churches in this kingdom. Several free negroes and some slaves regularly attend divine service. I could mention a family of the former, whose devotion is sometimes the object of what, in the present cant, is called *skit*, in the Barbadoes newspapers. The poor whites very seldom enter a church, except at elections or funerals; and are then, generally, in a state of intoxication.

'Barbadoes is almost the only colony where any tolerable degree of decency is preserved, respecting an established religion; and, though there be *many and grievous defects in its constitution and government*, yet this cir-
'cumstance

'cumſtance gives it conſiderable advantages, in point of
'decency and civilization, above *all the others*, eſpecially,
'the *new* Iſlands.'*

I have the honour to be, &c.

LETTER IX.

'——— *Deus almus, eandem*
'*Omnigenis animam, nil prohibente, dedit.*'
WILLIAMS, vid. tit. pag.

SIR,

WE have, hitherto, proceeded with as much ſecurity on the ſuppoſition, that the Africans are men co-ordinate with ourſelves, as if the apologiſts for ſlavery had not refuſed to grant us any ſuch poſtulatum; or as if they had not called in the joint aid of ſophiſtry and modern metaphyſic to wreſt humanity as well as liberty, from an injured and inſulted race of men. Shame on European pride, avarice, and tyranny, which, by wreathing the chains of ſlavery on their perſons, have ſunk the Africans to, or, at leaſt, have kept them in, a ſtate ſo brutiſh as to give ſanction to a doubt, whether the ſlave and his haughty lord partake of the ſame common nature!!

On this very difficult part of my ſubject, I cannot pretend to offer much that is original, though ſeveral thoughts and arguments I have, which, I think, I may call my own. A narrow plan obliges me to confine, to one letter, a diſcuſſion on which a volume might be written. My brevity is of the leſs importance, as the ſubject has been very fully handled by much abler writers—by Buffon, by Beattie, by Ramſay, by Clarkſon, and lately by a perſon who had uncommonly good opportunities for making obſervations, as well as ability to draw conclu-

* Ramſay's Eſſay on the Treatment, &c. p. 108, Note.

ſions

sions from them *. Are the *doubts* of some philosophers, whose means of information were very much circumscribed, to be put in the scale against the *arguments* and the *facts* of writers, one of whom (Mr. Ramsay) spent a great part of his life, and the other (Dr. Smith) I believe, his whole life, among different tribes of men? The motives of those philosophers for expressing such doubts are well known; but it is highly probable that the humane Voltaire, and the good-natured, benevolent Hume, would not have thrown them out, had they dreamt that their *conjectures* and their *assertions*, would have been magnified into *arguments*, by the apologists for slavery. With all due respect to these, and to some other great modern names, I cannot assent to this their doubt, any more than I can to some of their dogmas. Several of their literary productions are as admirable, as, in my very humble opinion, their philosophical, or rather unphilosophical chimeras are absurd: and, till their followers support the flimsy, tottering fabric of their untenable philosophy with reasonings more accurate and conclusive than any we have yet seen, I shall take leave to consider it, as a

---

* The Rev. Samuel Stanhope Smith, D. D. in ' An Essay on the ' causes of the variety of complexion and figure in the human species, ' printed at Philadelphia in 1787, reprinted at Edinburgh in 1788, with ' additional notes, by a gentleman of the University.' This gentleman is B. S. Barton, member of the Royal Medical Society of Edinburgh, &c. author of a very ingenious and interesting work, entitled ' Observations ' on some parts of natural history, to which is prefixed an account of ' several remarkable vestiges, of an ancient date, which have been dis-' covered in different parts of N. America.' (See Kalm's and Carver's Travels). This last curious account has already appeared, and the rest of the work will shortly be published. One part of it will be, 'An essay towards ' a natural history of the North American Indians,' in which Dr. Barton, from his own observation, will rectify several mistakes, respecting those tribes. He assures me, that Dr. Smith's account of the colour, &c. of the Indians, is perfectly just.——Dr. Smith, in my humble opinion, has, in a very masterly manner, refuted the arguments of Lord Kaimes, to prove that there are different species of men. See prel. disc. to his Lordship's sketches, which, in most other respects, is a valuable work. That a writer of so much ability and humanity should have reasoned so weakly on a subject, which leads, we fee, to such serious consequences, is only to be accounted for, from the well known effects of hypotheses, in misleading the mind. *Knowing*, as I do, how grossly *one* part of mankind have been misrepresented, I humbly think, no man is so fully competent to write on this subject, as he who has *resided* among the people he means to describe, long enough to receive the full and fair impression of their character; and, even then, he ought to be unbiassed by *interest*, or *prejudice*, which are still more unfriendly to mankind than hypotheses.

jumble

jumble of refined sophistry and heterogeneous paradox, which it is impossible for the human understanding (I know it to impossible for my understanding) to reduce to any thing like a consistent whole.

On the present subject, though I am not a match for those writers in argument, still less in the illusive semblance of argument, I may surely say, without vanity, that, in point of information, I have the advantage of them, having seen and *observed* more of the negroes, than any one of them, or, perhaps, than all of them put together. And God forbid, I should be guilty of insulting the wretched and the forlorn, by affirming that any single instance of their behaviour ever gave me the shadow of a reason to doubt of their *natural* equality, both in intellect and sentiment to the Europeans. Sir, I never did observe in them any mark of inferiority which might not very fairly be referred to those most powerful causes *the savage state*, which suffers not the faculties to expand themselves, combined with a *state of slavery* which, it is well known, debases and crushes every power of the human soul. Nay, since *Britons* have been insulted by an execrable comparison of their condition with that of negro *slaves*, I will ask (but without any intention of offending) Wherein the superiority of the poor Barbadian whites, over the negroes, consists? For my own part, though I have been at some pains to satisfy myself, on this disputed point, by purposely mixing with both, and putting their mental faculties to the test of experiment, I declare I never could discover, in the poor, uninstructed whites, any other mark of superiority than the very equivocal one of colour, and some slight differences in figure.

I call colour (the principal difference in the varieties of men) a very equivocal mark of superiority. I cannot tell, Sir, what passes in the minds of other men; but, in my own mind, I never could perceive any connection whatsoever between my idea of *intellect*, and my idea of *colour*. The white man reasons thus, The negro's *colour* is different from mine, *ergo* I am naturally *superior* to the negro. May not a copper-coloured man, or an olive-coloured man, or a tawney man, or a *black* man thus demonstrate the natural superiority of men of *his own* colour, to all others? By such sort of logic, we find the celebrated

Francis

Francis Williams attempting to demonſtrate the ſuperiority of the negro to the mulatto: 'A ſimple white or a ſimple black complexion was reſpectively perfect; but a mulatto, being a heterogeneous medley of both, was *imperfect*, ergo *inferior*.'† I ſuſpect, Sir, that the ideas of intellect and of colour have a mutual dependence in minds which pretend to be ſuperior to that of our black philoſopher.—The whites paint the devil black, and the negroes paint him white; but do ſuch chimeras prove the devil to be either black or white? A man may *aſſociate* his idea of *blackneſs* with his idea of the devil, or with his idea of *ſtupidity*, or with any other of his ideas he thinks proper; but he ought not to reaſon from ſuch arbitrary aſſociations.

The *truly important national* queſtion, which has been ſo long agitated by the Scotch and Iriſh antiquaries, ‡ will help farther to *illuſtrate* my meaning. Set aſide the ſophiſtry of both parties, and ſtrip their arguments to the bare thought; and, then, poſſibly, they may be found to amount to theſe. *My* country, ſays the Scotchman, lies to the *northward* of your's; therefore, *Ireland was peopled from Scotland*. Nay, replies the Iriſhman, but *my* country lies to the *ſouthward* of your's; therefore *Scotland was peopled from Ireland*. Now, what force is there, in theſe arguments, that is not reſolveable into the *prejudices* of the caſuiſts, couched in a *laughable* kind of emphaſis which they are apt to place on the word *my*, when combined with the word *country?* for, where is the connection between the *points of the compaſs* and the *antiquity* of a nation? Or where is the connection between the *colour* of the human ſkin, and the *faculties* of the human mind? And, if it appear, that there is no *connection* or *relation*, of any kind whatever, between ideas which, ſome prejudiced, and weak minds have abſurdly, unaccountably and unphiloſophically *aſſociated*; how, in the name of

† Hiſt. of Jamaica. vol. 2. p. 478.—This argument, abſurd as it is, has more of the appearance of logical connection than any other of the kind, that has been offered on this ſubject.

‡ See the Hiſtory of the Decline and Fall of the Roman Empire, vol. 2. p. 528.

common

common sense, is it possible to infer the one from the other?

Thus I have endeavoured to lay the axe of demonstration to the root of this most monstrous production of diseased imaginations. The same mode of reasoning is evidently applicable to all the other marks of distinction, which have been fondly assumed and confidently pressed upon the public as marks of inferiority in the negroes.

From a connection of ideas so very capricious and chimerical we cannot expect very legitimate consequences. Towards the equator in the eastern,* western, and middle parts of the old world, the human complexion is black; towards the northern extremity of the temperate zone it is white; and, in the intermediate latitudes, gradually verges from each extreme to the opposite, making some allowances for high and low, dry and moist soils, with other causes which act on the complexion, especially for civilization and mode of life, by which it is well known to be greatly influenced. Now, if intellect had any connection with colour, we should find the like gradation in the one as in the other. Thus, since we find the Dane is *fairer* than the Frenchman, we must conclude he is proportionably *more rational*; contrary to what would seem to be the fact, for Denmark has not produced nearly so great a proportion of men of genius as France. But genius—original inventive genius, hath shone in nations of a much darker hue than the French, or than any nation in Europe. Not to mention that the Chaldeans were the first astronomers, let it be remembered that the Ægyptians, who are themselves very dark, and who border on nations perfectly black, first instructed the proud Europeans in the rudiments of geometry; that the Arabians taught them arithmetic and algebra; and that the Indians,

---

* 'The people of Pekin are fair, at Canton, they are nearly black. The Persians, near the Caspian sea, are amongst the fairest people in the world; near the gulph of Ormus, they are of a dark olive. The inhabitants of the stoney and desart Arabia are tawney; while those of Arabia the Happy are as black as the Æthiopians.—The Jews are fair in Britain and Germany, brown in France and in Turkey, swarthy in Portugal and Spain, olive in Syria and in Chaldea, tawney or copper-coloured in Arabia and in Egypt.' Dr. S. S. Smith's Essay, p. 35. See also Buffon's Nat. Hist. vol. 3. Smellie's Transl.

who were also skilled in those sciences, invented the difficult and scientific game of chess.*

Again, if it be just to affirm that the blackest and the fairest nations had different origins, may not the same be as justly affirmed of those of the intermediate shades of colour? Must we not, then, conclude that the swarthy Spaniard and the fair German or Pole are descended from two original human pairs, of their respective complexions? At this rate, we shall have Adams and Eves without number—one pair, at least, for every country. The difficulty will be to find gardens of Eden in some countries, in Labrador, for example, or Lapland, or Kamtschatka.†—

But let us try whether analogy will throw any light on this subject. Hogs, in this country are very often white, and sheep are universally covered with wool. In tropical countries, the former are generally black, the latter have a slight covering of short smooth hair, and the rams in Barbadoes have no horns. No naturalist regards these as specific differences. Why then are the colour, and other peculiarities of the negro, regarded as specific differences?

Most animals are destined for, or, at least, thrive best in, particular climates. Man was intended to assert his dominion over the inferior animals, in all climates. Hence he can roam, with impunity, from the arctic to the anarctic regions, as the voyages of our late great navigator evince. ' Nous verrons evidemment qu'aucun des
' animaux n'a obtenu ce grand privilege; que loin de
' pouvoir se multiplier par tout, la plufpart font bornés
' et confinés dans de certains climats, et meme dans des

---

* Wallis's Algebra, ch. 12.

† — or *Scotland*, say certain *great wits*, whose *patriotic* aim ever has been to *unite* this *divided* kingdom, and whose *brilliant irradiation* have penetrated the gloom even of the western hemisphere. It is certain, nevertheless, that the paradise of that country was at or near *Edinburgh*, as the name plainly imports. To the men of profound *philological indagation* we submit, Whether *Paris* be not a mere contraction of the French word *Paradis*. *Nobis enim verisimile est, nomen proprium* PARIS *a* PARADIS *formari, elidendo, scil. literas* A *et* D. Having thus discovered the Edens of ancient Caledonia, and of her ancient, *great and good* ally, we leave other nations to find out their's.

' contrées

‘ contrées particuliers.'* Man, it will be allowed, is the moſt perfect animal, and his being leſs incommoded by local circumſtances, than moſt other animals, is undoubtedly one of his perfections.—This eaſy accommodation to climate, and the dominion man every where poſſeſſes over other animals, demonſtrate the ſuperiority of his nature. And ought the being who, in Africa, ſubjugates the *elephant*, and hunts the lion and the tiger, to be accounted inferior to him who, in Europe tames the horſe and the ox, and hunts the wolf and the boar?

From the comparatively ſhort experience we have had of the various climates of the earth, we cannot, or, at leaſt, ought not, to decide, with dogmatiſm, on the effects of climate, during a long ſeries of ages. We have ſeldom ſeen climate, and ſavage manners acting together on Europeans in tropical countries. But where thoſe cauſes have been combined, the effects have been very conſiderable. According to Lord Kaimes himſelf, A Portugueze colony, on the coaſt of Congo, in a courſe of time, have degenerated ſo much, that they ſcarce retain the appearance of men.† Another Portugueze ſettlement, in Sierra Leona, and the Spaniards in the torrid zone of America, afford farther proofs of the ſame effect. The former are aſſimilated in figure and complexion to the negroes‡, the latter are become copper-coloured, like the Indians.‖ With reſpect to the Anglo-Americans, ‘ a certain countenance of paleneſs and ſoftneſs (ſays Dr. ‘ S. S. Smith) ſtrikes a traveller from Britain, the mo- ‘ ment he arrives upon our (the North American) ſhore. ‘ A degree of ſallowneſs is viſible to him, which, through ‘ familiarity, hardly attracts our obſervation.—This ef- ‘ fect is more obvious in the middle and, ſtill more, in ‘ the ſouthern than in the northern ſtates.'§ The effects of climate and mode of living in America is farther proved by the whites, who have been captivated by the Indians, in their infancy, and by the Indian children, who

* Buffon Hiſt. Nat. tom xviii. p. 177.
† Sketches of Man, prel. diſc.
‡ Treatiſe on the Trade of Great Britain to Africa, by an African Merchant.
‖ Phil. Tranſ. No. 476. § 4.
§ Dr. S. S. Smith's Eſſay, p. 37.

have been brought up among the whites, and whose colour and features assume a very near resemblance to those of the people among whom they have been educated.*

Upon the whole, Sir, I am, by no means, singular in thinking, That as difference of soil and culture give rise to many varieties of vegetables, those of the potatoe, for example, or the apple; and as very considerable changes are known to be produced on some species of animals, as dogs, horses, sheep, &c. by domestication, climate, and other causes; so the varieties of the human species may be produced by the *slow* but *long continued* and combined operation of soil, climate and mode of living—by *physical* joined with *moral* causes. This doctrine is evidently favoured by the prince of naturalists, Linnæus. ' Afri
' pilos contortuplicatos, quamvis albos, in hoc miratus
' sum, *collatis, imprimis varietatum causis in plantis, et ani-*
' *malium generatione ambigena,* nec tamen quidquam de
' Mauris nigris et albis statui.' †

This opinion of Linnæus, I shall reinforce with an observation of one of the greatest physiologists in Europe: That most animals in their wild state are of a dark colour; and that, when domesticated, they generally assume a lighter hue, and often become perfectly white. Of this we have very striking examples in the duck, the goose, the dunghill fowl, the pigeon, the turkey, the cat, and others, perhaps, which may occur to gentlemen skilled in natural history. Let the apologists for slavery beware, lest they stir up naturalists to investigate this matter with redoubled ardour; for it seems not improbable that the result of their inquiries may be, That the negroes are the aborigines of mankind.

Thus, perhaps, this interesting problem may, one day, be compleatly solved. We may, at last, be able to account for the various colours of men in the old, as well as for their more uniform complexion in the new hemis-

* Of this Dr. Smith gives remarkable instances at p. 93, 94, and his editor Dr. Barton, at p. 39, note.

† Systema Naturæ, edit. 13. This great man, we see, speaks on this subject, with the caution which becomes a philosopher.

phere,

phere,* and for it's general resemblance to that of the Tartar hordes; for the dark complexion of the Samoieds, and the clear brown complexion of the Otaheiteans. But this supposes a knowledge of facts which we are not yet possessed of, a knowledge not to be obtained from the legends of ignorant, credulous, book-making travellers, many of which have been found by the great and justly celebrated philosophers, who, of late years, have explored distant regions, to be false—fables which scarcely deserve a place in the humourous itineraries of Captain Lemuel Gulliver! 'Nothing (says Dr. S. S. Smith, p. 136.) ' can appear more contemptible than philosophers, with ' solemn faces, retailing, like maids and nurses, the sto- ' ries of giants, of tailed men,† of a people without ' teeth, and of some absolutely without necks,' to which, I may add, the Formosan women, who, according to Struys, quoted by Buffon, have beards; and the North American (Indian) men who, if we believe some travellers, are absolutely without them.

It has been suggested, That the negro occupies a place in the scale of being, or forms a link in that chain which connects the white man with the Orang Outang; but, here, Sir, is a chasm, which it is impossible for any *one* link to fill up; and, I am apt to think that the modern manufacturers of systems will have hard work to forge links sufficient in strength and number to connect creatures so widely distant as a human being and a Kakur-

* The complexion of the North American Indians is, by no means so uniform, as has been imagined. ' In travelling from the great lakes ' to Florida or Louisiania, through the Indian nations, there is a visible ' progression in the darkness of their complexion. And, at the councils ' of confederate nations, or, at treaties for terminating an extensive ' war, you often see sachems or warriors of very different hues.' Dr. S. S. Smith's Essay, p. 159. note.

† ' Among these (people of Manilla) some have been seen who had ' tails, four or five inches long, like the islanders mentioned by Ptolemy, Les Voyages de Gemelli Carreri, v. 3, p. 87.——' Mark Paul says, that ' in the kingdom of Lambry, there are men with tails about a palm long ' only.'—Struys expressly declares that (in Formosa) he saw a man with ' a tail more than a foot long.' Les Voyages de Struys, tom. 1. p. 100. ' It appears (says Buffon) that Struys rests on the authority of Mark ' Paul, as Gemelli Carreri does upon that of Ptolemy.' See Smellie's Buffon, v. 3. p. 87, 88, 89.

lacko.

Jacko.* The external resemblance, however, in figure and motion of some of the monkey tribes, to mankind, is a striking and a mortifying resemblance. 'Simia quam 'similis, turpissima bestia, nobis!'‖ This circumstance it is, which misleads superficial observers; for their moral structure is totally different from that of mankind. Indocile, speechless †, and, consequently destitute of the power of abstraction and the moral and religious sense, in real and useful sagacity, they fall much behind the dog and the horse, not to mention what we have been told, of the 'half-reasoning elephant.'‡ The Creator, when he wisely allotted to every animal that portion of those mysterious faculties, instinct and sagacity, which was most proper for their condition, seems not to have impressed, on any being, inferior to man, the least signature of himself. Accordingly some philosophers chuse to characterize mankind by the religious sense, rather than by reason, the former being, in their opinion, the most unequivocal criterion of his nature. 'And God said, Let us 'make man *in our image*,' is the decision of revelation. 'Homo *solus* Deum contemplatur,'§ is the language of philosophy. Now it is certain, That the negroes have a just sense of right and wrong, and make the common moral distinctions, with much acuteness and accuracy.—They may even be said to ' draw a hasty moral ' —a sudden sense of right.'—If they do not, I ask *with*

---

* Linnæus's synonymes of this animal are troglodytes, homo nocturnus, homo sylvestris, *orang outang*, kakurlacko. Buffon's suspicion that Linnæus has confounded the orang outang with the albinoe would appear to be groundless from the passage we quoted at p. 66, '*Afri pilis* ' *quamvis albos*,' &c. *mauris nigris* et *albis*, &c. Perhaps the edition Buffon quoted did not contain this passage. ‖ Ennius.

† Mr. Camper, in Phil. Transf. for 1779, has demonstrated that orang outangs are, from the texture of their organs, inc.. ble of forming speech. See also Dunbar's Essays, p. 203.

‡ The elephant has a small brain. See Sparrman's Voyage to the Cape of Good Hope, vol. 1. p. 319. The skull of a rhinocero contained only a quart of peas, id. vol. 2. p. 106.

§ Linn. Syst. Nat. edit. 13.—Such too is the language even of infidelity. 'To believe invisible, intelligent power, is a stamp set by the 'divine workman on human nature. Nothing dignifies man more than ' to be selected from all the other parts of the creation to bear this ' *image*' (*Moses*'s word) ' of the universal Creator,' Hume's Natural History of Religion.

what

what JUSTICE *the pretended, superior race of men inflict on them* EXEMPLARY *punishments, and, sometimes, doom them to expire by horrible tortures?*—Like other men, too, they believe in, and often appeal to the great God, the acquitter and the avenger, who, they firmly and fondly believe, has prepared for them a better world beyond the grave. Nor, Sir, does either natural or revealed religion, so far, at least, as I understand them, teach us, that even such rude hopes, cherished, in the 'house of bondage,' by innocent, though ignorant, men, will be disappointed; for, to whom little is given, of them little will be required.'

Much stress hath been laid, by certain authors, on this external, and, to hasty observers, illusive, similarity of the Orang Outang to the human species. I, therefore, beg leave to adduce the very *greatest* authority, on this point— an authority in which we ought to acquiesce, till the *fullest* information be obtained, concerning an animal so very scarce, so very shy, and of which so little is known.
' Speciem *Troglodytæ* ab *homine sapiente distinctissimam*,
' nec nostri *generis* nec *sanguinis* esse, statura quamvis
' simillimam, *dubium non est*; ne itaque *varietatem* credas,
' quam sola membrana nictitans *absolutè negat, et manuum*
' *longitudo*.' * The eloquent Buffon too, though he differ from the great master we have just cited, in many particulars, yet agrees with him in this. ' Throwing
' aside therefore, this *ill-described being*, and supposing a
' little *exaggeration*, in the relation of Bontius, concern-
' ing the modesty of his female Orang Outang, there
' only remains a *brute* creature, an *ape*, of which we shall
' find more pointed information, in writers of *better*
' *credit*.' †

To the opinions of these great naturalists, I shall add those of some writers, whose authority, in the literary world, is, at least, as great as that of Voltaire, Hume, Lord Kaimes, or any other supporters of the contrary opinion.

One of the justly celebrated Doctor Johnson's biographers blames him for his prejudices against the inha-

* Linnæl Syst. nat. edit. 13.
† Smellie's Buffon, vol. 8. p. 80.

bitants of the northern parts of this kingdom.—Wherever we turn our eyes on human nature, we are shocked with its vices, or mortified by its imperfections; but that the sublime moralist we are speaking of, should have laboured under a pitiable narrowness of soul, which, far from embracing all mankind, could not find room for these *two*, I wish I could say, these THREE *united kingdoms*, appears to me so incredible, that I would willingly suppose his antipathy was more affected than real. Be this as it may, that prejudice in my opinion was more than compensated by a prejudice of a very different nature: I mean that '*favour to negroes*,' which the prejudiced biographer has thought proper to condemn.* In the Doctor's journal (Easter day 1779) we find him talking, with his black servant, on the sacrament. Would so able an observer of mankind have conversed, on such a subject, with a creature, who, in his opinion, was but a little above an ape, and was not endowed with a rational and immortal soul? If this be called an instance of weakness, it must be allowed to be a most amiable one.

' That a *negro slave*,' says Doctor Beattie, who can
' neither read, nor write, nor speak any European lan-
' guage, who is not permitted to do any thing but what
' his master commands, and who has not a single friend
' on earth; *but is universally considered and treated, as if*
' *he were of a species inferior to the human*;—that such a
' creature should so distinguish himself among *Europeans*,
' as to be talked of through the world as a *man of genius*,
' is surely no reasonable expectation. To suppose him
' of an inferior species, because he does not thus distin-
' guish himself, is just as rational as to suppose any pri-
' vate European of an inferior species, because he has not
' raised himself to the condition of royalty.'†———' It
' would be ridiculous,' says Dr. Ferguson, ' to affirm, as
' a discovery, that the species of the horse was never the
' same with that of the lion; yet, in opposition to what
' has dropped from the pens of eminent writers, we are
' obliged to observe, that men have always appeared
' among animals, a *distinct* and a *superior* race, that nei-

* Sir J. Hawkins's Life of Dr. Johnson, at the end.
† Essay on Truth, p. 462.

' ther

'ther the possession of *similar organs*, nor the approxima-
'tion of *shape*, nor the *use of the hand*, nor the continued
'intercourse with this sovereign artist, have enabled any
'other species to blend their nature with his; that, in
'his *rudest state*, he is found to be *above them*, and, in
'his greatest degeneracy he never descends to their level.
'He is, in short, *a man* in every condition; and we
'can learn *nothing* of his nature from the *analogy* of other
'animals.'*—Nor is the opinion of a writer, who appears to be rising fast into eminence, less favourable to the cause of humanity. 'Europe,' says he 'affects to
'move in another orbit from the rest of the species. She
'is even offended with the idea of a *common descent*; and,
'rather than acknowledge her ancestors to have been
'co-ordinate only to other races of barbarians, and in
'parallel circumstances, she breaks the *unity* of the system,
'and, by *imagining* specific differences, among men,
'precludes or abrogates their common claims. *According to* THIS THEORY, *the oppression or extermination of
'a meaner race will no longer be so shocking to humanity.
'Their distresses will not call upon us so loudly for relief.
'And publick morality and the laws of nations, will be
'confined to a few regions peopled with this more exalt-
'ed species of mankind.'†

But I must not omit a very notable argument against the Africans, from their hair, which is observed to be very different from that of the Europeans. But so is the *short* HAIR of the African sheep, from the *long* WOOL of the European. So is the hair of most rude nations from that of polished ones; and the hair of individuals often differs from that of other individuals of the very same family. The North American Indians and the Tartars anoint their hair; and the negroes, who inhabit climates incomparably warmer, do not anoint it. The hair of the former is long and lank, that of the latter short and curling. That climate, of itself, hath a very considerable effect on the human hair, is evident from that of the Anglo-

* Civil Society. p. 8, 9.

† Dunbar's Essays, p. 161. Surely those are *execrable theories*, which plainly give sanction to the *oppression* or *extermination* of a part of the human race.

Americans; 'for curled locks, so frequent among their ancestors, are rare in the United States.'* The hair of the negroes, with proper care, will grow to no contemptible length, as is evident from the queues of the black beaux and the toupees of the black belles.—But what, I pray, has the hair of the head to do with the intellect? Were the understandings of men to be estimated by the length of that excrescence, who could hope to equal the race of macaronies in intellectual endowments? But their diminutive sticks and their eye-sight, which has been lately so defective as to oblige the youths to wear spectacles, would, perhaps, be more proper measures of their understandings.

I have endeavoured to answer the preceding arguments, in the sense in which, I know, they are taken by the vulgar, in the West Indies; and in which, I suspect, they are understood by persons who rank themselves far above the vulgar, not in the West Indies only, but even in this country. Those reasoners infer natural inferiority from the peculiar colour and features of the Africans, *immediately*, or without interposing any connecting idea. Other defenders of this system, if I rightly understand them, state the argument thus. 'The external peculiarities of the negroes are so many specific differences. The negroes, then, are a species of men different from, and therefore, inferior to the whites.' But, by what logic can inferiority be deduced from difference of species, supposing it proved, any more than from the pretended specific differences? And, is it more agreeable to philosophy and to common sense to say, He is of a *different*, and, therefore, an *inferior* species of men, than to affirm, That he has a *black skin*, and is, therefore, *inferior?*— Some men may suppose it their interest to cherish such vulgar errors; but it is the business of philosophy to explode them; especially when, as in the present instance, they are evidently repugnant to the happiness of mankind.

Let it be observed, That, although the knowledge I have of the negroes forbids me to subscribe to the crude

* Doctor S. S. Smith's Ess.

theories

theories which have been fabricated in the closets of philosophers, to prove that there are different species of men; or to pay any regard to the very unphilosophical accounts of ignorant, partial travellers, on which such theories are generally founded; yet that I am far from arraigning the conclusions which may have been drawn by anatomists from internal peculiarities in the bodies of Africans.—But the *mores animalium*, are justly regarded, as more certain criteria of the mental powers, so to speak, of animals, than any conclusion that can be drawn either from the external or internal peculiarities of their bodies. If, by long observation, and a habit of comparing the actions and reasonings of the negroes, for example, with those of the whites, a man be satisfied that the one is as rational and intelligent, *cæteris paribus*, as the other, it cannot be expected that any contrary opinions of anatomists should shake his conviction. To the learned, I submit, whether such a conviction *ought to be* so shaken? And whether, if the *Houynhnhnms* were realized, we must not account them rational beings, notwithstanding they had the bodies of horses?

But, besides the conviction forced on my mind, by arguments from analogy and by the general behaviour of the negroes, it may be proper to mention some particular facts which have had their weight with me, and may have their weight with others, in proving the natural equality of the Africans to the Europeans. Many similar facts, I must have witnessed, which have slipped from my memory, though the conviction they worked remains; just as a man may forget the demonstration of a mathematical proposition, but may retain and be convinced of the truth of the conclusion.

It cannot be denied that the negroes, when put to a trade which happens to coincide with the bent of their genius, become as good, and, sometimes, better artificers, than white men. I have seen a white carpenter drudging with the saw, jacking-plane, &c. and who could not lay off his work properly, while a black one was employed in making pannel-doors, sash-windows, &c. I have known the carpenter's work of a good house of two stories, with a pavillion-roof, king-posts, &c. planned and conducted,
by

by a black carpenter—On the doors of some of the negro huts, I have observed wooden locks, at once simple and well contrived, and which it was impossible to open, without the wooden key, which had two or three square, polished prominencies, adapted to the internal parts of the lock, which I have also seen, but it cannot be explained without a model.—In the learned Dr. Burney's History of Music, there are figures of several ancient musical instruments, by a comparison with which, the banjay or coromantin drum would lose nothing. This last is a most ear-piercing instrument; but, being prohibited, is but seldom used, by the negroes, in Barbadoes. The black musicians, however, have substituted, in its place, a common earthen jar, on beating the aperture of which, with the extended palms of their hands, it emits a hollow sound, resembling the more animating note of the drum.—As silver-smiths and watch-makers, the negroes shew no want of genius. I have employed a black watch-maker who was instructed in the art, by a most ingenious mechanic and natural philosopher, in Bridgetown. That worthy person (now deceased) was bred a mathematical instrument maker, in London; and I knew him to be a person of too strict probity to have put people's watches into improper hands.—But, without enumerating such instances, I might, at once, have appealed, for a proof of African ingenuity, to the fabric and colours of the Guinea cloths, which most people must have seen.—By the word *mechanic* is generally meant a person who makes but little use of his rational faculty; but it must be remembered that *mechanical contrivance* is one of the highest departments of reason. Nor can this be otherwise; since, the science of mechanics depends entirely on mathematics, and hath exercised the genius of an Archimedes, of a Galilæo, of an Emerson, of a M‘Laurin, and, above all, of that great ornament of this island, and of the human species, the immortal *Newton*.

The fondness of the negroes for music, and the proficiency they sometimes make in it, with little or no instruction, is too well known to need support, from particular instances. This their taste for melody and harmony, if it does not demonstrate their rationality, ought, at least, to be admitted as an argument in proving their *humanity*.
—The

—The same may be said of their patriotism, a principle which glows in their bosoms, with an ardour which does them honour. That man must be callous, indeed, who can remain an indifferent spectator of a meeting of two poor Africans, who may have been dragged from the same district of their dear native land. On such occasions, after all parties had got fairly on their centers, I have affected to inquire into the cause of their emotion, and have generally been answered by another question, expressive of extreme astonishment, that I should be ignorant of it: 'Kai! we no *countrymen*, Massa?'[*] One of Voltaire's marks of the superiority of the Iroquois and Algonquins over those whom he affects to call European savages, is, That the former have a country, and that they love and revere that country, which he, too severely, perhaps, insinuates the latter do not.[†] If this be a just criterion, then are the Africans inferior to no nation upon earth.

I have heard the negro chaplain of a black corps preach to a large audience of whites and blacks. Though his dialect was, by no means, good; yet the weight of his arguments, and the native, untaught energy of his delivery were such as to command attention, and to repress ridicule. He had a colleague who gave out a hymn (I think from Watts) and prayed extempore. His dialect was even worse than that of the preacher; but his prayer was such as would have rendered laughter criminal, especially when he implored the Almighty Father of Mercies, with tears, to behold, with an eye of pity, the deplorable ignorance and debasement of his countrymen.——A black teacher, who is employed by several white families in Bridge-town, writes a variety of hands very elegantly. I do not say that this implies any great strength of reason; but it implies a taste for the beauty arising from the combination of flowing lines and accurate proportions, a faculty very nearly allied to reason. Yet more: he teaches English and arithmetic; and, I believe, assists a certain able geometrician and worthy man in instructing the pretended superior race, in mathematics. Above all, he has the

---

[*] Strange! Are not we *countrymen*, Sir?
[†] Phil. d'Hist.

reputation of being an honest man, and a humble, sincere Christian.

To these instances of African capacity, I shall add two remarkable ones. 'Wanted to purchase two negro car-'penters, one of *which* must be *able to carry on business by* '*himself,*' &c. Barbadoes Gazette, March 1st, 1786. —' To be sold two valuable negro carpenters, one of *which* ' is a *compleat wheel-wright*, WIND-MILL *and house car-* '*penter,*' &c. Barbadoes Mercury, Oct. 21st, 1786. Would not an European carpenter who could, with any propriety, be said to be *compleat* in these three branches, be accounted, rather an ingenious man?

Of nine negro ship-carpenters, now in his Majesty's yard at Antigua, three can read very well, four read in the bible, and two in the spelling-book.

I lately saw a section of the strata of a mine in Scotland, which was laid down by the proprietor's black servant, who is very ingenious, in other respects, and intirely self-taught. Among other arts, he excells in turnery. He plays on a very neat pair of bag-pipes which he himself made. They are tipt, at the ends, with common bone.

Doctor Barton tells me, that he was informed by a gentleman on whose veracity he could depend, that the best physician now in N. Orleans, is a Guinea negro, who gives a rational account of his practice, according to the reigning theories. *Anthony Benezet*, author of an account of Guinea, devoted much of his time and his whole fortune to the establishment of a negro-school in Philadelphia. That worthy person declared, in Doctor Barton's hearing, that, were he to make a comparison between the genius of the Europeans, and the Africans, it would be rather in favour of the latter.

To the Latin Ode of Francis Williams,* 'Denique ' venturum, fatis volventibus, annum,' &c. the beautiful

* Published in the 2d volume of the History of Jamaica, *cum notis hypercriticis*.

poetical

poetical pieces of Phillis Wheatly,* and the letters of Ignatius Sancho, we appeal for specimens of *African literature*.—Have their calumniators obliged the literary world with any such specimens?

But, for a decisive proof not only that the negroes *are*, but that, notwithstanding the late pretences to the contrary, they are *held and reputed* to be rational, moral agents, I appeal to every *black code* which, under the sacred name of LAWS, was ever compiled, by the Europeans, on the *other side* of the Atlantic. Laws—*penal laws*, dictated by the spirit of a Draco, if indeed, Tyranny, were she to appear upon the earth, would not claim them as her own—laws, in which harsh restraints are imposed on, and cruel punishments threaten, *helpless slaves*—laws which have reduced oppression to the grave formality of system, have been enacted to govern the negroes. But laws are enacted to govern rational, moral, accountable beings *only*. It follows, therefore, either that the negroes *are*, or that the legislators *were not*, rational, moral beings—or else, that those black codes are founded in the most consummate injustice.

But this argument may be carried a step farther. On the supposition that the negroes are not moral agents, co-ordinate with the whites, I asked with what *justice*, and I might have asked with what *sense*, the pretended superior race inflict on them *exemplary* punishments, and, sometimes, doom them to expire, by horrible tortures?——Those who direct the labours of cattle stimulate them to exertion by stripes. Dogs, being more sagacious, are punished, by the huntsman and the shepherd, with more severity, and with some little view to improvement. Every needless stripe, however, even on dogs or horses or asses, is accounted a mark of the inflictor's barbarous disposition. But no person thinks of inflicting *exemplary* punishments on *brutes*. Boys, convicted of crimes, are treated more moderately than grown persons. Extreme and unavoidable ignorance always weighs, or ought to

---

* For some account of this most extraordinary African girl, and some elegant specimens of her poetry, see the Rev. Mr. Clarkson's excellent Essay on the Slavery and Commerce of the Human Species, 2d edit. p. 121.

weigh,

weigh, more or less, in favour of an offender, except in cases of murder, or other very flagrant crimes. Even among the Hottentots, 'The murderer has his *brains beat out*, and is buried with the murdered person, if he be a *man of quality*; but a simple, *ignorant body* may pay a *ransom*.'* Thus punishments are, or, in general, ought to be, proportioned to the moral improvement of the offender. But *exemplary* punishments are inflicted on the negroes, *more severe* punishments than the whites, for the same crimes, are doomed to suffer; therefore, if their respective punishments be proportioned to their mental faculties, the negroes (for whose *instruction* the laws, by which they are judged, make no effectual provision) are moral agents of an order *superior* to the whites—*if not*, they are treated with a criminal degree of injustice and cruelty. Our adversaries are welcome to take either side of the alternative. Of all the figures in logic, none is so formidable to sophistry as the dilemma.

Again, it has been denied that the negroes are capable of carrying on a chain of reasoning; but it cannot be denied, that, even in Africa, they attain to the knowledge of the leading principles of morality, and even of that most sublime and exalted of all truths, the existence of the living and true God, the Creator and Preserver of all things, which, according to *Hume*, ' is a stamp, set by the divine workman, on *human nature*.'‡ Now, if the negroes arrived at this truth, in the ordinary way, then we must conclude their faculties to be equal to our's; but if, as their enemies insinuate, they be incapable of forming a chain of reasoning, they must have perceived that and other great truths, *intuitively*. If so, not their equality only, but their *superiority* to white men will be demonstrated. Of this faculty of arriving at demonstrable truths, *per saltum*, and of ' grasping a system by intuition,' *we* have no more idea than a man born blind has of colours. We humbly ascribe it to superior orders of beings, and, in a transcendent and infinite degree, to the Deity. This is nobly expressed by the great Dr. Barrow, in a pious

* Ogilby's Africa, p. 594.

‡ Natural History of Religion.

address

address to the Deity, prefixed to his Apollonius. 'Tu autem, Domine, quantus es geometra?—Tu *uno*, hæc omnia, *intuitu* perspecta habes, *absque catena consequentiarum, ne tædio demonstrationum.*' See also the *scholium* ge..le of the Principia, and the *conclusion* of M'Laurin's account of the Newtonian Philosophy.

Upon the whole, Sir, if I have failed in proving that the rational faculties of the Africans are equal, in every respect, to those of the Europeans, I must confess myself ignorant of those distinguishing marks, on which the latter found their claim of superiority.*

But, although it could be proved that the understandings of the Africans are weaker than those of the Europeans, it will, by no means, follow that the latter have a right to enslave them; since, on this principle, no such thing as national liberty could ever have existed in the world. And it may be asked what would become of the liberties of the lower orders even of Britons, were their title to those liberties to depend on powers of reason or of imagination, which bore but a small proportion to those of the great men who have done honour to this island and to mankind?

Let the European be superior in *reason*. Ought they not also to be superior in point of *justice* and *mercy*? And are they superior in justice, and mercy?—Let the Africans tell!

But, setting aside reason altogether, the *passions* of the negroes prove that they were not created to be slaves; any more than the fierce lion was created to ' abide by a ' master's crib, or to harrow the vallies after him,'† which appears to have been the destination of the horse and the ox. Those who complain of the passionate *vindictive* tempers of the Africans cannot surely be aware that they are demonstrating the utter repugnancy of slavery

---

* ' Upon the whole,' says Buffon, ' every circumstance concurs in proving that mankind are not composed of species *essentially* different from each other; that, on the contrary, there was originally but *one species*.' Smellie's Buff. v. 8. p. 206.
† Job.

to their nature. That a creature should have been *formed* for a state which he *abhors*, is an exception to the general œconomy of the universe. That beings created for slavery, should be endowed with stubborn, rebellious, unconquerable passions which spurn the yoke, and often prove fatal both to themselves and to their lords, is a paradox which we leave those of their lords who believe it, to explain, by the newly broached theories of slavery. The theories of scepticism, which have helped them out, on other occasions, will assist them on this.—It would be strange indeed, if there were not a close analogy, a certain sympathetic affinity, between the paradoxes of slavery and those of infidelity!

I am not so confident of the strength of my reasonings on this, or any other part of my subject, as to suppose that they will put sophistry to silence. The changes will no doubt be repeated on a set of battered and exploded arguments which, taken together, form such a group of absurdity, as has been seldom presented to the public—" Evils, it has been said, are permitted by Providence. It is vain for man to attempt to stop their progress. No reformation ought to be aimed at. ' Whatever is, is right.' —The Africans had got into a vile habit of cutting each other's throats. We pitied the poor creatures, and attempted to relieve them. For this purpose, we encouraged humane christians to drag, from their miserable native land, a set of ugly, black, flat-nosed, thick-lipped, woolly-headed, ignorant, savage heathens.——We DENY that we have shut out every ray of light from their minds; that we have caused them to serve with rigour; that our scourges have lacerated their bodies; that the iron of our chains hath debased their very souls. Dare any man affirm that ever we oppressed them?—Yet under every means of improvement and, although they enjoy all the advantages of *English peasants*, they still continue contemptibly stupid and ignorant, and incorrigibly thievish and obstinate?—They have, at times, even dared to question our right to enslave them, the *sacred right of the strongest*.—*Ergo* they are inferior to us, in their mental faculties. They are little, if at all, superior to the *Orang Outangs*, and were *created* to be our slaves.—*Ergo* the vast continent of Africa was peopled with one hundred

and

and fifty millions of the accursed *offspring of Ham*, to serve as a nursery of slaves, for a few little islands, at the distance of some thousands of miles: that, by means of their toil, the favoured posterity of Japhet, (who from *policy* were one day to extirpate the original inhabitants of those islands) might have—rum for their punch, and sugar for their tea.'—Q. E. D.

COR. Hence ' negro *slavery* is not only compatible ' with *sound policy*, but also with *justice* and *humanity*.'*— Q. E. A.

Such, in their primitive nakedness, are the arguments urged in support of negro slavery. Trusting, as I do, that they have no manner of weight with you—and GOD FORBID arguments for slavery should have weight with any member of the British Legislature!!

I have the honour to be, &c.

POSTSCRIPT.

I would sooner, Sir,
    ' —— undertake to prove, by force
    ' Of argument, *a man's no horse*,' †
than to answer, all the objections that have been urged against the bona fide *harmless* doctrine *That the Africans are men*. We shall, however, endeavour to apply the ' test ' of truth,' to some of these very pertinent and very profound objections.

The negroes, it is objected, have a fetid smell. I admit that some negroes have a fetid smell, and so has every man, more or less, who toils and sweats much, in a sultry climate, and neglects bathing. Many of the negroes, however, have no peculiar smell that I could ever discover.

---

* ' Apology for Negro Slavery, by the author of letters to a young ' planter.' This author has *seriously* quoted *The Spirit of Laws*, in support of slavery. Montesquieu has treated that subject in an admirable strain of severe, but deserved, irony; but it is impossible to press into his vile service a writer whose detestation of slavery the ridiculous arguments he uses, will be a lasting monument.

† Hudibras.

But,

—But, granting it to be universal, what connection has a fetid smell with the intellect? If there be philosophers, however, who can scent out men of parts, by power of nose, we felicitate our country on the acquisition. Such intellectual ferrets may have their uses.

But the negroes have flat noses.—How this became a national feature among the Africans, I cannot account, any more than I can account for the high cheek bones of the Scotch. But it is remarkable that it is yielding to civilization. The noses of native domestics are less flat than those of native field-negroes and the noses of these last than those of the Africans.*—We decline using any *Shandean* arguments on this subject; but we own we are mightily inclined to expose the absurdity of an argument imported, from the nasal promontory, not by *Slawkenbergius*, but by a certain French *apologist* for slavery, who has found means to insinuate himself into the good graces, even of Englishmen, to the great *danger* of the liberties of this land. He insists, that as ‘ the creatures are all over black ‘ and have *flat noses*; they ought *not to be pitied*.'† Admirable reasoning! just as if a man should say, A poor, old woman is full of wrinkles and, therefore, ought to be burnt as a witch; if, indeed, the guilt of *bewitching* be not oftener chargeable on *the charms* of young than of old women.

But a negro cannot lay a table even or square in a room. Hence an obliquity of intellect.—The streets of many towns in this kingdom, and even of this metropolis, are crooked. If our ancestors, who laid out those streets, were to be half as much calumniated as the negroes have been, it would probably be asserted, that they could not draw a straight line, between two given points, in the same plane.

Linnæus and Buffon asserted that there was no affinity between the Orang Outang and the human species. But we are happy in announcing to certain philosophers, that all *their* doubts, respecting this matter, are likely to

* See Dr. S. S. Smith's Essay. p. 92.
† See Montesquieu's *Apology* for Slavery, commonly called the Spirit of Laws, b. XV. ch. 5.

be foon cleared up. There is a purpofe of marriage between a *Troglodyte* gentleman and a *Caffrarian* lady.* If a match can be brought about between two perfons of rank, the vulgar will foon imitate their betters, in this, as in other, notable improvements. Certain goffippers who think themfelves amply qualified to negociate fuch an affair, have, for fome time, feduloufly laboured to effect it. Nor is this to be wondered at; for, as nothing improves animals fo much as croffing the breed, the Weft Indian market may, thus, come to be fupplied with choice *anthropomorphite* mules—animals likely to be more durable and better adapted for herding with and fuftaining the drudgery of, brute beafts, than the African *Anthropophagi*, who have fomething in them which too much refembles the old leaven of human nature, ever to be profitable, as labouring cattle. The philofophers too, who have long fearched for the aborigines of mankind among apes and drills, and fatyrs and monkeys and baboons, will become more intimately acquainted with their fpecies, and the Troglodyte ideas and language will become their own. In fhort, fo many good effects may be expected to refult from this match that we wait with impatience, for its confummation, which, we prefume, has been poftponed, till the youth fhall have finifhed his ftudies, and taken his degrees at the Univerfity.†—We are told that Jockoo's

—————— parts and ready wit
' Prove him for various learning fit;'‡

* ' Ludicrous (read *indecent* or *fhocking*) as the opinion may feem; I do
' not think that an *Orang Outang hufband* would be any difgrace to a
' *Hottentot female*.' Hift. of Jamaica, vol. 2. p. 364. It is mortifying to
fee an author, of fo much general merit, mifled by travellers, whofe only
aim feems to have been, to fill the world with monfters, of their own
creating. Linnæus and Buffon thought very differently. ' Inter Simias
' (fays the former from Apollodorus') ' inter *fimias verfantem* oportet
' effe *fimiam*.' Syft. Nat. edit. 13.—' Whatever refemblance takes place,
' therefore, between the *Hottentot* and the *Ape*, the *interval* which
' feparates them is *immenfe*.' Smellie's Buff. vol. 8. p. 67.——Doctor
Sparrman, a refpectable pupil of Linnæus, tells us he thinks it his
' duty to fhew how much the world has been mifled, and the Hottentot
' nation been mifreprefented.' He affirms that all the organs of the
Hottentots, of both fexes, are the fame with thofe of other people;
that their perfons are flender, their colour an umber-yellow, their hair
frizzled and that ' their *tout enfemble* indicates health and content.'
Voyage to the Cape of Good Hope, v. 1. p. 181.
† Hiftory of Jamaica, Vol. 2. Page 370.   ‡ Gay.

so that, when he shall emerge into the philosophical world, his name will, no doubt, be decorated with cabalistical combinations of the Roman capitals and his *knowledge-box* brim full of entities and quiddities, and the late admirable discoveries about the *materiality and mechanism of human and bestial souls*. Of the new theories of the *different species of men, and the near affinity of the black species to other monkies*, he is so perfect a master, that, for aught we know, he may have already composed some elaborate lectures, on that subject, in the Troglodyte language, and which, it is probable, he will publicly deliver, when an audience can be collected, who sufficiently understand that ' *hissing dialect*.'* To hear the honours of the race vindicated, by a learned and eloquent individual, will be a gratification of which no being can form an idea, who is unacquainted with the refined pleasure resulting from the establishment of a favourite *misanthropic, antimosaic,* or *antichristian* hypothesis.

If a certain philosopher formed his '*perceptions*,' alias *doubtful doubts*, into ' *bundles*,' why may not we pack up the *refuse* of our objections, in the same way, and thus dispatch them in the lump?

The calves of the legs of negroes are high; their faces concave; their nostrils tumid; their lips thick; their eyes round; their chins prominent, &c. &c. &c.—All the world knows, Sir, that honest *John Bull* has cheeks like a trumpeter; that his *Sister Peg*, poor girl! though, *now*, treated as she should be, both by her brother and

---

* ' Linnæus, upon the authority of some voyage-writers affirms that ' they CONVERSE TOGETHER *in a kind of hissing dialect*.' Hist. of Jam. Vol. 2. p. 360. It is not quite probable that, after Linnæus had pointedly delivered his opinion on this subject (which our author has, but we *have not* omitted) he should insinuate that Orang Outangs articulate any thing like human speech. The words of that great man are, " *loquitur sibilo*," that is, when *fairly* translated, HE *speaks, or* IT *speaks by hissing*,' just as a goose may be said to do, or as a turkey may be said to speak by *gabbling, &c.*—On what authority are we to rest the shocking practice with which the negroes in the heat of prejudice (for every man has his prejudices) are, several times, charged; and a particular instance of which *is said* to have happened in England, a few centuries ago (vide vol. 2. p. 313. Those stories disgrace a work, in many respects, valuable; especially as they stand, unsupported by any authority, or shadow of authority.

by *Mrs. Bull*, still has a thin visage and high cheek bones; that *Lewis Baboon* has a pair of long lanthorn jaws; that *Lord Strutt* has a sallow hide; and that the whole outward man of *Nic Frog* is clumsy and uncouth. Let the philosophers account for those striking differences, in the features and figure of such *near neighbours* and relations; and let them decide which of those personages is intitled to precedence, in point of intellect, before they set out on their travels, in quest of different species of men, which are already more than half formed, in their own plastic imaginations.

We cannot dismiss this part of our subject without animadverting on a passage of the French *apologist* before mentioned, in which he not only doubts of the human nature of the Africans; but, what is *worse*, most wantonly sneers at the Christianity of the Europeans; as if all the world had not *experienced* how conscientiously they practice their divine religion, and how grateful they are to the author of it, for that and all its concomitant blessings. ' It is impossible, says he, ' for us to suppose ' that these creatures are men; for the allowing them ' to be men, will lead to a suspicion that we are not ' Christians.'* If this be not irony, it is something very like it. But surely he does not mean it to be generally applied. Probably he alludes only to his own countrymen. Be that as it may, we *generous Britons* have the comfort to be conscious that no such illiberal suspicion is applicable to our countrymen.—Historians yet unborn in delineating the characters of certain nations, will be at a loss which most to celebrate, their enlightened zeal for their holy religion, or their entire conformity to her benevolent precepts, in their dealings with the simple, uncorrupted part of mankind; but particularly with the Africans. Language will sink under the DIGNITY of actions which totally eclipse all *Greek* and all *Roman* FAME.†

* See Montesquieu's *Apology* for Slavery, b. xv. ch. v. the title of which is ' Of the Slavery of the Negroes.'

† I have, somewhere, I think, in Hume's Essays, seen the modern French compared to the Athenians, and the British to the Romans. The former it is well known were mild, and the latter were rigorous masters of slaves.

LETTER X.

SIR,

OF the *African* Slave Trade, strictly and properly so called, I cannot undertake to say much that I have not learnt from others. The little I can say, however, is of the very last importance to this nation; for it tends to prove that that trade is carried on, at the expence of the lives, not of the slaves only, but of numbers of that most valuable class of men, British sailors. It is the practice of the masters of Guinea men, Sir, after their business is finished, and they are about to sail, to smuggle their sick sailors ashore, and to leave the poor creatures, generally in a most deplorable condition, emaciated and covered with ulcers, to beg in the streets. In Barbadoes, they are generally sent to the alms-house in Bridge-town; but the accommodations it affords are, by no means, such as to preclude the necessity of begging. While they are able to walk about, the hospitable inhabitants very readily administer to their wants, and the medical gentlemen dress their ulcers, and give them every humane assistance within their department.———One would think the loss of seamen in the slave trade would, *of itself*, be a sufficient motive for abolishing that trade. For my part, Sir, I have ever considered the great and peculiar hardships our brave tars undergo on the coast of Guinea and in the middle passage, as having a tendency to destroy the very sinews of the state.

Having no data to proceed upon, I can form no estimate of the numbers who perish by this and the other hardships and cruelties which seamen endure, in a traffic which is at once the reproach and the bane of British commerce. My want of information, on this head, is the less to be regretted, as the learned, humane and active author of the Essay on the Slavery and Commerce

merce of the human species * has been, for upwards of a year, employed, at the different ports, in collecting authentic vouchers of the *loss of seamen* and the other ruinous consequences of the African trade. When his work, the result of a very laborious but well conducted and successful inquiry, appears, the public will see the *impolicy* (as they have seen the *inhumanity*) of that trade demonstrated in a manner not only satisfactory, but *decisive*. †

The friends of humanity rightly conclude that the abolition of the African trade would insure a milder treatment to the slaves already in our islands. The planter, obliged to promote the natural increase of his negroes, would soon abandon his parsimonious or oppressive system; or, if he did not, his ruin would be certain. ‡ Thus the property would fall into more humane hands; and, in a few years, the system of slavery would be much reformed. It is incumbent on those who insist on the necessity of the African trade, to shew why our *old fully settled* islands still continue their demands for new negroes; why the many hundreds of thousands who have been imported into those islands, since the commencement of that trade, never have satisfied those demands; and why the negroes, far from multiplying like other men, never have kept up their numbers. It is well known that they are a prolific race,

---

* Translated from a Latin dissertation for which the author, the Rev. Mr. Clarkson, was honoured with the first prize, in the University of Cambridge, for the year 1785.

† Since the above was written the 'Essay on the *Impolicy* of the Slave Trade' hath been published.

‡ 'When the principal nations in Europe, Asia and Africa were united under the laws of one sovereign, the source of *foreign supplies* flowed with much less abundance, and the Romans were reduced to the *milder but more tedious method of propagation*. In their numerous families, and particularly in their country estates, *they encouraged the marriage of their slaves*. The sentiments of nature, the habits of education, and the possession of a dependent species of property, contributed to alleviate the hardships of servitude. *The* EXISTENCE OF A SLAVE *became an object of greater* VALUE; and though his happiness still depended on the TEMPER AND CIRCUMSTANCES of the master, the *humanity* of the latter, instead of being restrained by fear, was encouraged by the *the sense of their own interest*.' History of the Decline and Fall of the Roman Empire, Vol. I. page 48. When the elegant historian penned this apposite passage, we cannot suppose he meant to allude to *modern* slavery. Most probably he did not even think, at the time, that he was befriending the cause of humanity—Let the reader keep in mind that, among all the great writers of Europe, of all parties and persuasions, there is but *one* opinion on our subject.

and that the West Indian climate is perfectly congenial to African constitutions. Although they labour under every personal hardship; although no care has ever been taken to proportion the sexes among the imported *Africans* (among the *Creoles* the sexes are proportioned, by a wise Providence) although marriage is not known among them; and, above all, although, on attachments for debt, they are often sold, *individually*, at public outcry, and even bought up for exportation, which affects the total dissolution of their families, to the great *emolument*, no doubt of the respective purchasers of the disconsolate, separated parents and their orphans; yet, under all these disadvantages, there is a very great majority of *creole* slaves now in Barbadoes, and they are universally preferred, *cæteris paribus*, to Africans.

All our islands, except Jamaica, Dominica, and Anguilla have a greater, and some of them a vastly greater, proportion of inhabitants, than Britain and Ireland. In truth the reader will not err much in thinking, that some of them, at this hour, have a great many more people than, *communibus annis*, they can properly maintain. If Barbadoes hath not more people than it *can* properly maintain, sure I am, it contains a great many more people of all colours, than it *does* properly maintain. The whites are still so numerous as greatly to interfere with each other's means of subsistence, a circumstance which proves that there is much too great a proportion of *that* colour. This arose from the introduction of slaves. Were the use of *cattle and implements of husbandry* introduced, the present great numbers of negroes would be equally superfluous and useless.—Incredible as it may seem, Sir, there is, now, on that contracted spot, a body of people *far exceeding* the number of English who had arrived in all North America previous to the year 1751. ' There are supposed (says Dr. Franklin) to be now ' (A. D. 1751) upwards of 1,000,000 of English souls ' in North America; though, it is thought, scarce 80,000 ' have been brought over sea.' *——— Jamaica *alone* contains *more than thrice* 80,000 *slaves*, exclusive of whites, Marons, free negroes, &c.

* Thoughts on the peopling of countries.

There

There are, without doubt, many estates in Barbadoes, that require no supplies of African negroes; and I could, almost, venture to *affirm* this of several; but being anxious, *if possible*, to preclude contradiction, on this important point, I will not risque even my *opinion* on any particular estate.—The only instance, of any remarkable increase from the births, of which I can venture to speak positively, occurred in one of the towns.—About the year 1767, a gentleman married a lady who had a considerable number of negroes. They were represented to me, as having been, then, a very idle debauched set of people, and as having been in a fair way to ruin their too indulgent mistress. By her husband's prudent care, however, assisted by regular discipline, they were soon rendered an excellent gang of field-people. They have been chiefly employed in the holing of land at so much per acre. But they are not worked beyond their strength; and, when holing, a dinner ready dressed, is served out to them, besides the ordinary allowance. The children are most carefully attended to; and, in short, they are better treated, in all respects, than by far the greater number of plantation-slaves. The consequence of this management has been, an increase of about one third.

By meliorating the condition of the slaves, the abolition of the African trade would be an excellent preparatory step for the gradual annihilation of slavery itself in our islands.* Yes, Sir, I will not dissemble that I ardently

---

* The sentiments and conduct of the Polish and Russian grandees, and of our West Indian planters, respecting their vassals and slaves, are perfectly similar. The bugbear of emancipation is no less unreasonably terrific to the one than to the other. '*The generality*,' (says a late most intelligent traveller) '*of the Polish nobles are not inclined to establish or give efficacy to any regulations in favour of the peasants*, WHOM THEY SCARCELY CONSIDER AS INTITLED TO THE COMMON RIGHTS OF HUMANITY. A few nobles, however, of benevolent hearts and enlightened understandings, have acted upon different principles; and have ventured upon the expedient of giving liberty to their vassals. The event has shewn this project to be no less *judicious* than humane; no less friendly *to their own interests* than to the happiness of their peasants.'—' The first noble who granted freedom to his peasants was Zamoiski, formerly great Chancellor, who, in 1760, enfranchised six villages in the Palatinate of Masovia. These villages were, in 1771, visited by the author of the patriotic letters from whom I received the following information: On inspecting the parish registers of births, ' from

dently wish for the total annihilation of slavery, especially of *British slavery*. Yet notwithstanding the pointed detestation with which I have treated and ever will treat acts of cruelty and oppression, I am an enemy to all sudden and violent measures, an enemy to *anarchy*, though a friend to rational *liberty*. Without referring to the nature of the political relation which the British colonies bear to Britain, I have the very strongest reasons for thinking that any plan which might be adopted for extending liberty, *(protection* may be immediately extended) to the negroes, must be *gradual* in it's operation.

In the first place, our colonists, under the connivance, if not the express sanction, of the British legislature, in favour of the African trade, have vested a very great part of their property in the persons of slaves. The original settlers of our islands were the less to be blamed for this, as they never dreamt or suspected that their property in slaves was not as secure and ought not to be held as invio-

' from 1750 to 1760, that is, during the ten years of slavery, immedi-
' ately preceding their enfranchisement, he found the number of births
' 434; in the first ten years of their freedom from 1760 to 1770, 620,
' and from 1770 to the beginning of 1777, 585 births.—During the
' first period there were only 43—second period 62—third period 77
' *births each year.*——In their state of vassalage, Zamoiski was obliged
' to build cottages and barns for his peasants, and to furnish them with
' feed, horses, *ploughs and every implement of agriculture;* since their at-
' tainment of liberty, they are become so easy, in their circumstances,
' as to provide themselves with all these necessaries, at their own ex-
' pence; and they likewise chearfully pay an annual rent, in lieu of
' the manual labour, which their master formerly exacted from them.
' By these means, the *receipts* of this particular estate have been nearly
' *tripled*.'—Prince Stanislaus, nephew to the king of Poland, has warmly
' patronized the plan of giving liberty to the peasants.'—Coxe's Trav.
v. 1. p. 196, et seq. ' In *Russia* a peasant may obtain his liberty, 1. by
' manumission: 2. by purchase; 3. by *serving in the army or navy.*'—A
' century ago, perhaps no one in Russia would have ventured to debate
' the question, Whether the peasants ought to be free? But the science
' and learning which are now dawning upon these regions, have alrea-
' dy introduced such a spirit of enquiry, that similar subjects are not un-
' frequently discussed in public.'—In 1766, a prize was given at Peters-
' burgh for the best Dissertation (and 164 were offered) on this question;
' Is it most advantageous to the state, that the peasant should possess
' *land*, or only *personal effects*; and to what point should that property be
' extended, for the good of the public?' The prize-dissertation was
' *in favour of the peasants.*' The author of it ' recommends the legislature
' to confer upon the peasants a *gradual succession of privileges*, and to fol-
' low the slow, but sure method of *instruction and improvement.*' See
Coxe's Travels, v. 3. p. 175 and 178.

lable as any other part of their property.* The present generation of West Indians, who succeeded to that property, and some of whom, to my certain knowledge, very much dislike it, do not appear to me to be blameable merely as they are *owners* of slaves. My countrymen must not be offended, if I distribute the blame impartially. My very humble opinion is, that all persons who use rum or sugar, in other words, that the whole British nation, and ABOVE ALL, *the African traders*, ought to be considered as *participes criminis*; and it would be the extreme of injustice and cruelty that *one* class, and a very useful and valuable class of men, should absolutely be *ruined* for a crime (and a crime it certainly is) in the guilt of which *all* are involved.

In the second place I am convinced that liberty would be a curse instead of a blessing to beings so very rude and uncultivated as the field-negroes now are. We must here admit, with some limitation, the noble and generous sentiment of Sallust, ' Libertas juxta bonis et malis, stre-' nuis atque ignavis, optabilis est.† The field-negroes could not bear any great and sudden alteration of their condition. They must be made sensible of their value and dignity as *men* and, must be converted to *Christianity*, before they can be expected to act properly as *freemen*. Foolish profusion and low debauchery are the usual consequences of a very poor man being suddenly raised to affluence. Idleness, drunkenness, violence, in a word, every species of excess, would be the no less probable consequences of a numerous body of slaves, at least of brutish field-negroes being suddenly converted into freemen. Great, or, at least, improved and tried spirits alone are capable of bearing such sudden transitions. No man, in his senses, who knows any thing of the West Indies, would ever dream of any measure of the kind we allude to, which did not proceed by gradual steps. Of the vast body of slaves whom Moses conducted out of Egypt only *two* entered, or, probably, were *fit* to enter, into the

---

* I relate the fact; I do not attempt to justify the principle.

† ' *I cannot conceive what harm* LIBERTY *can do to* ANY *man*'!!
    A British Peer, in his place, in the House of Lords, in the year MDCCLXXXVIII.

promised

promised land. Perhaps the present generation of adult slaves, too, must be left to die in their chains, which are rivetted into and have irretrievably debased every power of their souls.—But, on this *most delicate* part of my subject, I dare not obtrude any opinions of my own. It belongs to the humane enlightened and enlarged policy of the present, auspicious period, to digest a plan, which may promote the interests of the owner as well as the happiness of the slave, which I contend are, by no means, incompatible.

But I am persuaded the friends of humanity have never entertained an idea of so dangerous a measure as the sudden emancipation of the slaves—a measure which would most probably prove ruinous to our sugar islands, and would be little short of disbanding legions of ignorant, lawless beings to destroy the property and the lives of a small number of settled inhabitants.

But, although I cannot, without horror, contemplate the probable consequences of a sudden emancipation of the slaves; yet I have good reasons for thinking that the Barbadian slaves, at least, would very well bear that improvement of their condition, which would result from the abolition of the African trade.

Barbadoes is our oldest, best established, and best cultivated West Indian colony. The majority of the slaves in that island are *creoles*, who are interested, as far as *slaves* can be interested, in the prosperity of that their native land; and are so well reconciled, even to their present debased condition, that nothing like an insurrection, has taken place there for many years. Not that I suppose that they, any more than other slaves, are destitute of a desire for liberty. The holy flame may be smothered up, but can never be extinguished, in the human breast. But I can conceive that custom, necessity, fear and it's offspring *mutual distrust* may produce a feeble kind of acquiescence in a condition against which human nature revolts. The very numerous free negroes and mulattoes, who are generally sober and industrious, are well attached to the whites, on their relation to whom the mulattoes very much value themselves. No island in the West
Indies

Indies has so great a proportion of whites as Barbadoes; and many white men are not ashamed to live in such habits of *intimacy* with the female domestic slaves, that it is next to impossible a revolt could be hatched and come to any dangerous crisis, without being discovered. In this, as in many other cases, by the wise appointment of Providence, order arises out of confusion.

But, so far as I can learn, no prophecies of war and bloodshed have been uttered by the people of Barbadoes. I must do the Barbadians the justice to say, that their general behaviour shows but little of that corporal dread of the blacks which seems to pervade some of the islands. The truth, I believe, is, that they are conscious their treatment of the negroes, on the whole, *less* deserves to be resisted than that of the panic-struck colonies. The general confidence between the whites and the blacks which reigns in Barbadoes, does honour to both. I have walked and rode, as I formerly said, at all hours of the day and night, often alone, always unarmed, and I never scrupled to take shelter, from a shower, in the first negro-hut I came to, often in a watch-house, at a distance from any other dwelling; though, sometimes, I knew not a negro on the plantation. Such humble cots, I ever did enter, with as little fear, as I entered my own chamber. Had the negroes been half so savage as has been pretended, I must inevitably have fallen a victim to their ferocity, having been many hundred times, absolutely in the power not of creoles only, but of *Africans*.—A conduct so irregular, as that many of the town slaves, before described, would never be permitted by a *suspicious* people. On Sundays and holidays it is common to see many hundreds of negroes and mulattoes dancing and making merry, without the superintendence even of a constable. If a well dressed white man wish to enter the circle, the cry is, ' 'I and á by, let Massa come ' forward!' when they immediately make way for him, respectfully bowing or court'sying as he passes, often with a ' God bless you Massa,' and, sometimes, whispering, loud enough for him to hear it, ' Da good Backra' (That is good white man). Such scenes, in the environs of the towns, where there is not a great mixture of poor field-negroes, would make a stranger believe there

is

is no such thing as oppression in the island. Nay, such excellent animals are the negroes, that if not too hardly treated, they enjoy the dance and the song on the plantations, where I have seen very large companies of fieldpeople making merry, sometimes at late hours on Sunday and holiday evenings. Curiosity, I own, when I first arrived in the island, has led me out of my way, to mix with such nocturnal meetings, both in town and country, when, sometimes, I did not know an individual present. In certain islands, I suppose, such meetings and such adventures would be looked upon, as very perilous indeed. Yet, I am here, alive, to testify, that the only mark even of disrespect, I ever experienced, was, that, on my going up, the music, sometimes, has ceased—a modest hint for an intruder to withdraw.—Gentlemen often ride with pistols; but more, perhaps, for ornament than use; for, I believe, they are seldom loaded.—On the other hand, *jumpers, negro-catchers*, &c. do not often go out, at nights, unarmed.—These facts, though apparently trivial, tend to evince that the negroes, in Barbadoes, are, by no means, so savage as those in some other islands have been represented to be.

Throughout the late war, large bodies of slaves in Barbadoes were armed with swords and spears. The free negroes had fire-arms, were well cloathed, at their own expence, and made a very good appearance. But no instance occurred of their abusing the confidence reposed in them. On the contrary, the negroes, both slaves and freemen, exhibited, on all occasions, an alacrity, which, there is good reason to believe, would have been very troublesome, if not fatal, to the enemies of what may be called by a bold figure *their country*. Indeed, I have often heard it affirmed, That, though the French might *take* Barbadoes, yet they could not possibly *keep* it; and one reason always assigned, was, *That the negroes would cut their garrisons to pieces*, which, I verily believe, would be the case. The very slaves in Barbadoes are inspired with something like loyalty. The same kind of contempt of the French, which actuates the bosoms of our soldiers and our seamen, hath taken possession of those of the negroes. Sentiment, rather than reason, will ever rule the bulk of mankind; and, of all sentiments, that of patriotism tifm is furely the moft proper to be cherifhed in the lower orders of a nation, who never will underftand the meaning of it's polite, modern fubftitute philanthropy.* In enlarged minds, the latter principle will grow out of the former; for philanthropy is no more inconfiftent with patriotifm than the love of one's neighbours is with the love of one's family. Addifon's admired character of Sir Roger de Coverley would be incomplete without 'a 'laudable partiality for his country;' and Lord Chefterfield was of opinion, that the perfuafion which every Englifhman entertains of being able to beat *ten* Frenchmen had often enabled him to beat *two*.

Loyalty and attachment to this country pervade every clafs of people in Barbadoes.†—When our brave, ably conducted and victorious fleet and army were languifhing with ficknefs, at St. Lucia, the white inhabitants of Barbadoes fent them liberal fupplies of live ftock and of corn to feed that ftock. The unanimous vote of the legiflature, by which thofe fupplies were raifed, was almoft unneceffary; for people of all ranks, feemed to vie with each other, in contributing even more than their quota. I was not in town, at that time, to obferve the conduct of any confiderable body of the negroes; but when the news of the glorious victory, of the 12th of April, arrived, the negroes in Bridgetown were almoft frantic with joy. Some gentlemen affected to call this a mere

---

* Thofe who wifh to retain their fellow-creatures in everlafting chains cant very prettily about 'warm *philantbropy*;' and 'fouls tuned 'to the finer' and fofter fenfations;' and the glutton 'Benevolence, 'indulging her *fweeteft gratification* and *enjoying* her *feaft of the foul*, her 'higheft, moft *delicious luxury*.' With what delicate languor do they drawl and lifp out 'liber-*a*-lity of fentiment,' and 'fenfibility—dear 'delicate, fweet, foft, fine *feeling* fenfibility! of heart?'—What pleafure can there be in beflubbering the virtues not with the milk, only, but with pailfuls of the cream and whole firkins of the *butter* of human kindnefs?—a compoft yet more naufeous and hypocritical than any in Whitefield's Journal!—But, let poor unlucky wight of an author only venture to differ in opinion from thofe men of feeling, and ftraightway they go to work, with the tar-brufh and the bag of feathers!

† There is nothing wonderful in this. Barbadoes was originally fettled by loyalifts; New England by independent republicans; Pennfylvania by Quakers; the eaft of Ireland had Epifcopalians from England; and the north of that kingdom Prefbyterians from Scotland; and the prefent inhabitants of each of thofe fettlements ftill adhere to the religious and political creeds of their refpective anceftors.

effufion

effusion of animal spirits; but I asked them from what source any man's joy, even a philosopher's joy flows—from his *head* or from his *heart?*—Are men, thus attached to Britain and to her Sovereign, to be, *for ever*, debarred from *tasting* British liberty, and from *enjoying* British protection?

The great hurricane, in 1780, put the whites *intirely* in the power of the blacks. The former could not leave the ruins of their houses, having been employed in searching for and burying their dead, in collecting the scattered fragments of their effects, and in providing for their immediate shelter and subsistence. The few troops then in the island having been similarly employed, were in no condition to act. Between 2000 and 3000 stand of arms were buried under the ruins of the armoury, and those in the forts were either buried or rendered useless. Yet the negroes remained peaceably with their owners; and shewed no signs of a spirit of mutiny. I well remember, that the white inhabitants were under greater apprehensions from about 1000 prisoners of war, than from the whole body of the slaves. This may seem incredible; but it is true.

Nothing, therefore, is to be dreaded from the slaves in Barbadoes; and *I do very much suspect* that the fears of insurrections in the other islands are exaggerated, if not groundless; but I expressly bar the effects of imprudence and ill usage.* I need scarcely add, Sir, that were the West Indian slaves converted to Christianity, were they

---

* Political prophets, always think themselves interested in the accomplishment of their predictions. And it is easy to see, that if owners upbraid their slaves with the favour of the people of England, or with ' Aldermen of London and Members of Parliament, having taken up the cudgels in their behalf.' (See an abusive paragraph in a Jamaica paper, which we shall afterwards quote) *if* such I say *should be* the imprudent conduct of owners, they may draw expressions of joy from the more imprudent slaves. Correction, perhaps brutal treatment, will follow. The jealousy of both parties, if thus roused, *may* produce ill effects, though scarcely dangerous effects; for it is next to impossible, such conduct should become general.—Let it be observed that the field-negroes can neither read nor write.—Yet they are shrewd enough to know that mutinous conduct would but tend to rivet their chains. They will dread that power which could cope at once with France and Spain and Holland and *North* America.

protected

protected from arbitrary violence, and, had they but the pleasing *phantom* of liberty to fight for, they would form a phalanx more than sufficient to repel any force which could be sent against our islands—a phalanx incomparably more numerous, hardy and *susceptible of discipline* than an ill established, ill armed, undisciplined, tattered rabble of poor whites; and such, if we except the town-companies, who were well trained and respectable, the *privates* of the Barbadoes militia were, during the imminently dangerous situation of that important island in the late war. The men are not deficient in personal courage; but very many of them have nothing to fight for, but the precarious possession of little spots of *bad* land, on which they barely exist. I may safely affirm, that they could not lose half so much by a defeat, as a numerous body of well treated, effectually protected and contented negroes, WHO WOULD SOONER DIE THAN PART WITH SUCH A CONDITION.*—The present white militia have no pay, and, when they meet with accidents, far from receiving any kind of compensation, *they receive not so much as* THANKS. This, in some cases, cannot but be peculiarly distressing. A poor fellow, from Britain, for instance, in endeavouring, by his exertion and example, to serve his country, in the hour of danger, or of serious and universal alarm, is mutilated in the Barbadoes militia. If he have no respectable friend to vouch for his character, he must return home, with as ill a grace, and he runs the risque of being as much despised by his old friends, as if he had lost his limb for a crime. Such, under those circumstances, will most probably be his reception in a country-place, where the very word *Indies*, east or west, commonly imports all that is opulent and splendid and *generous!*—To any such man, it might be some consolation, if, he could still serve his country, by promoting the security of her colonies, or, which is the same thing, the security and happiness of a body of men,

---

* 'The magistrates of St. Thomas and St. Cruz have more than once declared ' *That the baptized negroes are a greater security to them than their forts*.' Succinct View of the Missions, &c by the Church of the Brethren.—' As the Europeans lose vigour by the heat of the climate, the free negroes, especially those on the mountains, are the safeguard of the island (Jamaica); and it was by their means chiefly that a number of rebellious negro slaves were subdued, in the year 1760.' Lord Kaimes's Sketches, p. 22. Edin. 1788. See also Hist. of Jam.

whom a mistaken policy hath hitherto considered not barely as aliens, but as outlaws—as enemies.

Every Briton, who hath the true and lasting glory of his Sovereign and his Country at heart, must ardently wish to see the slave trade for ever annihilated.

To adopt this measure would be to transmit to posterity the mild and benign reign of GEORGE III. with a lustre unequalled by that of any Monarch who ever swayed the British sceptre. To save from slavery and from death the thousands of innocent victims, who are annually dragged, in chains, from their native land, and who either perish on the voyage, or are doomed to an ignominious, painful and perpetual bondage; by means so noble to effect a nobler purpose—to provide for the gradual extension of the blessings of civilization, liberty and religion to millions yet unborn; to exhibit to admiring nations an exalted and illustrious example of clemency, justice, and political wisdom: These are actions altogether unparalleled in the annals of this or any other nation, actions which the world would applaud and revere, and which future historians would celebrate as the greatest that adorned a prince who was distinguished, among his cotemporaries, as the promoter of morality and science, and the father of his people.

Happily for his country, the genius and integrity of her patriotic, illustrious and favourite statesman, survive in his offspring.—It is incredible, Sir, it is impossible that those talents which have improved the finances of this country, which, by treaties and alliances wisely formed, have secured her peace and extended her commerce, and which, on a late most critical emergency, foiled and appalled the House of Bourbon—it is impossible, in a word, that those consummate talents, which, under Providence, have RESTORED Britain to her wonted respectability among the nations, should be unaccompanied with that compassion for the miserable which characterizes every great soul.—The definition of heroic virtue consists of two inseparable parts—*parcere subjectis* et *debellare superbos.*

Certain

Certain illiberal suggestions might prevent a man from publicly avowing such sentiments, did he not know that *they are the sentiments of the nation.*—And is there not very great reason to think, That it would be *generally agreeable* that the statesman whose wisdom and public spirit have so largely contributed to the present prosperity of the country, should have the honour of contributing to wipe off the foulest blot on her character?

'Let it no longer be said, That slavery is counten-
'anced by the bravest and most generous people on
'earth; by a people who are animated with that heroic
'passion, the love of liberty, beyond all nations ancient
'or modern; and the fame of whose toilsome, but un-
'wearied, perseverance, in vindicating, at the expence of
'life and fortune, the sacred rights of mankind, will strike
'terror into the hearts of sycophants and tyrants, and
'excite the admiration and gratitude of all good men, to
'the latest posterity.'†

It hath been observed, that the conquered provinces of free states have, in general, been more oppressed than those of despotic governments.‡ The same observation will, perhaps, hold good with regard to their respective slaves. Without recurring to history, it is well known, and a mortifying truth it is, to Britons, that the NATIONAL *code noir* of our humane neighbours, affords the slave a greater degree of protection than can be expected

---

' De petits esprits exaggerent trop l'injustice que l'on fait aux *Afri-*
' *cains* ; car si ills étoient telle qu'ils les disent (scil. *hommes*) ne seroit il
' pas venu dans la tete de *Princes d'Europe*, qui font entr'eux tant de *con-*
' *ventions inutiles*, d'en faire UNE GENERALE EN FAVEUR DE LA MISE-
' RICORDE ET DE LA PITIE?' Esprit de loix liv. XV. ch. v.———
——————' Pour renverser l'edifice de l'esclavage, etayé par des passions si
' universelles, par des loix si authentiques, par la rivalité de nations si
' puissantes, par de prejugés plus puissans encore, a quel tribunal porte-
' rons nous la cause de l'humanité que tant d'hommes trahissent de
' concert. ROIS DE LA TERRE vous seuls pouvez faire cette revolu-
' tion.'——' En attendant cette revolution, *les negres* gemissent sous le
' joug de travaux dont la peinture ne peut que nous interesser, de plus en
' plus, a leur destinées.'
                             Raynal Hist. Phil. et Pol. tom. V. p. 289.

† Beattie's Essay on Truth, p. 464.   ‡ Hume.

to result from the narrow, partial, oppressive, PROVINCIAL *laws* of the English. *What a glorious emulation is it, for two great nations to rival one another in justice and humanity?*—Let it no longer be said, that in the practice of those virtues, *Britons* are inferior to *Frenchmen*.

Let it no longer be said that Great Britain, in point of justice and humanity, is inferior to the states of of America. The Americans, while they declaimed and contended and fought for what they fondly supposed would be *political liberty*, held the Africans enchained in that *worst* species of slavery, *personal slavery*; for, 'when men talk of liberty they generally mean *their own* liberty, and seldom suffer their thoughts on that subject to stray to their neighbours.'—'The treatment,' one of their writers tells them, with equal justice and spirit,—' The treatment we received from Britain is no more ' to be equalled to *our's* to the *negroes,* than a *barley-corn* ' is to the *globe of the earth*.* It would be unjust not to own, That the Americans have since endeavoured to obviate that unanswerable objection to their cause—an objection which transformed all their pompous oratory into the most ridiculous, contemptible bombast. The Quakers in Pennsylvania, by ' loosing the bands of wick-' edness, and undoing the heavy burdens,' † have converted sullen, reluctant slaves into diligent, faithful servants.‡ So desirable a change cannot be, immediately,

effected

---

* Serious address to the Rulers of America, respecting slavery.—The following advertisement exhibits a most lamentable instance of the truth of the author's assertion. From the ' *Constitutional* Gazette of Georgia, ' March 5th, 1788. The subscriber advises all people to caution their ' *slaves* to refrain their rendezvous on an island, situated on the marshes ' of Little Ogeechie, known by the name of May Island, otherwise they ' shall have *the treatment of* A WOLF, *without enquiry*.' W—— S——. *A Wolf* agrees not with the words *slaves* and *they*; so that Mr. S. himself must have meant to personate the *wild beast*.—Such was, and such, *in Georgia* I believe still is, *constitutional* liberty as it respects miserable slaves!!

† Isaiah.

‡ ' The late resolution of the Quakers, in Pennsylvania, to emancipate ' their slaves, seems to evidence a degree of pure and disinterested virtue ' in that people, beyond the example of the most virtuous communities ' of ancient times.' Dunbar's Essay; p. 411. Their brethren, in this country, have shown themselves to be no less sensible and zealous friends to mankind.——Since the foregoing letters were written, every

denomination

effected in the West Indies, where the proportion of slaves is much greater than it was in Pennsylvania. But the British legislature, by abolishing the slave trade, would adopt the measure most likely to effect it. This measure, like other public measures, may be attended with temporary inconveniencies to a few individuals; but could not fail to be ultimately beneficial to this country and to her sugar colonies—an effect which all measures, dictated by the enlarged spirit of political wisdom, will ever, in the end, be found to produce.

Sir, I have now finished every thing I intended to say on this most interesting subject.

From the dispassionate, merciful and, on every account, respectable, part of the little community of Barbadoes, I *know*, I shall have inward approbation; and some of them may, perhaps, reward and honour me even with public applause.

I write not for the praise of persons of the opposite character.—I would repel it as the vilest badge of infamy.

denomination of Christians in Britain, and particularly, respectable bodies of the clergy of both the national churches, have petitioned the Legislature for the abolition of the slave trade. If we except a few (and compared with the whole nation, they are but *a very few*) persons, who unreasonably suppose their interests to be in danger, all descriptions of the people seem to have but one wish, on this occasion. In a word, never was a measure, at once so glorious and so popular, recommended to the Legislature; and great and just applause will redound to the administration who shall adopt it.——Sooner would the author throw these sheets into the fire, than they should come abroad stained with any thing like flattery; but he will give praise where praise is due. He would not wish to be premature in applauding the conduct of his countrymen; but as he is not afraid to condemn the conduct of *some*, and throws a share of blame on *all*, it is but proper he should give the nation credit for the general and noble effort they are now making to wipe off the foulest of all blots from their character. Would to Heaven they could prevent it from having a place in future histories!——The General Assembly of the church of Scotland have appointed the *fifth of November* next, to be observed as a day of solemn thanksgiving to Almighty God, in commemoration of the GREAT AND GLORIOUS REVOLUTION, of which that day will be the first centenary—a day 'much to be remembered' by Britons of *all* ranks and persuasions. With great humility and respect it is submitted, *Whether a petition from the last General Assembly, to the Legislature, in favour of the innocent, oppressed, and benighted men who now groan under the yoke of* BRITISH BONDAGE, *would not have been peculiarly proper and well timed?* But, perhaps, such a petition, from the next Assembly, may not be too late.

My subject, I must repeat it, as well as my design in treating it, are entirely of a public nature. I have, therefore, most carefully avoided all *unnecessary* personal allusions. But, when the practice of individuals happens to coincide with that which may deservedly meet with public reprobation, it is not surprising that offence should be taken at expressions and passages with which it is altogether impossible the *innocent* should be offended. Let such persons seriously weigh the well known adage,

QUI CAPIT, ILLE FACIT.

In whatever manner my own little interests may be affected by this endeavour to inform the minds of my countrymen on a subject so generally interesting, I will say, with the poet,*

' Welcome for thee fair Freedom, all the *past*,
' For thee, fair Freedom, welcome—even the last.

I have the honour to be, &c.

* Pope.

THE FOLLOWING LETTERS

CHIEFLY RELATE TO THE

STATE OF SLAVERY

IN

JAMAICA.

> 'There is no sensible and ingenuous man, with whom I have hitherto conversed on the subject, who denies, that the NEGROES in this island are, IN GENERAL, OVER-WORKED AND UNDER-FED, EVEN ON THE MILDEST AND BEST REGULATED PROPERTIES. There is no man likewise who will seriously say, that negro population has yet become an object of sufficient magnitude, or that the best means have been adopted to produce it.' McNEILL's Observations on the Treatment of the Negroes in the Island of Jamaica, p. 44.

LETTER XI.

SIR,

AFTER some of the foregoing letters had been printed, and the following ones were ready for the press, I was agreeably surprized by the appearance of a pamphlet.

let intitled 'Observations on the Treatment of the Negroes, in the Island of Jamaica, &c. in a Letter to a Physician in England, from Hector M'Neill.' I was agreeably surprized, I say, by this publication; for what can be more agreeable to an author than to see his book confirmed, even before it comes abroad, by a writer of the adverse party? The disregard for the common sense and feelings of mankind, which is conspicuous in this piece, proves it to be of the apologetic kind; but I dare appeal to the public, whether it does not strengthen, instead of weakening, the proofs I now submit to their examination. Indeed the confirmation of some particulars and the confession of others which the rest of my authorities do not explicitly mention, together with Mr. M'N's *emphatic silence* or ambiguity concerning enormities which appear to be too common in Jamaica, are my only reasons for taking any notice whatever of an author who most decisively refutes himself. Thus like all the other apologies for negro-slavery, Mr. M'N's piece is, providentially, calculated to support the cause it is intended to subvert. At p. 13, the author says 'A negro in slavery, as I before mentioned, is supplied with *every* thing he has occasion for.' This is flatly contradicted at p. 44, 'There is no sensible and ingenuous man'. says our author, 'with whom I have hitherto conversed on the subject, who denies that the negroes, in this island (Jamaica) are, *in general, over-worked and under-fed, even on the mildest and best regulated properties.*' In the original, the word 'every,' in the affirmation, and the word 'general,' in the contradiction, are in italics; so that the expressions must have been deliberate. Again, p. 10 'I have already endeavoured to convince you by incontrovertible proofs, that the negroes, in this country, are generally protected,'—not very consonant to p. 31, where speaking of the *consolidated slave-law*, Mr. M'N. says, 'I am, therefore of opinion that something MORE EFFECTUAL, should be introduced *to curb the* WANTONNESS OF POWER, *and to prevent the* HAND OF CRUELTY *from being extended.*'

I shall not here insert any more of our author's incongruities. But I am so much convinced that his pamphlet, if read with common attention, will operate strongly in favour of the Africans, that nothing but the expence prevents me from having it bound up, *in statu quo*, with these sheets. If there should be room, I may insert, at the end, a few more glaring and palpable contradictions, from this pamphlet. In the mean time, let the reader compare what he will find in p. 2, ' But the happiness, ' &c.' *with* ' An action is brought, &c.' p 37.—' He ' would have seen,' &c. p. 3, *with* ' All this,' &c. p. 4.—' On a proprietor,' &c. p. 4. n , and 'I have ' been credibly,' &c. p. 9, and ' When he is seasoned,' &c. p. 25, *with* ' In the first place,' &c. p. 11.—' For-' merly,' &c. p. 4 and 5, *with* ' Unless it is,' &c. p. 5. —' I believe there are,' &c. p. 10, and ' That the bon-' dage,' &c. p. 45. *with* the declared end and aim of every apology for negro-slavery.

But I cannot omit some passages tending to exalt the planters of Jamaica at the expence of those of the Windward Islands. ' You may remember, says Mr. M'N. p. ' 1, that impressed with a keen sense of the *severities*, in-' *flicted on the helpless negro*, during my former residence ' in the WINDWARD ISLANDS, twenty years ago, I af-' terwards not only turned my thoughts seriously to a ' consideration of the subject, but *committed them to writ-' ing.'* What a pity our author has not published those written thoughts! ' On my leaving Britain the last time, ' those impressions were rather *strengthened* by the perusal ' of certain publications, which tended to rouse the indig-' nation and excite the pity of the public.'—P. 2. ' On ' my arrival in Jamaica, however, I found at the first ' view, the scenes appeared very different from those I ' was formerly accustomed to; for instead of severity, ' cruelty, and injustice, I observed in the towns of this ' island such a degree of lenity as often to occasion licen-' tiousness; and, in the country, a general attention ' and humanity to the welfare of the negro, sufficient to ' make bondage easy.'—P. 6, note, ' As to the article ' of *picking grass*, on which so much has been said by late ' writers, no such thing *now* exists in this island. I be-' lieve, however, that neither this alleviation nor that of ' the *plow* has yet been generally introduced in the other ' islands. In Grenada, I am confidently informed, that ' the old practices still prevail.' Thus our author expressly

pressly affirms or admits. 1. That the negroes in the Windward Islands were severely treated 20 years ago. 2. That their condition (in two very material particulars, at least) is not yet much meliorated. 3. That the publications on that subject (meaning no doubt Mr. Ramsay's, Dean Nickolls's, &c.) are founded in truth. 4. That the Jamaica bondage is 'easy,' and 'very different,' from that of the Windward Islands.—To the three first articles I most readily accede; but I cannot admit the last; because 1. It is contrary to the whole tenor of the following proofs which were penned in Jamaica, as well as Mr. M'N's pamphlet. 2. It is particularly contrary to the last sentence of the following description of a Jamaica scramble, 'Why not adopt the method pursued *at* ALL '*the Windward Islands.* 3. It is expressly contradicted by the author himself in the passage above quoted from his 44th page. 4. It unaccountably and widely differs from his own horrid description (p. 5.) of what slavery was 'formerly' in Jamaica, a description which, I am sorry to observe, is not very explicitly authorized by the history of Jamaica which delineates the state of things in that island about the period Mr. M'N. refers to. But we trust our adversaries will go on to contradict themselves, one another and *us*, till, independently of the writings which they vainly oppose, they divulge all the horrid facts which they labour to palliate or conceal. Be it observed, that Mr. M'N's 'confident information,' that old, bad practices still prevail in Grenada is directly in the teeth of the 'Apology for Negro Slavery' we cited at p. 81. Farther, Mr. M'N. affirms that the 'Cursory 'Remarks' 'accord perfectly' with the state of things in Jamaica. According to the other apologist, those same remarks fit Grenada to a title. Yet I have good authority to say that they are laughed at in the island to which they are professedly adapted.—If the deceased poor *Robin* blundered egregiously in his calculations for the meridian of St. K———, what sort of conjurers must they be, who contend that his farthing-almanack will equally suit Piscataquay and Tobolski? Why will not the obstinate bunglers compute by the *just* and universal canons we recommend to them, and which have been so successfully reduced to practice by that prince of philomaths, the sensible and worthy *friend Richard of Philadelphia?*

But

But to have done with such incongruous nonsense. It is not our business to reconcile the endless contradictions of our adversaries; nor can it be expected that any one writer should assign to each island in the West Indies it's degree on the scale of humanity; if, in truth, any one of them may be said to have advanced so high as the cool point of indifference. But my late researches into this subject have only tended to confirm me in the opinion I gave at p. 18, and which with leave of Mr. M‘N, I will repeat, That ' *severe as the treatment of the field-negroes in Barbadoes may appear, I have reason to think it is much milder than in most of the other, especially the* NEW *islands*,' and I will add, that, with regard to Jamaica, what was opinion is now conviction. Mr. M‘N's general charge against the Windward Islands, (and Barbadoes is the most windward island) renders it proper that my reasons for being of that opinion should be submitted to the examination of the public. 1. Barbadoes is our oldest colony; and the slaves are likely to be more reconciled to their chains there, than in the more modern islands, where there is a greater proportion of *African negroes*. 2. The very superior attention paid to religion, in that island (see p. 58.) 3. The much greater proportion of *ladies* (see p. 38.) 4. Barbadoes contains no mountains and woods in which runaways can so effectually secrete themselves, as in most other islands; and the longer and oftener a slave stays out, the more severe is his punishment when caught. 5. No island in the West Indies hath been so long exempted from insurrections as Barbadoes, the white inhabitants of which do not appear to harbour any considerable *suspicions* on that head. See page 93. 6. Small settlers, called ten-acre-men (whose slaves are employed in the comparatively easy culture of provisions, &c.) abound much more in that than any other island. 7. The vastly superior proportion of provisions raised in Barbadoes, not only by the ten-acre-men and the poor whites, but by the sugar planters. 8. The severest punishment, next to death, which can be inflicted on a Barbadian negro is to be shipped off the island. 9. I have been told by a certain worthy and respectable gentleman, that *the annual decrease of the Barbadoes slaves is only* ONE PER CENT. which is probably the least waste of human life in any European colony within the tropics. 10. I

have

have heard persons from St. Vincent, Grenada and Tobago, ridicule the Barbadian (or, as they sarcastically termed it, the *Badian*) discipline, on account of its lenity (see p. 18.) 11. *In particular*, my own observation enables me to affirm, that, on the whole, the slaves in Barbadoes are better treated than those in St. Kitts are represented to be by Mr. Ramsay; yet, as a general description, I still think his Essay applies very well to Barbadoes, and I must say, that the more I consider this subject, the more I am convinced that that valuable work was dictated by benevolence, candour and truth. The following proofs leave me not the shadow of a reason to doubt that the Barbadian slaves are incomparably better treated than those of Jamaica. 12. Lastly, I have ever heard it affirmed, without contradiction, in Barbadoes, and readily admitted in this country, that the slavery of that island, bad as it is, is the most tolerable in the British West Indies.—I protest the only evil I can think of (and a grievous evil it is) which I believe the slaves in Barbadoes suffer in a greater degree than those in the other islands is the injustice to which the *very partial laws* leave them exposed, from poor, starving, unconscionable whites, of whom that island has far more than its proportion.—The treatment of the slaves is undoubtedly less intolerable, in some of the islands than in others; and much alleviation of misery, might result from their comparative moderation being ascertained and made public, a point on which a careful examination of the news papers of the different islands would certainly throw some light. Emulation is known to be one of the strongest motives which influences human conduct.

In these kingdoms, so productive of all that is great in human nature, is there no man whose active and persevering virtue is equal to this arduous but glorious undertaking? Is there no benevolent, independent, intrepid HOWARD to explore the plantation-*dungeons* where forlorn slaves, for attempting to regain liberty or flee from cruelty, lie manacled in fetters, tyrannically rivetted on their limbs; to trace the lacerations of the whip on their bodies, to see ' the iron enter into their souls,' and to weigh in the scale of pity their ' bread of affliction'— perhaps to behold, with horror, a wretch broiling alive in the flames, or transfixed with tortures on a gibbet, for having been driven to an act of defperation by his oppreffor; and faithfully to reprefent to the nation and to the legiflature the degrees in which thofe enormous evils exift in the different Britifh iflands? Yes: The country which produced a HOWARD can alfo boaft of a SHARP and a CLARKSON; but their unwearied labours at home have been and are likely to be yet more valuable than they could have been abroad. To them, and the equally meritorious RAMSAY, the Africans owe much of that attention which is fo juftly and fo generally paid to their caufe.

I have the honour to be, &c.

LETTER XII.

SIR,

IN the beginning of the year (1788) the fubftance of the foregoing letters was fketched and fubmitted to the review of feveral judicious and refpectable gentlemen, who thought the facts and arguments worthy of being laid before the public. Added to the length of time fome of thofe gentlemen kept them in their hands, a circumftance occurred which contributed greatly to retard their publication, but which, it is hoped, will prove highly favourable to the caufe of the unhappy Africans. This was the procuring of an original letter from Jamaica which with extracts from fome late newfpapers of that Ifland, form the bafis of the following letters. I was willing to delay the publication, in hopes of getting fome farther information which has been promifed me; but which I have not yet received.

What reception this *new* kind of evidence (and evidence it certainly is, *in foro confcientiæ*, at leaft) may meet with from a humane and difcerning nation, it becomes not me to foretel; but every gentleman to whom I have imparted my defign, is of opinion, that, in the prefent

advanced

advanced state of the controversy, a more conclusive mode of treating the subject could scarcely have been thought of; since, in the newspapers, now in my possession, truths *stand confessed* which the most subtle sophist will in vain attempt to invalidate. Popular songs, and music, and proverbs, and diversions; but, above all, common advertisements in newspapers are perhaps some of the best criteria of the manners, taste, and character of any people.*

The authorities of which I am possessed will enable me to give a fuller account than I expected, when I first entered on this research, of the treatment of the slaves in Jamaica.—To begin with a description of a Guinea sale, otherwise called a *scramble*, as practised in that island.

From the supplement to the Jamaica Gazette of March 8th 1788, printed by Thomas Strupar and Joseph Preston, Kingston:

' The following description of a GUINEA SALE
' was handed to us, by a correspondent for publication:
' At length the hour arrives and the words are uttered
' with a loud voice, " The sale is opened!!" *The crowd*
' *in waiting immediately rush down upon the terrified Afri-*

---

* The following paragraph is taken from the supplement to the Savannah-la-mar Gazette of February 19th 1788. The author considers the scandalous licentiousness with which the most respectable characters are there treated, as a prelude to what he is to expect from that and similar quarters.—' A correspondent observes that as an *Alderman of the city* ' *of London*, and who, at the same time, is a *member of the* BRITISH *par-* ' *liament*, has, very humanely, taken up the cudgels in behalf of the *unfortu-* ' *nate people of colour*, and as *it is not doubted but that the rest of the Aldermen will* ' *tender their assistance*, he would recommend to them each to contribute ' his mite towards the purchasing a cargo of turtle, to be sent home as ' a present to those *deep waisted toad-eaters*, which would greatly induce ' them to *join heartily in the cause*, and strenuously endeavour to put those ' *oppressed people* on a proper footing, &c. &c. The piece concludes with something about ' *violent, wrongheaded, bigoted white men*,' epithets more suitable to the *enemies* than to the *friends* of mankind.—The writer of the following letter, inasmuch as he may not improperly be deemed a fautor of *the cause*, and has not, for a long time, tasted *green fat*, hereby puts in his claim to a share of the above promised turtle. But he begs he may be allowed to dress it in his own way, having a mortal aversion to the seasoning of such cooks as those of Savannah-la-mar, which scents powerfully of *Asa fœtida*, but contains not one single particle of *Attic salt*.

' cans,

' cans, who, at such a sight, are instantly struck with the
' most dreadful apprehensions. While many fall prostrate
' upon their faces, others are seen closely embracing their
' companions, expecting immediate death. Their cries, which
' are truly lamentable, are communicated through the ship,
' and they are overwhelmed with amazement, sorrow and
' despair. From the hurry and eagerness of those who
' are purchasers upon such dismal occasions, a person not
' acquainted with the *abominable etiquette* of a slave sale
' could have no other idea than that the wretches were to
' be had *gratis*. *The stated price of* SIXTY-EIGHT
' POUNDS AND THE DUTY, *for each of the trembling cap-*
' *tives would be thought a romance.* Some of the purchas-
' ers more active than others, jump over the barricade,
' the person who follows very often happens to thrust one
' of his feet into the coat pocket of him who leads, and
' the loss of a skirt is the consequence; whilst a third
' has his hat knocked off and trampled under foot, and a
' fourth loses one of his shoes. These casualties generate
' no small degree of ill humour among the parties and a
' boxing match ensues. But this is not all. Conse-
' quences of the most serious nature sometimes follow
' —a life is lost, perhaps also the life of a valuable mem-
' ber of the community—not in the implacable vehe-
' mence of passion; but coolly and deliberately after rea-
' son has resumed the throne. Fatalities of this kind
' are owing to one of the parties supposing himself in-
' sulted by the other; a challenge is therefore offered
' and accepted, and it has been known that two worthy
' citizens have been lost to society, the survivor being
' obliged to decamp, in order to avoid making that dread-
' ful compensation, which is due to the violated laws of
' his country. I shall instance the case of the unfortu-
' nate Mr. I——, who fell in a duel with Mr. B——,
' which was occasioned by a paltry misunderstanding, of
' the nature above described, on board of a Guinea-man.
' Is not this sufficient to point out the absolute necessity
' of changing the shocking ceremony practised at slave-
' sales? Why not adopt the method pursued at all the
' *Windward* Islands?'

As we are yet, in some degree, in the dark, as to the end and meaning of this brutal affray, I shall subjoin a
passage

passage which explains it, taken from a piece intitled 'An *Apology* for Negro Slavery, or the West India Planters *vindicated*, London 1786.' 'In this place,' says the author, 'it is certainly proper to observe, that a mode of selling negroes is sometimes practised which ought to be abolished by a law of the islands where it prevails, as being repugnant to decency, and, *in some measure*, to humanity. The custom I mean to reprobate is the selling a cargo of slaves by what is called a *scramble*. This is shutting them up in the merchant's house, or the area adjoining, and, at the beat of a drum, or some other signal, all those who intend to become purchasers *rush on suddenly* or, to use a *military* phrase, *dash* upon the astonished and frightened negroes, and endeavour to get hold of or to incircle in a cord, as many of them as they can. Although the negroes are generally prepared for this by being preinformed of what is to happen, yet some of the *women and children have been known to expire* from an excess of terror, which is incited by a scene of such confusion and uproar. Nor is it uncommon for the purchasers themselves to go by the ears and quarrel about the objects of their choice.' Such is the language even of an *apologist* for negro slavery.*

'To compleat your idea, Sir, of this infernal uproar, you must be informed that some of the Africans, as is understood from those who afterwards speak English, are so possessed with the apprehension of their being bought up to be fattened and roasted and eaten, that they pine to death, or commit acts of desperation, from that cause alone. The effect of such an idea on their minds must be the same, as if the whites really fed on human flesh; and, no doubt they look upon their purchasers as so many furious cannibals 'rushing down,' to devour them. We are told that they are 'generally preinformed of what is to happen;' but who is the interpreter? A sailor who has made more than *one* voyage to Guinea may understand some words he hears on the coast; a captain may know many such words; but is it possible that any man,

* Mr. M'Neill is *totally silent* on the subject of a Jamaica scramble.

white

white or black, should be skilled in the endless variety of dialects, spoken at the distance of many hundred miles up the country?

I suppose it impossible to increase the execration with which the reader must contemplate the scene of ferocious violence above described, which, taking in *all* the shocking circumstances, can have no parallel on this side of *New Zealand*. Humanity has no place at a scramble. Even common sense is excluded: and *where is the sense of* INTEREST *which hath been triumphantly extolled as the guardian angel of the slave?*—Come forward sophists! and explain to the world, how the interest of the seller or the buyer is consulted, at a slave-sale, when mothers and their babes elude the clutches of brutal monsters, by expiring at their feet!!

I pretend not to reconcile the word 'islands,' in the last account of the scramble, with the concluding sentence of the first 'Why not,' &c. The truth, I believe, is that the practice of scrambling prevails in more than one island. Certain I am *it is not now practised*, I had almost affirmed that it never was practised, *in Barbadoes*; for I never so much as heard of it, till, having a mind to see what shadow of argument could be offered in support of slavery, I read the above passage cited from one of our *adversaries*.

I have the honour to be, &c.

LETTER XIII.

SIR,

HAVING seen what kind of reception the African strangers meet with, on their arrival in Jamaica, let us next proceed to enquire into their subsequent treatment in that island.

In the Gazette of St. Jago de la Vega (or Spanish town) of Jan. 24, 1788, published by the printer to the Council and Assembly, I find the following paragraph, which is one of the

'Clauses in the St. Jago de la Vega police-law, passed the 22d day of December 1787.

'No person, to expose to sale, in or at the doors or piazza's of any shop or house, or in places adjacent thereto, any *putrid salt-fish* or other provisions, *rancid butter*, oil, or other *offensive commodity*, or keep the same in any dwelling-house or out-office, to the annoyance of any of the inhabitants under the penalty of *twenty pounds* for every offence, one moiety thereof to the poor, and the other to the informer: A justice upon view, forthwith to cause the same to be seized and immediately destroyed or burnt.'*

From this clause and the penalty, which will appear hereafter to be a very heavy one, I conclude that the provisions in question are so utterly spoilt as to be a great public nuisance; that, in this state, large quantities of them are exposed to sale in Spanish town; that those large quantities are purchased by famished slaves (for I know of no other animal which would feed on such trash) and consequently that *there are great numbers of famished or* 'under-fed'† *slaves in Jamaica*, a fact which I will presently confirm, by other authorities.

Had I thought of it, I might have proved, by this fact *alone*, that great numbers of the slaves in Barbadoes are most grievously pinched in their food. Rotten provisions are not destroyed or burnt, in that island; but are bought by the starving negroes, with the price of the trifles they bring to market. Before the late war, though vast, and sometimes superfluous, quantities of *sound provisions* were imported, several whole streets in the towns stunk pestilentially with the abominable effluvia of substances, which had been provisions, but which were often so far dissolved

---

* Mr. Long says, That 'the greater number' of the Jews in St. Jago de la Vega 'deal in *damaged salt butter, herrings, beef, cheese,* and train oil, a congregation of stinking commodities, which is enough to poison the air of their habitations.' Hist. of Jam. vol. 2. p. 29.   † M'Neill.

by

by putrefaction, as to be exposed to sale in tubs. Most of the lower kind of huckster-shops still emit no very agreeable odours.

I now beg leave, Sir, to lay before you, an extract of a private letter, which will throw very considerable light on our subject. The authenticity of the original, I am authorised to say, can be established, beyond the reach of cavil.

'Jamaica, March 10. 1776.'

————' Then I went up to my new habitation, which
' is a very agreeable place. You at home form a wrong
' idea of Jamaica. I will assure you the *white* people
' hath great indulgence; neither is it so hot as you may
' think it is. I have had a good state of health since I
' have been here. I hope I shall be able to do better
' for myself than I could expect in England, if God spare
' my health. Here are no taverns nor no public-houses.
' Every estate is our home. The white gentlemen are
' very respectful one to another; so there is no way to
' spend my money, as usual, in this part of the world.
' We set the least store by the Sabbath-day. It is hard
' to know this day from the rest. We are just within
' 20 miles of the church. There is one in every parish;
' but the parish very large. The living here is different
' from home. The bread groweth upon the trees, which
' I like very well. It groweth like a cucumber; when
' roasted eats very well. I live better than half the far-
' mers at home. I seldom sit down to dinner without a
' dish of fish, fowl and beef, &c. with rum and water,
' or punch to drink and a slave to attend us. I have
' done no ploughing yet.* The ploughs are come from
' England; but the horses all died, in their passages—
' six fine ones, cost 40l. each in Lincolnshire.————Dear
' father, *the greatest hardship I meet with is to see poor*
' *negroes flogged so bad. I have seen them worse whipt*
' *than ever ploughman whipt his horses.* We have a negro
' to drive them; one driver to every thirty negroes,
' which stand by them at work with a *large whip*; and,
' if any misdemeanor, *they lay them down naked* and whip
' them according to their crime—*thirty lashes, sometimes*

* Mr. M'NEILL (obs. p. 6, note) says the plough ' answers extremely
' well in Jamaica.'

' SIXTY, *which will cut them raw*; and, if they make any
' refiftance, DOUBLE THE QUANTITY. They have but
' *five falt herrings a week*,* which is the *beft* allowance,
' and beft tradefmen have no more—fometimes *nothing*
' *for fix months together, but what they can produce in their*
' *own lands, which they have only Sunday to work it.* They
' have about 200 acres of wafte land to clear and raife
' their food in, which produce them yams, plantanes,
' coco and coffee, tobacco, and moft forts of vegetables
' you have at home. You will think this *very hard to*
' *have flefh and blood ufed fo as the poor negroes are*; yet
' they look as fat as any working man at home. This
' is the time they take off their crop of fugar; which
' *they have but four hours fleep out of the twenty-four.*
' They work in the field all day, then boil fugar at night.
' —So I think I have given you a good account of our
' management here. Now I will give you an account of
' my own employ at prefent—to look after the cattle,
' and go with the wain-men to fee them load their wains
' properly, at night to fit in the boiling-houfe to *attend*
' *the negroes till twelve o'clock, then call another up.* My
' work is nothing, only attendance. I expect going to
' plough every day with the oxen, as we have no horfes.
' Here is *ninety good ftrong oxen*, all able to work and
' do work in the wains. We work *eight fteers* in

* ' *Tradefmen* and *chief negroes* receive a ftated weekly allowance of beef,
' herring, or falt fifh, THE REST OCCASIONALLY.' Hift. of Jam. v.
2. p. 490.—I am *particularly well* informed that the following were *all*
the *foreign* provifions, confumed in 1781, on a Jamaica eftate, the proprietor of which is allowed to be both regular and liberal in his fupplies.
—30 cwt. of flour at 15s.—4 cwt. do. at 17s. 6d.—4 bufhels oatmeal—
4 bufhels grute—120lb. barley—1 bufhel fplit peas—8 barrels *mefs*-beef—
4 barrels pork—2 cwt. 1 qr. 6 lb. rofe butter—70 *barrels of herrings* at
32s. per barrel, is 112l. fter. The whole coft of thefe provifions was
286l. 7s. 6d. fter. On the eftate there were, in all 320 negroes, 20 of
whom were employed about the houfe. Here 70 barrels of herrings
were the allowance of *animal* food, for 300 field-negroes, for a whole
year. A barrel contains from 600 large to 1000 fmall herrings. Thefe
laft are preferred for plantation ufe. Say, therefore 1000, which will
give nearly *four fmall herrings and a half* for the *weekly allowance* of each
negro.—It does not appear that the field-negroes, on this eftate, had
any fcraps of falted meat, on the holidays. Eight barrels of beef and
four of pork will not be thought too much for the whites, their guefts
and the houfe favourites. Befides *mufs* beef is not given to field negroes.
All the other articles were for the ufe of the houfe and the fick.

' one

' one wain, without any horses before them. They go
' like dogs,' &c.
                                    ROBT. BROWNE.

' Mr. P—— I hope you will communicate this to
' *Edw. Browne* my father; so I have the honour to be
' your most humble servt.
                                    ' *Robt. Browne.*'
' Direct to me at J— G— K—, Esq. Plantane-gar-
' den River estate, St. Thomas in East Jamaica.'

Sir, the heroic and justly ennobled Scotch ploughman, HAY,* was not more formidable to the Danish invaders of his country, than this honest and humane English ploughman is to the invaders of the rights of mankind. He alone is more than a match for a legion of such antagonists. If a British peasant, aware of no contradiction, dreading no persecution, cramped, embarrassed and appalled, by no CRITICAL terrors, and biassed by no prejudices but those generous ones which do honour to a man and to an *Englishman*†—if such a person, I say, should draw a picture of *slavery*, ought we to doubt that it represents the life? His letter is worthy of a large commentary; but I must content myself with making a few cursory observations on it.

FIRST then, according to R. B. little or no attention is paid to religion in Jamaica, see p. 58.—2. It appears that the white servants in Jamaica fare, or at least, that R. B. fared, incomparably better than men of his station in Barbadoes. Alas! they ' seldom or never sit down to
' a dish of (fresh) fish, (fresh) beef or *fowl*. Let the reader judge whether or not a man can be said to live
' better than half the farmers at home,' whose diet consists of herrings, salt fish or *cargo* beef, often of a bad quality, to say nothing of the quantity. Fowl is intirely out of the question. Their vegetables, indeed, are ge-

---

* See Henry's Hist. of G. Britain, v. 2. p. 82; also the New Peerage, art. ' Hay Earl of Errol.'

† ' *Slavery* is so *vile* and *miserable* an estate of man, and *so opposite to the
' generous temper and courage of our nation*, that it is hardly to be conceived
' that an *Englishman*, much less a *Gentleman*, should plead for it.' Locke
on Govern. B. 1. ch. 1.

nerally

nerally good; but not sufficient in quantity, as I myself have seen.—3. R. B's account of the ordinary punishments in Jamaica is truly shocking. *Thirty, sixty* and sometimes ' *double the quantity*' of lashes inflicted with a '*large whip,*' on a wretch laid ' *down naked !*' Sir, I scruple not publicly and positively to aver, that regular discipline in Barbadoes, is mildness itself, compared to this! R. B. specifies the *number* of lashes, which shews that they are *regularly* inflicted, see p. 15. et seq.*—4. The *best* allowance in the large, rich and fertile island of Jamaica is ' five salt herrings, a week'—much about the *best* allowance in the poor, little island of Barbadoes. ' *Best* tradesmen have no more' in the former island; in the latter *all* tradesmen are treated better, in every respect, than the field-people.———5. ' Sometimes nothing for six ' months together, but what they can produce in their ' own lands.'†—This, I have very great reason to believe, is sometimes the case in Barbadoes.‡—6. In Jamaica ' they have only Sunday to work it'‖—just as in Barbadoes.

* Mr. M'NEILL (Obs. p. 22.) talks of negroes ' receiving *so many* ' lashes;' but mentions no particular *number*.

† See our motto, p. 103.

‡ My reasons for believing this are of a very cogent kind. Not to repeat the general report respecting the starved and *gibbetted* wretches mentioned at p. 19, I have been *officious* enough to ask some complaining slaves, What need they had for any other allowance, when they had plenty of cane-juice? and have been answered, ' *Water* won't 'tand in a ' pond without *mud* Massa?' shrewdly intimating, That something more solid than cane-juice was necessary for their support. Others, whose looks evinced the truth of their assertion, have said to me, ' Massa no ' gie we no 'lowance' (Master gives us no allowance).—Why should I hint at the bruised tin pint-pots and the tin pint-pots with thick wooden bottoms which I have seen, or the ' deceitful weights' which I and others have *experienced*?—for short weights and measures are to be found in *all* countries.

‖ Mr. M'NEILL (Obs. p. 3.) says that ' Every negro is allowed, ' independent of Sunday, which he has to himself, throughout the ' year, one day in each fortnight, *for eight months*, for the particular purpose ' of working his grounds.' This supposes the crop season to be only four months. In Barbadoes it is five or six. I remember that, on one estate, in St. Andrew's parish, sugar was made, almost during the whole year. If ' *every* negro' in Jamaica has a day in each fortnight, I can only say that I know of no regulation, in favour of the negroes in Barbadoes, that hath any thing like an *universal* operation. After all, I have does.—7. On the estate from which R. B. wrote, they had '200 acres of waste land to clear and raise their food 'in'—an extent of land this, which perhaps no ten estates in Barbadoes can afford for *negro-grounds*. But the cultivation of provisions for the negroes in this last island always was a part, and is now a very serious part of regular *plantation-business*.—8. R. B. mentions no other vegetable food than what the negroes could produce on their own grounds. Indeed his expression '*nothing* for six months 'together' and his mentioning *herrings only*, gives us much reason to believe that the negroes immediately under his eye, had no allowance of grain or roots but what they so produced. On the other hand, we shall presently see a Jamaica estate abounding in ground-provisions. *Probably*, some Jamaica planters do, and others do not, follow the salutary and, in the end, œconomical, Barbadian practice of feeding their negroes, chiefly, with provisions which they themselves raise.—9. ' It produces them ' yams, plantanes, *cocers*' (as he spells it, qu. the *cocoa-nut*,* or the *coco*,† or chocolate-nut? probably the latter as it is followed by) 'coffee,' &c. That a common field-negro worn down with daily and often with *nightly* labour, should, on Sunday, be able to *clear* waste land, to raise shrubs and trees which yield only an annual crop, appears, to my little Barbadian ideas, so very incredible, that I must take it for granted, those luxuries belong chiefly to the principal negroes, or perhaps to some hardy rogue of a field-negro, who braves every hardship, or has the address to get others to work for him. Probably what R. B. calls waste land may be partly situated in gullies, &c. where canes cannot be planted, and where trees of the slowest growth get leave to come to maturity. If so, some such spots may be seen in Barbadoes. But Qu. Whether, on *new* estates, *at least*, the negroes, be not, sometimes, deprived of the land they have cleared, if proper for canes, and wood-land assigned them in lieu of it?—10. No sooner has R. B. mentioned these seeming luxuries, than he uses this strong language 'You may

have learnt, since these letters were penned, that the indulgence in question, is in effect, taken away, by the lately passed consolidated slave law.

* Cocos nucifera: † Theobroma Cacao.

' think it very hard to have flesh and blood used so as the
' poor negroes are.' This I call strong language; for
when the whole man is roused by some intolerable treatment received or observed, is not ' flesh and blood' very
often used to signify the outraged feelings of human nature?—11. ' Yet they look as fat as any working man
' at home;' but then he adds, ' this is the time they take
' off their crop of sugar,' March 10, about the middle of
the most plentiful season of the year.—12. ' They have
' but four hours sleep,' &c. This is too often the case
in Barbadoes, (see p. 11.) I have seen negroes collecting
mill-trash, which had been spread out, in the mill-yard,
to dry for fuel, at eight at night, when they had not
nearly finished their work. I have often been in a boiling-house, where they were at work *at least*, as late as
nine o'clock; and, at almost all hours of the night and
morning, I have observed the flames issuing from boiling-house chimneys, a certain proof that they were then at
work.*—13. ' At night to sit in the boiling-house,' &c.
—exactly the employment of men in similar stations in
Barbadoes.—14. ' I expect going to plough every day.'
R. B. an unseasoned European, approved of the climate
of Jamaica (see the beginning of this extract) and talks
here very coolly of going to plough. This is *one* strong instance that white men, were it necessary, as it is not, might
work in the fields of that island (see p. 41.) especially
such as do not excessively indulge in pleasures too much
followed there. R. B. had ' rum and water and punch,'
and something else, at his command.—15. ' Here is
' ninety good strong oxen,' &c. We shall, hereafter,
prove how well cattle thrive in Jamaica, which is a point
of some consequence. I am almost tempted here to make
a bold affirmation—That there are scarcely the above
number of what an English ploughman would call ' good
' strong oxen,' in the island of Barbadoes (see p. 10.)
Sure I am, that the united flocks of many estates there,
could not furnish ninety such oxen.

---

* Mr. M‘Neill (p. 5.) says that during crop time ' every person
' takes his *spell* or watch in the boiling house or mill *one night in three*.'
But, on estates which are weakly handed, (of which he says p. 36, there
are many in Jamaica) do they not take such spells *oftener*?

I cannot

I cannot dismiss this valuable extract, without adding a few words to shield it from the arts of sophistry of which it's author was happily ignorant. 'Their lands,' says 'R. B. produces them yams,' &c. This bill of fare of excellent vegetables, dressed in a certain way, * might fascinate the senses, and make us believe that

'On candied plantanes and the juicy pine,
'With choicest melons and sweet grapes they dine,
'And with potatoes feed their wanton swine: †

But the 'putrid salt fish and other offensive commodities' mentioned in the St. Jago de la Vega police-law, and R. B's, expressions 'five herrings a week,' and 'nothing 'for six months together,' undo the spell, and prove that the Jamaica slaves often pine with hunger.

'They look as fat as any working man at home,' *ergo*, says certain reasoners, their condition is as eligible. Sir, I cannot away with this gross insult to the laws and constitution of my country, which I have learned to value and to revere, by observing the dire effects resulting from the want of them. I might now, with the help of this *English peasant*, draw a parallel infinitely nearer the truth—but I forbear. I must ask, however, a question which cannot be too frequently or urgently pressed home, Why the West Indian negroes, (who, as animals, are not inferior to any of their species) if they really are as happy as English peasants, do not, like English peasants, keep up their numbers by procreation?

I have the honour to be, &c.

---

* See Mr. M'NIELL's obs. p. 3. where he describes 'groves of plan-
'tane, banana, and orange trees, loaded with fruit.'—'Styes filled with
'hogs, and flocks of fowls, ducks, and turkies.' But he immediately
adds (p. 4.) 'All this, 'tis true, although often, is *not generally* met
'with.'

† Waller.

LETTER

LETTER XIV.

SIR,

I believe you and the public are yet to be informed, That the negroes in Jamaica are BRANDED with their owner's *marks* and the *initials* of their names, and, in one instance before me, with the owner's firname at full length on four parts of the body. This is quite a new discovery to me; for the practice of branding slaves does not disgrace the island of Barbadoes. The full names of the owners, answering to the initials, are generally inserted in the several Jamaica newspapers, in which I find such lists as the following; but, for an obvious reason, I omit those names, inserting those of the slaves only.

From the Gazette of St. Jago de la Vega, of October 11. 1787.
RUNAWAYS in Westmoreland work-house Oct. 2. 1787. Cuffie marked R W or H W diamond at top.—Ned marked P within a diamond—Anthony appears to be marked W and WL in one—Cuffie marked TH in one.

RUNAWAYS in St. James's work-house, Oct. 5. 1787. Swanfey marked WM—Fortune marked PB diamond between.

'RUNAWAYS in Spanish town work-house, Oct. 10.
' 1787. Daniel marked on *both shoulders* MD—Amba
' marked AF—Candis marked LG—Oroonoko marked
' WF—Jasper marked BWB—Ned marked PE—James
' marked with a triangler stamp—James marked B—
' Downer a *mulatto* marked GC, C at top—William
' marked, on the *right shoulder* RA *(heart and diamond be-*
' *tween)* and on the *left* RA *heart at top*—Will marked
' IT—Batty marked *on both shoulders* HP in one—Toby
' marked DG—Molly and her child marked MF—Quaco
' BC on left breast.

RUN-

' RUNAWAYS in Spanish town gaol, Oct. 2. 1787.
' Rosie and child marked CP heart at top—Mimba
' marked SK—Billy DB—Peggy IT—Fidelia W—
' Cuffie TR, C at top—William WP, PG at top—
' Walker MF—Mary F—Jasper WG, heart at top—
' Hunt RC—Industry WI, C at top—Romeo B.'

' RUNAWAYS in St. Mary's work-house, Oct. 3.
' 1787. Rebecca CP, heart at top—Nancy *ditto*—Old
' Eve *ditto*—Thomas CH—Phœbe IH, S at top—Eletta
' U—Ben S—Billy WG—Bryan BE—Guy on the
' *right shoulder* WD, and on the left IH—Bacchus EB,
' diamond at top.'

' There are besides, in this paper, fifty runaway slaves,
' with ' no mark,' and *two* who are said to have no
' BRAND mark.'—That you may be able to compare the
marks (for the word *brand* occurs not in the stray-lists before
me) on the cattle with the brands on the slaves, I subjoin the following advertisement.

' St. Catharine's pound, Oct. 11. 1787. LIST of
' STRAYS sent in.'

' A bay stallion, marked IN on the off buttock and
shoulder—A dark bay mare marked ҘҘ—A bay gelding
mule EBL in one on near buttock—An English sorrel
horse, marked SI—Two sorrel horses marked IB, diamond between, on the off buttock—A bay mare marked
AC, 8 at top—A bay mare marked on the off buttock
W, diamond at top—A dark bay mare marked 3, and
diamond reversed. There are besides three horses and
one mule which are said to have Spanish marks, and four
with no visible mark.

In all, *seventeen stray horses* and *ninety-seven runaway
slaves* are advertised in this paper.

In the Gazette of St. Jago de la Vega, dated Nov. 8.
1787, I observe these remarkable brands.—Apollo, alias
Jack, marked WS *on his face and breast*—Robert marked
RP *on each cheek*, and, above all, Kingston marked
YORKE *on each shoulder and breasts.*

In this paper there are besides twenty runaways branded, thirty-eight unmarked, and five with ' no BRAND-
' mark'—also sixteen stray-horses marked, six with no
marks, and five with Spanish marks—In all, *twenty-seven
stray horses* and *sixty-six runaway slaves* are advertised in
this last paper.

In

In the Cornwall Chron. of Dec. 15. 1787. *Nine stray horses*, marked and unmarked, and *eighty-four runaway slaves* with and without *brands*, are advertised.

It would be tedious to enumerate the branded and wretched fugitives advertised in the large collection of Jamaica newspapers before me. But I hazard little in affirming, That, though there are not many more than thrice the number of slaves in that island, that there are in Barbadoes, yet that, in the Gazette of St. Jago de la Vega alone, there are at least, ten times the number of runaways that appear in the Barbadoes Mercury and Gazette taken together. This circumstance and that of their not being branded must be added to those I formerly adduced (p. 107) to evince the comparatively happy condition of the slaves in this last island.

That the Jamaica slaves are not always to be blamed for running away (my firm *belief* is, that, nine times in ten, they are not blameable) would appear from the following advertisement, in the Gazette of St. Jago de la Vega, for Nov. 8. 1787.

‘ To be sold a plantation and sugar work called Dover
‘ Castle, situated, &c. It consists of 1100 acres of
‘ land’——‘ well timbered with all kinds of hard wood,
‘ mahogany in great plenty, abounds with *ground pro-*
‘ *visions*, plenty of *Guinea grass*, a very fine set of works
‘ lately compleated, 100 negroes well disposed and ac-
‘ customed to the property, for a number of years. *They*
‘ *are strangers to running away*, &c.

DAVID HENRIQUES.

If Mr. H's account of his plantation be tolerably just, we must conclude him to be a very humane man. Notwithstanding he is so weakly handed, has a great part of his land uncleared, and has lately built a set of works, all frequent occasions of oppression; yet, we see his people are ‘ strangers to running away.’ But then, he has plenty of ‘ ground provisions’ for his people, and plenty of Guinea grass; so that those people are not harrassed in *picking grass* for his cattle.

I men-

I mentioned the building of a set of works, as an occasion of oppression; and I will give an instance in point. A manager of a Barbadoes plantation, in the same year that he made a large crop, erected some buildings. The slaves, after toiling in the field during the day, carried stones and mortar, &c. for a great part of the night. When the masons, on leaving off work, had worked up all the materials, they still found a fresh supply, on the spot, the next morning.

The consequence of this management was that shortly after a great number of the prime field negroes died. The tyrant who thought by such forced exertions to recommend himself to his employer, (now deceased, but who then lived in England) was, by the next packet, ordered off the estate. As he could not find employment in Barbadoes, he set sail for Jamaica, where he now exercises his genius, and is what they call a topping manager. A gentleman lately from that island, now in London, tells me, that he is still famous for *large crops and deadlifts*. Of this œconomy he gave an instance, in an estate which was offered for sale. In order to enhance the price, it was necessary that a large crop should be made and sworn to. Accordingly such an one as a Mr. I. was sent for, who made an uncommonly large crop; but it cost a great number of the slaves their lives. The gentleman very humanely and properly reprobated this conduct by the name of MURDER.

Let us next, if you please, Sir, see what treatment the negroes in Jamaica often receive, in the evening of their lives, and what are, too frequently, their rewards for exhausting their health and strength in the service of their owners.

In the supplement to the Cornwall Chron. of March 1. 1788 (Montego Bay Jamaica, printed by James Fannin) I find this paragraph.

‘ A certain gentleman, so we are given to understand,
‘ shortly means to lay before His Honour the Custos and
‘ the other magistrates of this parish, the outlines of a
‘ plan for building an hospital, at the West end of the
‘ town, for the reception of *disabled negroes abandoned by*
‘ their

‘ *their owners*, which, it is hoped, will be properly at-
‘ tended to.’

I have already (see p. 34.) observed that the practice of turning out and abandoning aged, worn out,
and leprous slaves utterly disgraces the island of Barbadoes. In every instance, I have taken care, That no
man shall justly charge me with partiality. But, as
no person, so far as I can learn, hath fully exposed the
infamous practice in question, I have been *particularly*
careful in anticipating every thing that can possibly be
urged to palliate it. I can most conscientiously declare,
Sir, That, were it possible for me to sit down to write
an *apology* for that practice, I could not think of, I had
almost said, I could not *invent*, any circumstance having
the smallest *tendency* to extenuate it, which I have not
thrown with its full weight into the opposite scale. But,
sorry I am to say, the opposite scale kicks the beam; nor
can all the feathers of extenuation, that can be collected,
however advantageously disposed, restore the equilibrium,
far less sink the scale. The last expiring breath of an exposed negro, will dissipate such feathers, like chaff before
the whirlwind.

A list in the Jamaica Gazette of Nov. 21. 1787,
will enable us to form some idea of the extent in which
this shocking practice prevails in that island.

‘ Account of negroes *interred* in the parish of King-
‘ ston, by order of the *Coroner*, during the year 1786.’

" Jan. 12. a man	" July 31. a man	" Oct. 11. a man
Feb. 1. a man	Aug. 10. a man	15. a man
3. a woman	24. a man	22. a woman
4. a man	Sept. 6. a man	30. a man
Mar. 2. a man	10. a woman	Nov. 15. a woman
4. a man	12. a woman	16. a man
21. a woman	13 { a man	27. a man
Apr. 15. a woman	{ a woman	Dec. 4. a man !
27. a man	22. a girl	10. a man
May 24. a woman	25. a man	20. a man
June 19. a man	27 { a woman	24. a *mulatto* girl
24. a man	{ a man	26. a *negro* ?
Jul. 25. a man	Oct. 4. a man	27. a *negro* ?

" Total 39 bodies."

‘ FEES

"FEES ON EACH."

" To the Coroner	L. 3	— —
" Constable for warning the jurors for the inquest	— 7	6
" Conveyance of the body to the grave	— 10	—
" Burial	— 10	—
	4 7	6
" Multiplied by the number of bodies (39)	170 12	6

I am willing to allow that some of the wretched subjects of those inquests died suddenly, or from unavoidable casualties. In the sequel, we will have abundant reason to believe that others were *actually* murdered. But I am of opinion, that the majority of them perished from being worn out or otherwise disabled in the service of, and afterwards abandoned by, their owners. My reasons for being of this opinion are, That *all* of them appear to have been buried at the expence of the parish, and that only *sixteen* of them perished during the first *eight* months of the year, which include the plentiful crop-season; whereas *three and twenty* perished during the remaining *four* months, which, in Barbadoes, at least, (see p. 7.) is the time of the year, when the greatest number of such wretches may be expected to drop into the grave.

I cannot compare this list with any similar one in Barbadoes; for, as I before observed, no coroner's inquest sits on the body of a slave, in that island. Why such inquest takes place in Jamaica I pretend not to say; for, before the late consolidated act passed, the murder of a slave was not capital there. But I may venture to say, that *thirty-nine* exceeds the *proportion* of exposed slaves who annually perish in Bridgetown, whither the majority of such wretches resort. This they may easily do in the small island of Barbadoes; but, in the large island of Jamaica, such a majority cannot easily resort to Kingston.

That thirty-nine is a most enormous number of coroner's inquests for Kingston and its neighbourhood, will appear, by considering, that it is rather more than *one eighth* of the average of deaths which annually happened
within

within the London bills of mortality,* for eight years, from casualties of *all* kinds, many of which require no coroner's inquests. Voltaire, in a passionate effusion to D'Alembert, dated June 29. 1762, mentions with very severe reprobation, ' Sixty assassinations or frightful mur-
' ders, considered in all their circumstances,' which had happened in France in a month, which is at the rate of 720, in a year. What would he have said had he been told, That *coroners* had sat on *one eighteenth* of that annual number in *a single district* of a West Indian colony, which *altogether* did not contain *one sixtieth*† of the population of that kingdom? He would have been ten-fold more severe than, in this very letter, he was against his countrymen for executing Callas. He had just warmed his fine imagination, with that tragical affair. In such a moment, few men are accurate calculators; and it is probable that his number sixty includes Callas, and perhaps others, whom he might have thought unjustly executed.

I have said nothing of the tempting fees which are paid for warning the jurors, to the constables, who, if they have any resemblance to the constables in Barbadoes, must often, but I do not say always, be both poor and worthless. But the coroners are generally very decent men. The late coroner of Bridge-town died, of an apoplexy, in the very act of supporting the cause of a negro, or a mulatto, with a warmth which probably was fatal to him.

I have the honour to be, &c.

* The only bills of mortality I have now at hand are those of 1752, 1753, 1756, 1757, 1780 (when the *riots* happened) 1781, 1782, 1783; and the average of casual deaths, in those years, is 309.—Bit by mad dogs, broken limbs, bruised, burnt, choaked, drowned, excessive drinking, executed, found dead, killed by falls and other accidents, murdered, overlaid, poisoned, scalded, self murder, smothered, starved, suffocated.

† The population of Jamaica, of all colours, falls short of 300,000, which is but one *sixty sixth* part of 20,000,000, the population assigned to France.

LETTER

LETTER XV.

SIR,

Having proved, I trust, to the satisfaction of every impartial person, that the yoke of slavery, in Jamaica, is altogether grievous and intolerable ; let us now, if you please, take a view of the laws which have been lately enacted to alleviate it, as far as those laws appear, in the papers, before me.
From the Supplement to the Cornwall Chronicle of Dec. 29th, 1787, printed, at Montego Bay, Jamaica, by James Fannin.

'The following clauses, we understand, have been
' proposed as an amendment and addition to the consoli-
' dated negro-bill now before the Honourable House of
' Assembly, and do much honour to the head and heart
' of the gentleman who introduced them.'

' And whereas the *extreme cruelties* and *inhumanity* of
' the Managers, Overseers and Book-keepers of estates
' have frequently driven slaves into the woods, and occa-
' sioned *rebellions* and *internal insurrections* to the great
' prejudice of the proprietors, and the manifest danger of
' the lives of the inhabitants of this island; For preven-
' tion whereof be it enacted, and it is hereby enacted,
' by the authority aforesaid, That any Manager, Over-
' seer, or Book-keeper of any estate or plantation who
' shall or may hereafter be convicted of inflicting any
' *unnatural* or *inhuman punishment*, on any slave or slaves,
' shall be liable to prosecution and to such fine and im-
' prisonment as the Judges of the Supreme Court, or the
' Judges of any of the Assize Courts may think fit. And
' whereas also it *frequently* happens, that slaves come to
' their *death by hasty and severe blows*, and *other* impro-
' per treatment, of overseers and book-keepers, in the
' heat of passion, and, when such accidents do happen,
' the victims are entered on the plantation-books, as hav-
' ing

'ing died of convulsions, fits or other causes not to be
'accounted for, and to *conceal the real truth of the cause
'of the death* of such slave or slaves, he or they is or are
'*immediately put under ground,* without the inspection or
'knowledge of the doctor or doctors of the plantation
'whereon such accidents do happen. For prevention
'whereof, *as far as possible,* and the better to enable the
'doctor and doctors of every estate to take the oath pre-
'scribed by this act, as to the increase and decrease of
'slaves annually on the estates or plantations under his
'or their care, be it enacted by the authority aforesaid,
'and it is hereby enacted, by the authority of the same,
'That, from and after the passing of this act, no slave or
'slaves actually dying suddenly, on any plantation or
'estate, whether by fits, convulsions or any other causes,
'shall be buried or put under ground, on any pretence
'whatever, until the doctor or doctors of such planta-
'tion or estate hath been called to and hath actually
'viewed the body of such slave or slaves so dying sud-
'denly as aforesaid. And for the more effectual preven-
'tion of *murders* and *inhuman treatment* of slaves, be it
'enacted by the authority aforesaid, and it is hereby en-
'acted accordingly, That the Manager, Overseer and
'Book-keeper or Book-keepers of every plantation do or
'shall, on the 31st day of December, in every succeed-
'ing year, after the 31st day of December instant, make
'oath of the increase and decrease of slaves on the planta-
'tion or estate under his care, setting forth the causes of
'such decrease, the nature of the diseases whereby the
'decrease had accrued and arisen to the best of his or
'their knowledge and belief.

'The member (Mr. GRAY) who introduced the a-
'bove premised, That to *his own certain knowledge* un-
'common and VERY UNNATURAL PUNISHMENTS were
'*often* inflicted on negroes; and that, in several instances,
'he had been obliged to interpose, as a magistrate, to
'prevent ACTUAL REBELLION, from such inhuman
'treatment.'

This extract discloses *a horrid groupe of* CAUSES of
the INSURRECTIONS in the island of Jamaica. 'Inhu-
'man treatment' and 'actual rebellion' necessarily and
mutually

mutually produce one another.—But I must leave you, Sir, to form your own reflections on this delicate subject. The following citations will help you to form some idea of the punishments in question.

'For rebellion,' says Sir Hans Sloane*, 'the punish-
'ment is burning them by nailing them down to the
'ground, with crooked sticks on every limb, and then
'applying the fire by degrees, from the feet and hands,
'*burning them gradually up to the head*; whereby their
'pains are extravagant. For crimes of a less nature,
'*gelding* or *chopping off half the foot*, with an axe.'—
'For negligence they are usually whipped, by the over-
'seers with lance-wood *switches*.'—'After they are
'*whipped till they are raw*, some put on their skins *pepper*
'*and salt to make them smart*: at other times, their mas-
'ters will *drop melted wax on their skins*, and use several
'*very exquisite torments*.'—We find a similar account in a history of Jamaica, written about the year 1740, by a person then residing in that island.† 'The most trivial
'error,' says he, 'is punished with most terrible whipping.
'I have seen them treated, in that cruel manner, for no
'other reason, but to satisfy the brutish pleasure of an
'overseer, who has their punishment *mostly at his dis-*
'*cretion*. I have seen *their bodies all in a gore of blood*,
'the *skin torn off their backs* with the cruel whip; beaten
'*pepper and salt rubbed in the wounds*, and a *large stick*
'*of sealing wax dropped leisurely upon them*. It is no
'wonder if the horrid pain of *such inhuman tortures*
'incline them *to rebel*.'—According to Mr. Long,‡ in consequence of the rebellion, in 1760, 'Two of the St.
'Mary ring-leaders, Fortune and Kingston were *hung up*
'*alive in chains* on a gibbet erected in the parade of the
'town of Kingston. Fortune lived seven days, but Kings-
'ton survived till the ninth.'—Gracious Heaven! what a spectacle, for nine days, in a public parade!!§

Before

* Nat. Hist. of Jam. Introd. p. 56.
† See Benezet's Guinea, p. 68.
‡ Hist. of Jam. v. 2. p. 458. n.
§ Mr. M'Neill, either expressly or tacitly confirms all the above extracts.—'Were I to advance' (says he, p. 19.) that punishments, in 'this country, are trifling and unfrequent, I should not only draw on 'myself the imputation of gross misrepresentation and prejudice, but
'in

Before I go farther, Sir, I muſt declare, in addition to what I ſaid at p. 16. and elſewhere, That the drivers (or overſeers) and book-keepers, in their ordinary treatment of ſlaves, in Barbadoes, are not permitted to inflict, and do not inflict, the ' very unnatural puniſhments,' much leſs ' haſty and ſevere blows' cauſing DEATH, againſt which the above cited clauſe provides, and which the praiſe worthy propoſer of it affirms are ' often inflicted on ne- ' groes' in Jamaica. In Barbadoes, ſuch perſons are obliged, on pain of abſolutely ſtarving, as ſome of them, from their great numbers, do, for want of employment, to ſtop far ſhort of ſuch horrid exceſſes. The powers delegated to them are, comparatively ſpeaking, very much limited, and never do extend beyond the uſe of the whip, which, however, if not ſtrictly looked after, they are but too apt to abuſe.

From the Supplement to the Jamaica Gazette of March 8. 1788.
' Extract from the Conſolidated Slave-law.'

' And be it further enacted by the authority aforeſaid,
' That on the 28th day of December in every year (the
' time of giving in as aforeſaid) the doctor or ſurgeon em-
' ployed on ſuch plantation, penn or other ſettlement, or
' where there is no doctor or ſurgeon employed thereon,
' then the owner, overſeer or manager ſhall, under the
' penalty of *ten pounds*, to be levied on the owner of ſuch
' plantation, for every neglect, give in, on oath an account
' of the decreaſe or increaſe of the ſlaves of ſuch plantation,
' penn or ſettlement, and the cauſes of ſuch decreaſe, to
' the beſt of his knowledge, judgment and belief.'

* in fact aſſert what is not founded in truth. *Puniſhments are certainly*
* *very frequent*; and to a mind actuated by compaſſion alone, thoſe pu-
* niſhments are a ſource of conſtant pain. To me, I freely confeſs, they
* were very diſtreſſing, on my *firſt coming to this iſland*.' [N. B. Our author had been in the Windward Iſlands] ' and, even at this time, after
* having reaſoned on the neceſſity, and (let me add) the propriety of
* CERTAIN *puniſhments*, the crack of the whip ſeldom fails to operate
* on my nerves like an electric ſhock.—But let us not be carried away
* by mere ſenſibility; let us for a moment *ſet ſlavery aſide*.'—Here our
author enters on the beaten track of other apologiſts for ſlavery, in which
we have not time to follow him. At p. 27. *torments* are confeſſed—
* The *ſlothful* and *unfeeling* wretch will purſue his crimes, and remain in
* a ſtate of apathy, EVEN IN THE MIDST OF TORMENTS.'

The

The words 'where there is no doctor or surgeon em-
' ployed thereon' plainly imply that there are estates in Jamaica on which no doctor or surgeon is employed, see
p. 11.

I before promised to prove the penalty of *twenty pounds* for exposing putrid salt fish to sale, to be a heavy penalty. To do this, we have only to compare it with the penalty of the present clause, which is no more than *ten pounds* for neglecting annually to give an account upon oath, of the decrease or increase of slaves on every plantation. TEN POUNDS! for not exposing to view, an account, in which we are warranted, by the preceding extract, to suspect that *actual* murder may be included, as one cause of such decrease. What owner, what overseer, or what manager would not sooner pay ten pounds than run the risque of being tried for his life for murdering a slave or slaves? Tried for his life, I say; in the sequel, we may be able to estimate the risque of his being convicted and executed for such a crime. I ask any man of common sense, Whether he can bring himself to believe, That a man who (like a murderous I. see p. 125.) hath diminished the number of slaves, on a plantation by oppression, or hunger, or cruelty, or all of them conjoined, be likely to give in the *true* cause or causes of that diminution? Still the real annual increase or decrease of slaves, if they can be obtained, may lead to beneficial consequences.

From the supplement to the Cornwall Chron. of March 1st, 1788.

" Extracts from the consolidated slave-law *which is to* " *take effect this day.*"

These extracts are so long that I am under the necessity of abridging them.

" Work-house keepers, and goal-keepers, under the penalty of 10*l.* for every neglect, to advertise runaways in three of the newspapers, once a-week; to keep them in custody until payment of the reward for apprehending them, with 2*s.* 6*d.* in the pound *extra*, the expence of advertising, at 1*s.* 3*d.* per month for each paper, and 6*d.* for every 24 hours such slave shall have been in custody."

' Owners

"Owners, &c. under the penalty of 10*l.* for each offence, to be recovered, in a summary manner, before any justice, not to turn away any sick, aged or infirm slaves. Any justice is impowered to lodge any such slave in the nearest work-house, to be fed, at the owner's expence, but not worked until trial. If any owner refuse to pay the penalty of 10*l.* with charges, the justice, under the penalty of 20*l.* is to commit such owner to gaol, till he makes payment. One moiety of the 10*l.* to the (*white*) informer, the other to the poor of the parish."

"Owners, &c. mutilating slaves, to be indicted in the supreme court of judicature, or in any of the Assize courts, and, on conviction, to be punished by fine not exceeding 100*l.* and imprisonment not exceeding 12 months, and still be liable to an action at common law for damages. In very atrocious cases, the mutilated slave may be declared free. The fine of 100*l.* in such case, to be paid to the parish, who are to allow the negro (now free) 10*l.* a year, for life.* Any justice, on application of a mutilated slave, is empowered to send such slave to the nearest work-house to be kept and attended till there can be a meeting of the justices and vestry of the parish, ' which ' justices and vestry so met are hereby created and ap-' pointed a council of protection of such slave or slaves,' and are impowered to make farther inquiry into the commitment of the mutilation, and to prosecute the offender at the expence of the parish, and, in case he shall appear capable of paying the costs of such prosecution, to commence suit against him for recovery of those costs. The keeper of the work-house to deliver up the mutilated slave to the said justices and vestry under the penalty of 20*l.*"

The first clause above quoted makes the expence and trouble of recovering runaways considerable, which will help to prevent owners and others from driving slaves into the woods, by cruelty and oppression. Yet the greater the trouble and expence of recovering him, the harsher will be the treatment of the fugitive when caught. The

---

* "By the law of this island (Jamaica) every person who manumits a negro slave is required to pay him annually 10*l.* currency to prevent his becoming a burden or nuisance to the community. *This is far from being regularly complied with.*" M'NEILL's obs. p. 14. note.

chains,

chains, pot-hooks, and boots will be heavier, and the dungeons more crowded.

On the next clause, I must observe, First, That I do not see how even the *name* of the owner of an infirm and exposed slave can always be discovered. It is true, the names of the owners, as well as of the slaves, are generally inserted in the runaway-lists before me. How the work-house keepers find out those names, whether by punishment or not I cannot tell; but, in Barbadoes, runaways are commonly very unwilling to discover their owner's names; and the confused sounds used by Africans, are often as unlike the real names as the Otaheitean *Toote*, *Tapane*, and *Torano* are to those of the great navigator and philosophers Cooke, and Banks, and Solander—In the next place, I scarcely see a possibility of convicting an owner of abandoning his worn-out slave. Gentlemen detest the invidious office of informers. Besides, it is absurd to suppose that they know every individual field-negro on the neighbouring estates. The bread of the white servants on the estate to which the wretch belongs, will often depend on concealing the truth. Should a poor settler, tempted by the £5, *dare* to inform, he must lay his account with persecution.— Lastly, an abandoned slave is to be lodged in a workhouse until trial; but it does not appear that, after trial he is to have any other asylum than his owner's estate. Let us suppose his owner convicted, fined and perhaps imprisoned. I ask, what sort of treatment the slave is to expect from an oppressor who had before turned him out to perish, who is now *compelled* to take him home; and is exasperated by the trouble and expence he has been put to, on account of an *useless* wretch? To the humanity and common sense of my reader I must the answer.

Under such circumstances, he will particularly deplore the fate of *leprous* negroes, who cannot safely be allowed to mix with healthy people. A paragraph before inserted (p. 125.) mentions the *outlines* of a plan for building an hospital for 'disabled,' but it takes no notice of leprous slaves 'abandoned by their owners.' This hospital, we presume, is yet, *in contemplation*. Such hospitals, will be be built, over all the West Indies, and endowed, and well managed and fully adequate to their end—when slavery shall change it's nature.

The humane intention of the third and last clause above cited appears on the face of it; but, if persons who mutilate their slaves are to be regularly convicted by the evidence of *whites* only, then I scruple not to express very great doubts of the efficiency of this clause in protecting slaves from such heinous abuses of the owner's power. The council of protection may be useful in very flagrant and *notorious* cases, which alone laws like the present are calculated to reach. While the testimony of a slave against a white man remains wholly invalid, no law can secure him from the cruel fangs of private tyranny. Indeed it is not pretended, that the justices and vestry of an extensive Jamaica parish will enter a man's premises to inquire why such a slave of his is reduced to a skeleton, why he practised some secret and, 'very unnatural punishment' (which might not have left very evident external marks) on another, or in a word, why his whole gang is 'over-worked and under-fed.'* The idea of a slave complaining to a justice against his owner is quite new to me. I say woe to that slave who shall *dare* to lodge such a complaint!! Besides how is a wretch who can neither read nor write, to know that there is such a law in his favour?

Mutilation is very seldom indeed inflicted by owners on their slaves, in Barbadoes. But miscreant drunkards and desperadoes, who sometimes murder slaves, do not much hesitate in committing less atrocious acts of violence on them.———An elderly negro woman, who worked out in Bridgetown, for her owner, a friend of mine, looked up to me for protection. One evening, she came to me, bathed in her blood, from a very large gash in her head. The piece hung over her ear, and had not the cutlass slanted off the bare skull, her ear, at which the stroke had been aimed, must have been cut off. Her life was in the more danger, as she was subject to violent attacks of the fever and ague; and she was confined for several weeks. She said she knew (and I am

* McNeill.

pretty sure, I know) the white man who cut her, and that *a great many negroes* saw the deed done. This was *no proof*. Her owner, therefore, was obliged to bear the expence and the loss of her labour. The very able surgeon who attended her is now in London.—A valuable and inoffensive negro man, belonging to an acquaintance of mine, was attacked, one evening, when going on his owner's business, by a white man, who, with one stroke of his cutlass, severed one of his hands from his body. His owner, who could produce no *white* evidence, was obliged quietly to put up with the damage, and the poor fellow with the loss of his *precious limb*.

The establishment of work-houses does credit to Jamaica. How the negroes are fed in those work-houses does not appear; but their employment is pointed out in the St. Jago de la Vega police-law quoted at p. 114. ' Corporation of the work-house to employ the negroes ' received into the said work-house to cleanse the streets ' lanes, &c. leading to the town; and to cultivate such ' pieces or parcels of land, belonging to the parish, as ' the justices and vestry shall direct, for the use of the ne- ' groes in the work-house.' The labour and discipline of a Jamaica work-house cannot be expected to be very moderate. By the same police-law ' slaves found gal- ' loping, or riding or driving furiously, &c. the master or ' mistress shall forfeit 40 s. &c. provided that if the ' master or mistress shall deliver up the slave offending ' to be publickly punished by receiving 39 lashes at the ' 4 most publick streets of the town, or *six days hard la- ' bour*, at the work-house, in such case the master or ' mistress shall be excused from paying the said forfeiture, ' &c.' ' If the offender shall be a free person of colour, ' he shall pay such fine as the justice shall think fit to im- ' pose, not exceeding *five pounds*, or be committed to hard ' labour in the work-house for *one week*.'

The only buildings, in Barbadoes, which bear any analogy to the Jamaica work-houses, are the cages, in the towns, so called from their fronts being composed of open frames of hard timber. In those miserable receptacles, which, next to the plantation-dungeons, are the most lively emblems of slavery, runaways are confined

fined in irons or in stocks, till they are claimed by their owners.

The Alms-house in Bridgetown for the reception of the (white) poor is the only apology for an hospital, belonging to Barbadoes. But, from the Barbadoes Mercury of October 28, 1786, I perceive that a subscription was opened on July 7, for establishing ' THE BARBADOES ' GENERAL DISPENSARY, *for the relief of the sick poor.*' To this charity, His Excellency Governor PARRY and his lady, with a considerable number of other ladies and gentlemen, liberally contributed; and the active humanity of that able physician DOCTOR HENDY was particularly useful in promoting it. Be the effects and the *duration* of this charity what they may, the public spirit and humanity which actuated the founders of it, do them much honour.

From that honour far be it from me to detract; but justice to a humble remnant of a once highly favoured state calls upon me to observe, That, of the sum subscribed to this charity, upwards of one tenth was contributed collectively and individually by the HEBREW NATION; though their numbers perhaps fall short of one twentieth of the white inhabitants of Barbadoes, and not one hundredth part of the property of the island is in their hands. Sir, this despised, (not to say *oppressed*) but peaceable, loyal and, I will add, *venerable,* people, still remember, as they were commanded, the affliction of their forefathers, in the land of Egypt. This surely is an amiable principle; and, for the peculiarity of their other tenets, while they disturb not society, they are not accountable to man. It is remarkable that they were enjoined to ' spoil the Egyptians'*—their oppressors, in order, no doubt, to vindicate for themselves the wages due for their servitude. To spoil *oppressors* who ' muzzle — not oxen but— men " while they tread out the corn," must, in *all* cases, be allowed to be a very venial trespass, if not an indifferent action.———Gracious God! The Africans now groan in worse than Egyptian bondage. They too are thy ' offspring.'† ' Though

* Exod. ch. iii. ver. 22. † Acts ch. xvii. ver. 28.
' Abraham

'Abraham be ignorant of them, and though Israel ac-
'knowledge them not; yet doubtless thou art their Fa-
'ther,' and in thy appointed time and way, maugre the
little, sordid *policy* of man, thou wilt be—' their Re-
'deemer.'*

West Indian worse than Egyptian bondage!—This, to some people, will sound like a very empty and a very bold figure of speech. But what would those people think, if it could be proved to be strictly and literally true?† This discussion we humbly recommend to some abler hand; but we may, hereafter, convert to some use the well-known fact, That the Israelites *increased* and multiplied under Egyptian bondage.‡ The negroes it is confessed, *decrease* under West Indian slavery.

I have the honour to be, &c.

POSTSCRIPT.

Sir, I have, very opportunely, received information, That a negro woman, far gone in her pregnancy, was shot dead by a white man (whom I shall not name) in Bridgetown, Barbadoes, in May 1788.

By the same channel I learn, That a Bill making the murder of a negro capital, has passed the *Assembly* of Barbadoes, which consists of 22 members, with only *one* dissenting voice. It was introduced by a gentleman of the law who possesses a plantation, and, with some others, does honour to the profession, to that his native

---

* Isaiah ch. lxiii. ver. 16.
† This is clearly evinced by these texts, 'Would to God! we had 'died by the hand of the Lord, in the land of Egypt, when we sat by the '*flesh pots*, and when we *did eat bread to the full*.' Exod. ch. xvi. ver. 3. *Every family* of the Israelites had *a lamb* to celebrate the passover. id. ch. xii. ver. 3. The Israelites had ' flocks and herds, even *very much cattle*.' id. ch. xii. ver 38.——I submit to the learned, whether an Egyptian was not capitally punished for murdering an Israelite. ' Apud Ægyptios, ' si *quis servum sponte occiderat* eum *morte damnari* æque ac si liberum ' occidisset, jubebant leges.' Diod. Sic. l. 1.
‡ Compare Gen. ch. xlvi. ver. 27. with Exod. ch. xii. ver. 37.

Island

Island and to humanity. I shall not comment on the 'broad hints' of some of his constituents:* nor shall I name that Member who could stand *alone* in opposing such a bill.

I am also given to understand, That ' worn-out superannuated and leprous negroes do not, *at present*, disgrace the streets of Bridge-town;' but I may venture to affirm, That the evil is only removed from that place, not remedied; since it is altogether incredible, That an owner who can turn out a slave to perish will be conscientious in providing for him at home, whence the wretch had before been driven, by famine or, perhaps, by brutal usage, (see p. L35.) ' A public lazaretto' should be built for the reception of *leprous* slaves.

LETTER XVI.

' *Je ne puis tuer mon esclave; mais je puis faire couler*
' *son sang goute à goute, sous le fouet d'un bourreau.*'
RAYNALL.

' *The law prohibits a master from killing or cruelly pu-*
' *nishing a slave; but how is a* SLAVE *to go to law with his*
' MASTER?'
SPARRMAN's Voyage to the Cape of Good Hope.

SIR,

I AM sorry I cannot lay before you the clause in the Jamaica consolidated slave law which makes it death to murder a slave. The only traces of that clause, which appear in the papers before me, are contained in the following paragraphs.

From the Jamaica gazette of Dec. 1. 1787.
' Thursday Nov. 29. The House went into a com-
' mittee on the consolidated slave-bill, and continued to

---

* The Assembly of Barbadoes is annual;

'sit upwards of three hours. We understand that by the bill, the whole system of the law respecting negroes is entirely changed. A council of protection is established in each parish, and many humane provisions are introduced for rendering their condition as easy and happy, as possible. It is also made *felony without the benefit of clergy to murder a slave*—a clause which, to the honour of the house, *passed without a single dissenting voice*.'

The unanimity, of so numerous a body as the Assembly of Jamaica *, in *restoring* or endeavouring to restore to injured men one of their violated rights, undoubtedly does them great honour. I am truly sorry the Barbadoes Assembly was not unanimous; yet I still adhere to my opinion of the comparative humanity of the inhabitants of that island. I am well assured they never have been, and I *know* they *will not be* inferior, in the practice of that virtue, to any island in the West Indies.

From the Jamaica gazette of Dec. 5. 1787.
'However the profligate and unmerciful may arraign the policy which urged our present Assembly, to secure the lives of the poor slaves by making it felony without the benefit of clergy to commit wilful murder on any of their persons, our correspondent views it as a most noble exertion of legislative power in the cause of humanity, which cannot fail of being highly acceptable in the eyes of that Almighty and beneficent Being, who is the fountain of justice and mercy. The patriotic, learned and eloquent Mr. EDWARDS, *who is so great an ornament and blessing to the country*, it seems, was one of the most ardent supporters of this sublime benignity.'
"GOD who hath made the world hath made of *one blood* all the nations of men that dwell on all the face of the earth."†

* Forty-three members. The times of their meeting and their duration are at the Governor's pleasure. An attempt was once made to appoint their term triennial, but the bill miscarried. A Governor has been known to dissolve several times in the same year.' Hist. of Jam. vol. 1. p. 57.

† Acts ch. xvii. ver. 26.

Sir,

Sir, I most chearfully subscribe to these just encomiums on the conduct of the present Assembly of Jamaica, and particularly on that of one of it's distinguished and praise worthy members. Those gentlemen, I most firmly believe, have done every thing within the compass of their power (consistent with the present state of things, and the attention they owe to their constituents) to secure the life and promote the happiness of the slave. Would to Heaven I had grounds to speak in the same language, of the efficiency of this clause, as of their laudable endeavours to render it efficient! But I fear that, like the rest, it must be understood with a salvo for one of the peculiar prerogatives of white men. It no where appears by what sort of evidence the murderers of slaves are to be convicted. 'There's the rub!' Till I shall be certain that something more than the evidence of white persons is admissible, in this case, I will not, I *cannot* believe that this clause will protect the life any more than the others will secure the good usage of the slave. Those who know that too many of our colonists 'scarcely consider' the negroes ' as intitled to the common rights of humanity'* will not be very confident of the rigorous operation of this law against rich and powerful offenders. Against a poor, friendless fellow, it may, however, now and then, operate; by way of convincing the people of this country how very sacred the life of a slave is esteemed in Jamaica. The islands of Grenada and Antigua have already something to boast of, for each of them hath hanged her white man for slave-murder.† Of the Antigua instance I know nothing; but Preston, the Grenada victim, I have heard mentioned in Barbadoes as one of the worst of men. His Christian name or nickname was Backhouse or Bacchus, probably the latter, from his drunkenness. Some twelve or thirteen years ago, Bacchus Preston fled from Barbadoes; and, in Grenada, met with the punishment his crimes, most probably, had deserved in his native island. Yes, Sir, this *white* man, it seems, was actually, hanged by the neck till he was dead— *only* for killing a negro, as hath been triumphantly pub-

---

* See the note p. 89.
† Apology for negro slavery by the author of letters to a young planter, p. 37.

lished

lished to the world. But, Sir, are two or three forlorn victims sufficient to answer the demands of justice? Are they sufficient—for where the lives of men are concerned, I must and will speak out—Are they sufficient, I say, to atone for the ocean of human blood, which under the description of virtual and actual murder, hath deluged our colonies, ever since the commencement of negro slavery? Sir, that atonement never will be made, nor will an effectual check be put to such horrid enormities, till the wretched outcasts of law and humanity shall be received into society, and shall enjoy that protection which is the undoubted birthright of every unoffending subject of Great Britain.

From the supplement to the Jamaica Gazette of March 8. 1788.

' And be it enacted, by the authority aforesaid, that, ' if any slave shall offer any violence, by striking or ' otherwise, to any white person; such slave, upon due and ' proper proof, upon conviction before two justices and ' five freeholders, be punished with DEATH or confine-' ment to *hard labour* for life, or otherwise, as the said ' justices and freeholders shall, in their discretion, think ' proper to inflict; provided such striking or conflict be ' not by command of his or their owners, overseers, or ' persons intrusted over them, or, in the lawful defence ' of their owners' persons or goods.'

The former law was to this effect, ' Striking or doing ' violence to a white person (except by command of their ' master or employer, or in defence of his person or ' goods) punishable at the discretion of two justices and ' three freeholders according to circumstances.* Why did the present law make the foregoing unmerciful, and (supposing the Jamaica negroes to be as well disposed as those of Barbadoes) *unnecessary* addition to the former powers of the justices and freeholders, which, though termed discretionary, I take it for granted, did not extend to life? It will be said that it would be imprudent to relax *penal* at the same time that *protecting* laws, or rather the *semblances* of protecting laws are enacted. This

* History of Jamaica, vol. 2. p. 485.

may be partly true, in Jamaica; but I contend that, in any case, it is unjust to increase a punishment to a degree so infinitely disproportionate to the offence. And who will say, that DEATH, or, for aught that appears, a worse punishment, even confinement to *hard labour* (in the Jamaica sense) for life, is not infinitely disproportionate to the crime of barely striking, perhaps only lifting a hand to ward off the stroke of a tyrant, in the very act of cruelty? From what I know of the general tempers of slaves, I am persuaded, that the rigid execution of this bloody clause will but tend to aggravate the evil it is intended to remedy.

By the law of Barbadoes (with the same exceptions as above) ' If any slave shall offer any violence to a Chris-
' tian, by striking, or the like, such slave shall be, for the
' first offence, severely whipped, by order of the justice
' complained to; the information to be given upon
' oath: for the second offence he shall be whipped, his
' nose slit, and be branded in the face with a hot iron; for
' the third offence he shall receive such *greater punishment*
' as the Governor and council shall think meet to in-
' flict.'* None of these punishments, whipping perhaps excepted, have been inflicted in Barbadoes, I had almost said, in the memory of man. But we have seen (p. 21.) that, in a certain other island, a negro *lost his right hand* for striking a sailor, though no such offence had, for many years, been committed. Sir, the man who would attempt to justify this punishment deserves not to breathe British air! The unmerciful tyrant who pronounced the horrid sentence ought himself to have experienced *the unspeakable loss of a right hand!*

But why, it may be objected, do I mention the mitigation of laws which, *in Barbadoes*, except in capital cases, I own are generally executed with mercy? And ought not those laws, for prudential reasons, still to hang, *in terrorem*, over the lives and limbs of the negroes? These objections I might answer by asking, Whether the Barbadians ever had any good reason to repent of their lenity? And whether *fear* be the only principle which actuates

* No: 82, cl. 5. Hall's abridg. p: 60.

the breasts of slaves? But where bad laws are in force, bad consequences will follow them; for there will always be found men disposed to take advantage of them. Witness the case of M. against A. in which, under the sanction of a barbarous and half forgotten law of Barbadoes, a violent attack was made on the personal liberty even of a *free born Englishman*, who had long supported a good character in that island, and in whose behalf that most promising young barrister, Mr. SKEETE, so nobly distinguished himself. If such statutes can be proved to be unnecessary, no cause can be shewn why they should not be repealed, or accommodated to the milder spirit of those who are interested in their execution, and the *consequent* civility of those on whom they are to operate. The black code of Barbadoes was evidently enacted by men less humane than their present posterity, and whose minds were incomparably less enlightened. The negroes, then mostly Africans, would be refractory, or 'savage,' in proportion to the harshness with which they were treated. Hence harsh laws were thought necessary to restrain them. The crime and the punishment of witchcraft were the offspring of ignorance and cruelty. What an age was that which saw the gravest characters of a nation enact laws against phantoms of crimes conjured up by their own barbarism! The reason, if some of them ever had any reason, of certain laws of Barbadoes, hath evidently ceased; and those respectable persons, in that island, who wish them to give place to statutes more becoming the most ancient, humane and polished West Indian colony ever possessed by the freest nation upon earth, do certainly consult the safety, as well as the honour of their little community.

We trust, the day is fast approaching, when, adopting the maxims of a milder policy, the legislatures of all the British islands, in the West Indies, will voluntarily purge their codes of injustice and cruelty. 'Necessity, 'the tyrant's plea,'* which is urged in support of some of their laws, exists only in the timid imaginations, not to say the guilty consciences of those who oppose a more

---

* '———And with *necessity the tyrant's plea*
 'Excus'd his dev'lish deed.' MILTON.

humane system. To repeat the *significant* words of the humane editor of the Barbadoes laws, 'if slaves were 'treated with more humanity than they *generally* are,' even the expediency of all sanguinary statutes would quickly vanish.

I have the honour to be, &c.

LETTER XVII.

SIR,

ONE great obstruction to the operation of the consolidated law professedly calculated to protect the persons of slaves, is that (so far as I can learn) it allows not the evidence of negroes, even of such as may have *seen* a murder committed, to have any place at all in convicting white criminals. I beg I may not be misunderstood. I do not think it would be prudent, in the *present* state of things, to make the evidence of a negro equivalent to that of a white person; but, is there no medium between allowing the evidence of negroes *that* weight, and allowing it *no weight* at all? Are those unhappy men never to be considered in any other light than that of 'brutes who 'want discourse of reason?' Might not the testimony of two or more negroes be made equivalent to that of one white person? They are known to believe in, and on solemn occasions, or when suffering unjustly, they never fail to appeal to 'the great God above, who knows the 'truth.' They universally look, beyond the grave, for a state of retribution, with a steadiness which may put many of their oppressors to shame. Their oath, on a negro grave, is so very sacred among them, that, in cases of perjury, they absolutely pine to death, a consequence which does not always follow that crime, in the most enlightened nations. Such are the principles they have brought with them from Africa. Those of them who profess Christianity might swear on the evangelists, and for farther security, on a negro grave.—This doctrine,

though

though tacitly favoured by a very sensible writer in one of the Barbadoes papers before me, I know will generally be reprobated as very wild and very dangerous doctrine; and it must be acknowledged that while owners have the power of extorting from their slaves by torture or by threats, any declaration which may be agreeable to themselves, it would not be safe to reduce such doctrine to practice.—Miserable, horrid condition, which to be thoroughly reformed, must be utterly annihilated! if indeed a man, in the midst of this great and free metropolis, and in the year *eighty eight*, may venture to mention the gradual annihilation of BRITISH SLAVERY.

To what extent it is practicable to reconcile validity of testimony with a state of unconditional slavery, it is not my province to determine; but I am clearly of opinion, That, till the evidence of negroes against whites, shall be allowed *some degree* of force, all the laws which the wisdom of man can devise will be found incompetent to protect them; and That till they shall be effectually protected, every plan calculated materially to improve their condition and their minds will be found inadequate to it's end: for it cannot be expected that any *oppressed* and injured people will readily embrace the religion of their *tyrants*.

To the extension of some other rights or rather *preparatory* semblances of rights to the West Indian slaves, I think it impossible for any man to object, who does not wish that they should always be considered and treated merely as passive instruments of labour. It has ever been my opinion, Sir, that negro-evidence should not only, as at present, be valid against negroes; but that all crimes of negro against negro should be tried by a jury of negroes; their verdict, *in all cases*, to be confirmed or reversed by a white jury. In many cases, negroes would come more easily at the truth than white men. I do not say, That this would disseminate among them the seeds of moral distinction, for those seeds are already implanted in their breasts, as in those of all other men. It would do more: it would make them feel their dignity as rational beings, and render them extremely solicitous of improvement; for none but regular men and *christians* should be admitted as jurors. I do not see why some of the enlightened free negroes, and there are many of that description, might not act as constables, in the above cases, in subordination to white constables. But this office, as it now stands, some of them would dislike, as considering themselves (though they dare not say so) the superiors of many of the whites who exercise it. *Many*, I do not say all, for very decent men are sometimes forced to act as constables, by ill-natured justices.

Black jurors and black constables! This proposition I know will be considered in the West Indies, as treason to the sacred Majesty of a white skin. I see the sarcastic grin of ridicule and the malignant scowl of asperity already formed. Asperity to individual men (not individual cruelties and absurdities) I will not willingly deal in; but ridicule I will not scruple to retort. I dare, however, promise my proposition a candid hearing from several respectable persons in Barbadoes; and particularly from a certain humane and enlightened gentleman, on whose estate all black offenders are regularly tried by a black jury, and, I have been told, with the best effects. Their sentences, which are sometimes very severe, are occasionally moderated by their owner, or changed into disgrace, of which negroes are not naturally more insensible than white men.

I have the honour to be, &c.

LETTER XVIII.

SIR,

IN case the slave trade is abolished, the public may expect to hear very lamentable accounts, indeed, from the West Indies. It will be affirmed, that, for want of new negroes, the estates are abandoned and that agriculture is rapidly declining in the Islands, just as it was some years ago affirmed that they could not exist without the American trade. *The suspension and diminution of the American*

American trade obliged the planters to be at some pains in raising provisions; the abolition of the African trade will oblige them to raise negroes. With what justice the decline of agriculture will be attributed to the abolition or restriction of the slave trade we may judge, before hand, by attending to the following paragraph taken from the Jamaica gazette of Dec. 1. 1787.

'A gentleman of veracity, who lately left the north
'side, assures us that no less than *three new sugar estates*,
'which have been settled within these few years, in the
'neighbourhood of Buff-bay, were lately *thrown up and*
'*abandoned*, and that the *same number underwent the same*
'*fate*, within these few months, near Port Antonio, a
'striking proof of the decline of agriculture, which will,
'most assuredly, draw after it a decline of shipping and
'navigation.'

To what cause or causes, the evil here mentioned may be owing, I pretend not to say. Certainly it is not owing to the *abolition* of the slave trade. Whether it may not rather be ascribed, to the *toleration* of that trade, the public will be able to judge, when they peruse the following quotation from the judicious author so often before referred to.—'To *augment our negroes therefore by procre-*
'*ation*, we must endeavour to *remedy* those *evils*.' (N. B. not *irremediable* evils) 'which *impede* or *frustrate* it's na-
'tural effect. And, to conclude, *if the waste of those men*
'*should become less, the price of them would fall*; and the
'same annual demand might be kept up, by extending
'our plantations, which is now produced by the *mortality*
'of these people; estates would be gradually well stocked
'and rendered more flourishing, and the circumstances
'of the planter would be totally changed for the better.
'*The purchase of new negroes is the most chargeable article*
'*attending these estates, and the true source of the distress*
'*under which the owners suffer*; for they involve them-
'selves so deeply in debt, to make these inconsiderate
'purchases, and lose so many, by disease, and *other* means,
'in the seasoning, that they become unable to make good
'their engagements, are plunged in law-suits and anxiety,
'while, for want of some prudent regulations in the hus-
'banding of their stock, and promoting it's increase, by

' *natural means*, they entail upon themselves a necessity of
' drawing perpetual recruits of unseasoned Africans, the
' expence of which forms only a new addition to their
' debts and difficulties.'*

As, in Algebra, the addition of a negative quantity to an affirmative, diminishes that affirmative, and as, in Swift's time, in the arithmetic of the Customs, 2 and 2, instead of making 4, frequently made only 1; so, in the arithmetic of slavery, every *addition of new negroes* hath, by long and fatal experience, been found to operate as a *diminution* of slaves, and consequently of *property*. Barbadoes, for example, in 1676, contained about 100,000 slaves. The *addition* of Africans, since that period, hath only served to *reduce* their numbers to about 80,000, that is (supposing only 1000 Africans to have been annually imported, for 100 years) $100,000 + 100,000 = 80,000$, an equation which no rule given by Newton or M'Laurin will reach; but which may easily be solved by the principles laid down by Doctor Franklin and Mr. Hume.† It would be ridiculous to ask when, at this rate, the islands will be stocked with slaves. The truth is, that the abolition of the slave trade, by removing the primary cause of depopulation, will promote the increase of negroes in the West-Indies. On the planter's property it will operate as the *subtraction of loss*, which is the same thing as the *addition of gain*.

Happy is the people who see their own interests in the proper point of light; but such is the imperfection of human nature, that there does not, perhaps, exist, that nation or that class of men, who have never been terrified by chimeras engendered in their own imaginations. It is well known that the happy union of these kingdoms was dreaded by many, as a measure pregnant with ruin. Many real and many pretended patriots predicted or affected to predict the downfal of Britain and the aggrandizement of America, from their separation—events which, for aught that has since appeared, are yet at a very great distance,

* History of Jamaica, vol. 2. p. 437.
† See Franklin's 'thoughts on the peopling of countries,' and Hume's 'Essay on the populousness of ancient nations,' to both of which we have been so much indebted.

and

and which the present phœnomena of the commercial and political, worlds evidently contradict. The conduct of the West Indians, who, overlooking the fertile soil they trod, cried out, some years ago, that they would all be starved, for want of the American trade; that of the parties, in both kingdoms, who were dissatisfied with the late well concerted commercial treaty between Britain and France; that of our ancient Barons and of the present Polish grandees respecting their vassals (see p. 89.) in a word the present dread of immediate ruin which dictates all the measures of the planters and the Liverpool merchants, respecting the slave trade, are all instances of popular infatuation, only to be equalled by the former mad fits of *Knocking John*,* who, on every trifling occasion, would run wild about the city crying out ' Oh! Sirs, we ' shall all be destroyed. Maid, wife and widow will be ' ravished; for the Great Mogul has got as far as White ' Chapel, and I saw the Pope in a brandy-shop in Wap-' ping!!'

I have the honour to be, &c.

LETTER XIX.

SIR,

I AM sorry I forgot to communicate to you earlier, a passage which comes pointedly home to our present subject, and perfectly coincides with the remarks I have made on the consolidated slave-law of Jamaica, and which I am happy to find are agreeable to ' the opinion of one ' of its framers.' This passage is taken from the supplement to the Kingston Journal of March 8, 1788, printed by Bennet and Dickson.

' We should be happy to witness the efficacy of the ' lately passed consolidated slave-law. That it would ' prove contradictory was the opinion of one of it's framers;

* See Tale of a Tub.

' and

' and that it will be found *most lamentably deficient* is our
' firm belief. *The wretched negroes who have so long
' disgraced our streets still continue a thorn in the side of hu-
' manity.* They cannot be received at the work-house
' among healthy slaves from principles of self-evident
' policy; but that, for this reason, they should be *exposed
' to every extreme misery* is not quite so clear. This law,
' *incompetent as it is*, impowers the justices and vestry to
' lay a tax on the inhabitants for the purpose of building
' a place for their reception. Till this can be done,
' we think no sensible mind would object to the hire of
' some house for their present shelter.'

You see, Sir, the papers before me furnish both text and comment of this law. I intirely agree with the spirited printers of the above passage, and I sincerely thank them for their humane attention to the most wretched of the human species. That all laws which can be enacted to protect creatures whose testimony against their oppressors is wholly invalid, who are considered and treated as mere beasts of burden, and whose places, when they sink into an untimely grave, *can speedily be filled up from a distant country*—that all such laws, I say, will ever be found ' most lamentably deficient, incompetent, and contradictory,' is not only my ' firm belief,' but it is my firm conviction, a conviction produced not so much by theory as by fact and observation. To suppose it otherwise would be to give our colonists credit for a degree of virtue which the experience of all ages and nations tells us is seldom or never to be found among men. It would be to believe them when, in effect, they say, ' We own that no man ought to be trusted with unlimited power. The power of kings themselves ought to be strictly defined and limited by the laws; but it is not proper that the power of us planters over our negroes should be thus limited. We have a law within our own breasts † which supersedes the necessity of any such limitations. This breast-law, aided and inforced by the impending terrors of the consolidated slave-law, will protect negroes as effectually as negroes ought

---

* Mr. M'NEILL says not a syllable about ' wretched negroes', disgracing the streets of Kingston, or any other town in Jamaica.
† Apology for negro slavery, p. 56.

to be protected.' But such pretences will scarcely satisfy a discerning public, who will judge for themselves of the degree of protection which *slaves* can expect from laws framed by their inveterately prejudiced *owners* who are at once *legislators, executors, judges, jurors, parties and witnesses*. The little protection slaves enjoy must depend, and does depend, more on the spirit of particular owners, than on such laws as we have been considering, which are better calculated to make a transient noise in the world and afterwards to lie dead or dormant in a statute-book, and perhaps to mislead inattentive persons, who never have resided in the West Indies, than to afford any effectual, any tolerable, degree of security to the persons and to the lives of slaves.

I have now extracted from the Jamaica papers in my possession, every material particular I can find relative to the treatment of the slaves in that island.

The causes of the rapid decrease of the slaves in Jamaica, assigned by the very intelligent historian of that island are—1. 'The venereal taint.' I never understood that this disease is more fatal to negroes than to whites: but of this and the other physical causes of decrease candid physicians are the only competent judges.*—2. 'Yaws.' The author says that 'experience proves that when left 'to nature, and the use of flour of brimstone to keep the 'humour in a constant elimination towards the skin, it 'gradually wears off in about three years." I cannot 'say to what precise extent this disease prevails; but cleanly, creole people are not much subject to it, in Barbadoes; nor can it by any means be justly reckoned

---

* Of the few things peculiar to this disease in the W. Indies, it is 'perhaps the most singular that it should at the present day, be *much less* 'frequent, in a country supposed originally to have produced it, than in 'any part of Europe.'—' In 331 patients admitted into the hospital of 'the 62d regiment there were only two with venereal complaints; and, 'in the other hospitals, the disease was not more frequent.' Obs. on the diseases of the army in Jamaica by JOHN HUNTER, M. D. F. R. S. and Phys. to the army, p. 284.

' The venereal disease is frequent in Africa; but is always easily 'cured.' Matthews's voyage to Sierra Leone, p. 136.

a general

a general cause of depopulation.*—3. 'The small-pox.' I never, in my life, understood that the negroes suffer more from the small-pox than the whites. A friend of mine brought thirty negroes through this disorder, by inoculation, without any loss, and comparatively with little medical assistance. I have heard of incomparably greater success. Our author indeed only mentions ' this as one principal cause of depopulation which existed here before inoculation was brought into general use, which was not long ago.' His book was printed in 1774, and refers to the state of things about the year 1768.— 4. 'The removal of negroes from a dry to a damp situation, from a south side to a north side parish.'— 'Even the creoles do not bear those removals from places where, perhaps, they have resided from the time of their birth.' And it is inconceivable what numbers have perished in consequence of the *law for the recovery of debts, which permits negroes to be levied on and sold at vendue. By this means they are frequently torn from their native spot, their dearest connections, and transferred into a situation unadapted to their health, labouring under discontent, which co-operates with change of place and circumstances to shorten their lives.'* This destructive evil prevails also in Barbadoes: and proves how little the feelings of the negroes are consulted by the West Indian laws. Thus the being ATTACHED TO THE SOIL a most grievous circumstance attending the Polish and Russian

* 'The yaws ' is infectious, and, like the small-pox, never attacks a person a second time. It is communicated by contact, most commonly in the same way that the venereal disease is'—' If a negro that has contracted this disorder, be put in circumstances favourable to general health; *if he be not obliged to work, if he be allowed a good diet*, and 1° he be kept clean by frequent washings, it will run it's course and, after a time intirely disappear.'—The ' yaws is a disorder not peculiar to the negroes; for several of the soldiers were afflicted with it.' Dr. Hunter's Obs. p. 306, 308.

'Though they (the negroes) are not entirely exempted from them (fevers) they suffer infinitely less than the Europeans. There was the strongest proof of this in the negroes who were sent along with the troops against Fort St. Juan, of whom scarcely any died, although few or none of the soldiers survived the expedition.' Dr. Hunter's Obs. p. 24.——' *Pulmonary consumptions* rarely originate in Jamaica.' id. p. 301.

vassallage

vassallage, would actually be a great relief, a great blessing to near half a million of men existing within the British dominions!—5. 'Some planters think it good 'policy to quarter their new negroes among the old 'settled ones; but these hosts generally make their guests 'pay dear for their lodging and maintenance, forcing 'them to be hewers of wood and drawers of water, and, 'in short imposing on their ignorance without measure 'or mercy, until they sink under the oppression.'—6. 'The introduction of too many recruits at once has 'often proved fatal to them.'—7. 'The women do not 'breed here as in Africa; for, in short, it has never 'been the planter's care to proportion the number of 'females to males.'—8. 'Worms are extremely fatal to 'children in this climate, and destroy *more than any other* '*disease*.' Are worms more fatal to children in the West Indies than in Africa, or to negroes than to whites?— 9. 'Others frequently perish by what is called here *jaw-* '*falling*, which is caused by a retention of the meconium, '*by not keeping the infant sufficiently warm.*' Infants are not kept sufficiently warm in Barbadoes any more than they are in Jamaica, at least, after the month.—10. 'Most of the black women are very subject to obstruc-' 'tions, from what cause, I will not presume to say; but 'perhaps they may be ascribed in part, to their using 'restringent baths or washing themselves in cool water, 'at improper periods.' Let the faculty determine, whether the diseases here alluded to, if indeed they be more common among black than white females, may not be 'ascribed in part,' to their *getting wet* or sleeping in damp huts, after *excessive toil*, in a hot and moist climate. In the wet season the negresses very frequently suffer these unwholesome vicissitudes.—11. 'Child-birth is not so 'easy as in Africa, and many children are annually des-' 'troyed, as well as their mothers, by the unskillfulness, 'and absurd management of the negro midwives.' Then why are not skilful midwives or *accoucheurs* employed?— 12. 'Thus we find there are various causes which pre-' 'vent the multiplication of negroes on the plantations; 'not but that *unseasonable work* may sometimes be added 'to the list.' I trust my readers are convinced, as I am, that downright *oppression* and *cruelty* may very often be

added

added to the list. 'I will not deny' continues our author, 'that those negroes breed the best whose labour is least and easiest. Thus the *domestic* negroes have more children than those on the penns; and the latter than those employed on sugar plantations.' I will add, that the domestic slaves in Barbadoes and those belonging to the middling and the lower classes of whites are as prolific, as healthy and long lived as any people I ever saw.*

Of these causes of depopulation the 1st, 2d, 3d and 8th may be called physical: the 4th, 5th, 6th, 7th and 12th are owing wholly to mismanagement and a bad law; and of these the 5th and 6th affect *African* negroes only. In the 9th, 10th, 11th disease and mismanagement are combined. The physical causes must be left to the faculty, who will scarcely be of opinion, That, independent of mismanagement, hunger, oppression and cruelty, the diseases to which Africans are more particularly subject are sufficient to account for the unparalleled and enormous waste of the species in the West Indies. If it should be pretended that African diseases depopulate the West Indies, we would have a right to ask, Why they do not depopulate Africa itself?

* There are many negroes in Barbadoes with all the marks of extreme old age, gray hairs not excepted, which are thought by some, to be rare among the blacks. I cannot exactly ascertain any of their ages; but I knew a hoary headed negro woman a great grandmother, who, I think, nursed, and who survived, her very indulgent mistress who died about the age of 63. In the same family there was an ancient African matron who, by the bye (for I have just recollected the circumstance) when she got up in the morning, used to trace a circle round her, on the floor, with her finger, at the same time, muttering something. On my asking her the meaning of this ceremony, she replied, 'Da for God' ('That is for God.') 'How, Mama, said I, does God live in Africa?' 'Kai! Massa,' said she, 'God no all about' ('Strange! Sir, is not God every where?') On the estate of a certain humane and respectable person, I remember an old African man, from his form of benediction, which was, 'God in a' top, God in a' bottom bless you Massa.' Do our fashionable philosophers speak more nobly of the Being who fills all space; or will their favourite orang outangs ever attain to so sublime an idea? I particularly recollect several other venerable *Struldbrugs* who certainly do infinite credit to their owners. Sir Hans Sloane knew blacks in Jamaica 120 years old. ' When old age has rendered his farther exertions useless, *the hoary headed bondsman* becomes often the partaker of liberty.' M'NEILL's Observ. p. 9.

The

The propagation of vegetables, of the inferior animals and of men, in favourable circumstances, universally proceeds in *geometrical progression*.* By an unvaried law of nature they continue to multiply till countries are so fully replenished, with people, for example, that they interfere with each others' means of subsistence. Then, but not till then, is a natural limit put to the farther increase of the species in such countries. Heavy taxes and bad laws also check that increase. The difficulty of maintaining families discourages marriage. Thus many persons remain single, and leave no issue, or they emigrate to countries which want people, and which, in their turn, become replenished with inhabitants.

Hence

---

* ' Nor is it necessary' (says Dr. FRANKLIN) ' to bring in foreigners ' to fill up any occasional vacancy in a country; for such vacancy (*if the* ' *laws are good*) will soon be filled by natural generation. Who can now ' find the vacancy made in Sweden, France or other warlike nations, by ' the plague of heroism 40 years ago; in France by the expulsion of the ' protestants; in England by the settlement of her colonies, or in GUI-' NEA *by* 100 *years exportation of slaves that has blackened* half America?' —' Was the face of the earth vacant of other plants, it might be gra-' dually sowed and overspread, with one kind only, as for instance, with ' fennel; and were it empty of other inhabitants it might in a few ages, ' be replenished, from one nation only, as for instance, with English-' men.—Thus there are supposed to be now (A. D. 1751) upwards of ' 1,000,000 of English souls in North America, though, it is thought, ' scarce 80,000 have been brought over sea. This million doubling, ' suppose but once in 25 years, will, in another century, be more than ' the people of England.'—In fine, a *well regulated* nation is like a poly-' pus; take away a limb, its place is soon supplied; cut it in two, and • each deficient part shall speedily grow out of the part remaining.' Thoughts on the Peopling of Countries.

' The people of New England have all along doubled their numbers ' once in 25 years.'—' DOCTOR HEBERDEN observes that, in Madeira, ' the inhabitants double their own numbers in 84 years.' PRICE on Annuities, p. 204. See also SP. OF LAWS, b. 23. ch. 16. and Smellie's BUFFON, v. 2. p. 36.

About 70 years ago, a Guinea ship was stranded on the island of St. Vincent. The posterity of the negroes who got on shore, known by the name of the BLACK CHARAIBS, notwithstanding the wasting wars they have sustained to maintain their independence, still amount, as I am credibly informed, to between 2000 and 3000.

' After the decisive victory gained over the Spaniards in Jamaica, ' their negroes' (the MARONS) ' still continued very troublesome.'— ' *The* ENGLISH *procured some blood-hounds and hunted these blacks like wild* ' *beasts*. Having *augmented their numbers by procreation*, and by fugitive ' slaves, they continued to distress the island for about 47 years, held

' out

Hence the world was originally peopled from one human pair,* and, after the deluge, from the family of Noah. Hence the vast increase of the Israelites, even in a state of bondage. † Hence, in modern times, the astonishing multiplication of European men, animals and vegetables in America, and of the potatoe, and perhaps other American vegetables, in Europe. Hence an overplus of people in some countries, as in Switzerland and other European countries, and, in spite of all obstructions, in AFRICA. Hence black cattle, sheep, &c. afford so vast an overplus for the food of man. Hence the great *increase of stock in Jamaica* ‡ and, to give no more instances of so notorious a truth, hence the increase of the

BLACK

‘ out against forty times their number’—‘ and at length were able to put an end to the struggle by a treaty of peace the more *honourable* to them, as it confirmed the full enjoyment of that *freedom* for which they had so long and so obstinately contended.’—‘ These negroes, although inhabiting more towns than at first, are diminished in their number by deaths, and *cohabitation with slaves on the plantations*, instead of intermixing with each other’—‘ The whole number (of Marons) in all the towns, is *not augmented much* beyond the above list in 1749.’ LONG's Hist. of Jam. v. 1. p. 124, 278, 279 and v. 2. p. 339, 340, 347, 349.

* By calculation, it appears, that 953,000,000 of people (supposed to be about the present number of the whole human race) might be produced in 721 years (nearly) from *one* pair, uniformly doubling their numbers every 25 years, or, which is the same thing, increasing, uniformly, at the apparently slow rate of (nearly) 3 per cent. per annum.

† The Israelites, shortly after their egress out of Egypt and 430 years after the vocation of Abraham (see Josephus b. 2. ch. 5. Bp Patrick on Exod. and Playfair's chronol. p. 34) amounted to 603,550, ‘ from twenty years old and upwards, all that were able to go forth to war,’ (Num. ch. 1. ver. 46.). If, following Dr. Halley and Mr. Kerseboom, we account the fighting men to have been about one-fourth of the whole, we may estimate their number at about 2,400,000 men, women and children. If so, the posterity of Abraham, by his grandson *Jacob*, must have doubled their numbers in 21 years and 3-10ths of a year, nearly. But if, with Bp. Patrick, we suppose, that they amounted only to 1,500,000, of all ages, we shall still find that they doubled their numbers in 22 years.——— This approximation to what we know hath taken place in modern times, at the same time that it evinces the comparative mildness of the Egyptian bondage, is a good internal proof of the truth of the Mosaic history. In this last view, the author humbly thinks this and similar inquiries worthy of the attention of the learned.

‡ The increase of stock in Jamaica, exclusive of about 8,000 head slaughtered annually, is computed at 28,000 head per annum. See the Cornwal Chron. of Jan. 5. 1788. Thus, we see, there is no want of cattle in Jamaica for food and labour; but we fear the plough is not so universally

Black Charaibs in St. Vincents, of the Marons in Jamaica, and of negro slaves when well treated on many of the estates in the West Indies.*—That, on the whole, negro slaves decrease, is a deplorable exception to the general procedure of nature.

I cannot collect authentic data on which to found a comparative view of the waste of human life in the different European colonies in the W. Indies; and I indulge not in conjecture: But the following particulars will convey a general idea of that melancholy subject. According to a French account, published by authority, no less than 800·000 Africans had been imported into the French part of St. Domingo, in 96 years ending in 1774, of whom there then remained only 290·000, viz. 150·000 Africans and 140·000 creoles, these last being the whole posterity of 650·000 Africans. During the six years, immediately preceding 1774, the number imported into the same colony was 103·000 and 61·000 had been born, making together 164·728, of whom, in that year, there remained in all, only 40·000†. A certain gentleman has favoured me with a copy of a M. S. account in his possession, of all the negroes and cattle, with the taxes raised on them, in the several parishes of Jamaica, in the

---

universally adopted, as it should be; and who would think of feeding negroes on fresh meat, while indifferent salt provisions can be imported, at any price?' 'The island is well supplied with provisions of every 'kind, and could *easily* raise more than sufficient for the inhabitants; 'but the cultivation of the sugar-cane is so lucrative, that every exer-'tion is turned that way, and many articles are imported, which might 'either be produced in the island, or their room supplied with others 'equally good.' Dr. Hunter's Obs. on the diseases of the army in Jamaica, p. 10.

* Mr. M'Neill (Obs. p. 35.) owns that ' there is certainly no ' denying the fact, that negroes, *with proper attention*, will *multiply* con-' siderably; for, upon many of the old estates in this island' (Jamaica) ' which have not experienced *revolutions from debts or change of property*, ' there are TEN, nay sometimes TWENTY *natives* for ONE *African*; ' but that the supply from propagation alone, *in any circumstances*, should ' preclude the necessity of importing new slaves, is an idea, which, ' pleasing as it may appear, cannot, I am afraid be admitted.' I leave the reader to form his own judgment of this and similar passages.

† This decrease is at the rate of 21 per cent. per annum, which, in 78 years (nearly) would reduce the whole inhabitants of the globe to *ten*.

years

years 1734, 1740 and 1745; also of all the slaves imported into that island from March 28, 1713 to Dec. 1, 1745, specifying the number of slaves and vessels each year. From this paper, which is much too long to be inserted, it appears that there were in Jamaica,

		SLAVES.
In 1734,	— —	86,546
Imported, from 1734 to 1739, inclusive, in 154 vessels,		
Negroes	— 36,996	
Indians	— 41	
	—	37,037
		123,583
Deduct on the island 1740	—	99,239
Decrease in 6 years	— —	24,344
On the island, in 1740	—	99,239
Imported from 1740 to 1745, inclusive, in 163 vessels	— — —	36,493
		135,732
Deduct on the island in 1745	—	112,428
Decrease in 6 years	— —	23,304

It does not appear what number of slaves were on the island in 1713; but supposing there were *no slaves* then on the island, the number imported in 33 years, in 949 vessels, is

Negroes	— · —	221,534
Indians	— —	115
Total	— —	221,649
Deduct on the island in 1745	—	112,428
Decrease in 33 years	— —	109,221
——— every six years	—	19,858

No

No less than 27,000 slaves were introduced into Jamaica in two years and a half ending in July 1766.* In 1761 there were on the island 146,000; in 1768 the number was 166,904 †, increase 21,000; but in two years and a half of this period 27,000 had been imported, and, if it be considered that the period including 1768 was the most flourishing period of the slave trade, 27,000 more will probably be much too small an allowance for the other four years and a half. Here then is a *decrease* of at least 33,000 in 7 years.

According to Raynall ‡ 8,000,000 or 9,000,000 of Africans had been imported into all the European colonies, in the new world previous to the year 1774; and their wretched remnants did not then amount to more than 1,400,000 or 1,500,000. The former number is very probably equal to the whole population of G. Britain, or to about one hundredth part of all mankind—the latter alas! falls short of the population of Scotland alone.—What a horrible picture of European iniquity is this! The foremost groupe composed of the surviving Africans, famished, covered with scars, and loaded with chains— the gloomy back ground besmeared with the blood of the extirpated American tribes!

These rates of decrease far transcend the effect of any known cause of depopulation; and, if universal, would, in a few ages, exterminate the human race. The wretched policy of the feudal system, unfavourable as it was and, in some countries, still is, to their multiplication,‖ did not exterminate, or threaten to exterminate, the vassals whom it oppressed. Scarcity, tempests, volcanoes and earthquakes have not depopulated those countries to which they have been most fatal. ' Men,' says a learned writer, ' will even INCREASE *under circumstances* ' *that portend to* DECAY. The frequent wars of the ' Romans and many a thriving community, even the ' PESTILENCE and the MARKET *for* SLAVES' (par nobile fratrum!) ' find their supply, if, *without destroying the*

---

* Long's Hist. of Jam. vol. 2. p. 442.
† Id. p. 432.
‡ Hist. Phil. et pol. t. 5. p. 261.
‖ See Coxe's Travels into Poland, &c.

' same,

'same, the drain become regular.'*—Strange that Africa is not exhausted by *selling* slaves, while the islands are exhausted by *buying* them!—Thus it would appear, that all the ordinary and extraordinary causes of depopulation are not nearly so destructive to the lives of mankind as the present WEST INDIAN SLAVERY and it's sweeping train of worse than pestilential mischiefs. These, with fatal, because *incessantly* corroding, malignancy, can alone blast the strong principle of life. In this one instance hath the depravity of man been permitted wholly to counteract the great law of Creation which said, ' Be ' fruitful and multiply and replenish the earth,'—a law which pervades the universe, and preserves, in the most admirable order, every species endowed with vegetable or animal life.

That a diminution of population may be, nay, actually is, speedily supplied, by natural means, hath been clearly evinced: but, from whatever cause such diminution may have arisen, it confers no right of supplying the defect by methods incompatible with justice and humanity. A great number of the inhabitants of Sicily and Naples perished by the earthquake in 1783. Was the king of Naples, therefore, intitled to supply the deficiency, by dragging into exile the people of a distant land? Would not even the attempt have been wicked? And would a similar mode have been innocent in our unfortunate colonists who survived the great hurricane, in 1780? † If this would have been iniquitous, how unspeakably nefarious must it be to replace by violence and perfidy in Africa, those whom mismanagement, bad laws, oppression and cruelty have destroyed in the West Indies?

Having thus proved that the Africans, on their arrival in Jamaica are, at the *Guinea sales*, treated worse than brutes; that they are ' *branded*' like cattle; that they are pinched in their food; that their drudgery is

---

* FERGUSON. civ. so. ed. 5. p. 236.

† Suppose *five per cent.* of the inhabitants, white and black, perished by that dreadful visitation, which, in Barbadoes, where it was most fatal, was, I believe, pretty near the truth. Such a deficiency, it is plain, would be supplied *in less than five years*, by a people increasing at the rate of only *one per cent.* per annum, or doubling their numbers in about 70 years.

incessant;

incessant; that the punishments and 'torments' inflicted on them are shockingly severe and often 'very unnatural;' that, in the decline of life, they are often 'exposed to every extreme of misery;' that they are often killed, and 'immediately put under ground;' that the laws lately enacted for their protection are 'most lamentably deficient and incompetent; and that, 'with proper attention,' they increase and 'multiply,' by procreation—having demonstrated, I say, all these truths, and having had reason to think myself called upon to take up my pen in this interesting controversy, I now, in my turn, ask the advocates for slavery and the slave-trade how they dare clank their accursed chains in the ears of Britons, by avowedly attempting to justify a traffic and a domination so execrable in themselves, so peculiarly hateful to the great body of the people, so subversive of the rights and so destructive to the lives of mankind—so utterly repugnant, not to say dangerous, to the laws, to the liberties, and to the religion of this nation?

The foregoing facts and arguments will, I humbly hope, meet with attention from you, Sir, and from many other respectable and conscientious inquirers into the state of slavery, in the British sugar islands. But well established facts, and cool reasoning and warm expostulation will, I fear, equally fail of working conviction in minds preoccupied by inveterate prejudices, or by interest or policy ill understood.

I have the honour to be, &c.

CONCLUSION.

WITH becoming humility, and with all that respect which an obscure individual may be supposed to entertain for a nation whose interests it is his bounden duty, and his most ardent wish, to promote, the author would now intreat the serious attention of *all ranks* and descriptions of Britons, to a few considerations which seem naturally to arise out of the present subject.

Every man who does not disregard and revile the religion of his country, will allow, that 'The Most High 'ruleth over the kingdoms of the earth,' and that nations can only be punished *as nations*, that is, in this world. Most dreadful plagues were sent, by a just and offended God, to chastise the Egyptians for exercising a tyranny *comparatively* mild in itself, and which was not supported by a murderous *slave trade*. The scene of that disgraceful traffic; 'That AFRICA which is not now more fruitful 'of *monsters* than it was once of excellently *wise and* 'learned men; that AFRICA which formerly afforded us 'our Clemens, our Origen, our Tetullian, our Cyprian, 'our Augustine; that *famous* AFRICA, in whose soil 'Christianity did thrive so prodigiously, and which could 'boast of so many *flourishing churches*, alas! is now *a* '*wilderness*. "The wild boars have broken into the "vineyard and eaten it up, and it brings forth nothing "but briars and thorns," to use the words of the prophet. 'And who knows but God may suddenly make this 'Church and Nation, this our ENGLAND, which Jes-'hurun-like, is waxed fat, and grown proud, and hath 'kicked against God, such another example of his *ven-*'*geance?*'*

Now let Britons call to mind the many distinguished blessings they have enjoyed, and the many dangers from which their peculiarly favoured country hath been pro-

---

* See the Sermons of ARCHB. SHARP (grandfather of that friend to his country and to mankind, the present Granville Sharp, Esq.) vol. 1. sermon 1. which was delivered before the House of Commons, April 11th 1679.

vedentially

videntially delivered. Let them remember, in particular, the alarming situation of their affairs in the year 1780, when, without a single ally, Britain maintained a noble struggle against the powerful nations, which were combined, with her revolted colonies, for her destruction; when faction embarrassed her councils; when a lawless multitude of desperate men carried fire and desolation through the streets of her metropolis; and when a tempest, as if sent by Heaven to point out *one* cause of all those calamities, 'swept' some of the West Indian Islands 'with the besom of destruction'* Let Britons seriously contemplate that awful crisis, and then blame a fellow-citizen, if they can, for humbly recommending to their consideration these striking passages of scripture, selected from a very great number which, alas! are but too applicable to the present subject. '*The nation to whom they shall be in bondage* WILL I JUDGE SAID GOD: and, *after that shall they come forth and serve me.*'† 'What mean ye that ye *beat* my people to pieces, and *grind the faces of the poor*, saith the LORD GOD OF HOSTS?‡ Among my people are found wicked men. *They lay wait, as he that setteth snares—they set a trap—they catch men.* As a trap-cage § is full of *birds*, so are their houses full of deceit; therefore, they are become great and waxen rich—they are waxen fat—they shine—yea they overpass the deeds of the wicked. They judge not the cause—*the cause of the fatherless*—yet they prosper—the *right of the needy do they not judge.* SHALL I NOT VISIT FOR THESE THINGS? SAITH THE LORD—SHALL NOT MY SOUL BE AVENGED ON SUCH A NATION AS THIS?'**

Such are the tremendous denunciations of the Almighty against avarice, injustice and oppression. Similar crimes deserve similar punishments—greater guilt, more terrible visitations. *Esto perpetua* is the prayer of every patriotic soul: yet the hour of Britain's dissolution, as a nation, must—must arrive. Let us no longer provoke indulgent

---

* If. c. 14. v. 23. † Acts, ch. 7. v. 7. ‡ If. c. 3. ver. 15.
§ See Blayney's Jerem.
** Jerem. ch. 5. v. 26 et seq. 'The *sins of oppression* are called CRYING SINS—such as cry to Heaven for vengeance.' Lowth's com. on this passage.

Heaven to hasten that awful event. Let not Britain, in her present prosperity ' say in her heart, I sit a Queen and ' shall see no sorrow.'* But let her remember that she herself hath experienced calamity—that she too hath *groaned under the yoke of* TYRANTS! and that *her own* liberties have been fully established only during one short century.————But away with all mean ideas of a great, a magnanimous nation! There is yet virtue in Britons, and the memory of the GLORIOUS REVOLUTION † will call it forth into action. A jubilee will be celebrated; and PRINCE and PEOPLE will gratefully commemorate the final delivery of Britain from arbitrary power.‡ The temple of BRITISH LIBERTY will be opened. The sacred fire, so fatal to tyrants, which burns in its hallowed recesses, will blaze—will fulminate: and AFRICAN SLAVERY, bound in her own execrable chains, will be utterly blasted and consumed on the altar!‖

* Rev. ch. 18. v. 7. ' SLAVES *and souls of men*' are among the ' *merchandize*' of the city threatened in that awful chap.—By the bye, it is wonderful what some people find to laugh at, in the Rev. of St. John. Sir I. Newton and Lord Neper, the greatest men, even Hume being judge, (see Hist. of Eng.) that ever Britain produced, were so far from ridiculing, that they wrote comments on that sublime book. The first 6 v. of the 10th ch. contain such a groupe of exalted images, as is no where else to be found, in the same compass.

† ' God seems, in this last deliverance, in some sort, to have united ' and brought together all the great deliverances which he hath been ' pleased to work for this nation, against all the remarkable attempts of ' POPERY, from the beginning of our reformation. Our wonderful deliver-' ance from the formidable *Spanish invasion*, designed against us, happened ' the year 1588. And now, just 100 years after, God was pleased to ' bring about this *great and most happy* DELIVERANCE. That *horrid* ' *gun-powder conspiracy*, without precedent and without parallel, was de-' signed to have been executed on the *fifth day of November*, the same day ' upon which his Highness The Prince of Orange landed his forces here ' in England. So that this is a day every way worthy to be solemnly set ' apart and joyfully celebrated, by this church and nation, throughout ' all generations; as the fittest of all others to comprehend, and to put ' us in mind to commemorate, all the great deliverances which God ' hath wrought for us, from POPERY *and it's inseparable companion* ARBI-' TRARY POWER. Archbishop Tillotson's Thanksgiving serm. for our deliverance by the Prince of Orange,' preached Jan. 31st 1689, from Ezra, ch. ix. ver. 13, 14. ‡ See p. 101. note.

To the WHITE INHABITANTS in general and, in particular to the LEGISLATURE of the Island of BARBADOES.

"*I must be cruel, only to be kind.*" SHAKESPEARE.

I Confess I am entirely at a loss in what terms to address you, or how to express myself with that freedom which becomes my cause, without offending you, which, whatever you may think, is very far from my intention. My sentiments respecting slavery are, and, as some of you know, ever have been, so diametrically opposite to the unreasonable prejudices and the apparent interests of very many of you, that I expect to be *generally* considered as the enemy, if not traduced as the *calumniator* of the island of Barbadoes. Such a charge will give me but little pain, while I am conscious of the rectitude of my intentions; and that I have incurred your displeasure, by a well meant endeavour to discharge what I *know* to be my duty to God, to my country, and to an injured and oppressed race of men.

Yet a very respectable number of you possess a large share of that good sense, candour and humanity which happily characterize the present age. Your virtues, in many instances, compensate for the glaring defects of laws enacted by your less enlightened ancestors; and have rendered the galling yoke of slavery confessedly lighter in Barbadoes, than it is in any other British colony.

Still, it must be owned, this is but a faint, a negative kind of praise. Go on to merit greater encomiums,—to preserve the eminent character for comparative humanity you so justly possess, and which, you need not be told, that strong incentive to generous actions, emulation, will stimulate the other colonies to equal, if not to surpass. I cannot bring myself to believe, that, in this glorious strife, Barbadoes will yield to any colony in the W. Indies.

L 4   Could

Could I hope that my advice would be attended to, I would humbly and earnestly exhort you to begin your reforms by driving away every slave-ship from your coast, as the best means of giving efficacy and stability to your future regulations.

For your own credit, as well as for the sake of humanity, I would respectfully intreat you to expunge, for ever, from your statute-book a few laws which I have blushed to hear mentioned and see quoted in this country, as a reproach to human nature. 'Would to God' exclaims a certain well informed, respectable and elegant writer, 'that the stain which the savage ordinance of Barbadoes has stamped on the spirit of colonial legislation could be, for ever blotted from the page of history.' And again 'Contemplate, if you can, Sir, without horror, the spirit which could dictate the following law of Barbadoes.'* The only circumstance I can urge in defence of the statutes here alluded to, is that when enacted they were, no doubt, *thought* necessary; and that, at present (except in punishing capital crimes of negroes against whites which very seldom occur) your penal laws are, generally, executed with a moderation which does you honour. But it is to be lamented that the lenity of your magistrates is far from being universally imitated.—To your own good sense I appeal, Whether it be proper, or expedient, or just, that the power of private individuals over their slaves should, in fact and in practice, be absolutely unbounded, while that of publick magistrates is defined and effectually limited by the law; that the former, for example, may, or, at least, does inflict as many stripes or blows as he thinks proper, and for any or no fault; while the latter, for a real fault or crime cannot, and does not, exceed a certain number of stripes. This may be agreeable to the dogmas of slavery; but, you are conscious, it is repugnant to common sense, propriety and justice. You know too that, by restraining the abuse of power, you oblige men to consult their own *interest*, which you are sensible is very far from affording sufficient protection to many a miserable slave. In a

* Remarks on the slave trade and the slavery of the negroes, 4to, p. 77 and 85. See also SHARP against the toleration of slavery, p. 67, and BENEZET's Guinea, p. 70.

word,

word, 'the punishment by *whipping* should be brought within some limit; so that owners or managers might not, *with impunity*, transgress, through the *heat of rage*, a fit degree of *just* correction.'* For trampling on the rights and claims of men every transgressor ought to *suffer*; for the murder of a human creature, of whatever condition or complexion, and whether it be by hunger, by oppression, by repeated cruelties, or by immediate violence, every criminal ought to DIE.

The present language of your law, and, I am sorry to add, of your practice, is, 'If a white man murder a white man, he ought to die for it;' if a black man murder a white man he ought to expire by slow and barbarous tortures; but if a white man murder a black man he ought to be acquitted. Is not the negro led to espouse the very same principles and creed, *ex converso?*†

Lay your hands on your hearts, and declare your own conscientious opinion of those principles and that creed, Whether you seriously think that God and nature or justice, or *sound policy*, ever dictated such principles or such a creed? And whether the civilized state of your community renders an adherence to such barbarous doctrines, any longer necessary, or even expedient?

Another island hath copied and practised the severity of your negro-code.‡ It is now incumbent on you, to compile a code which, in point of moderation, justice and *efficiency*, may serve as a model to *that*, and to every other British colony in the West Indies:—a code which may fix the quantum of food and cloathing, and the periods of labour and rest, abridge the exorbitant power of owners

---

*LONG'S Hist. of Jam. b. 3. ch. 5. which contains many judicious and spirited remarks on the negro-code of that Island. † Id. Ibid.

‡ 'The negro-code of this island ([amaica) appears originally to have been copied from the model in use at *Barbadoes*; and the legislature of this latter island, which was first planted by the English, resorted to the English *villeinage-laws*, from whence they undoubtedly transfused all that *severity* which *characterizes* them.' id. ibid. The *old* legislators of Barbadoes endeavoured to apologise for the severity of their laws by affirming that 'negroes and *other* SLAVES are of barbarous, wild and savage nature.' But to what cause are we to attribute the severity of the English villeinage laws? Was it owing intirely to the *barbarity* of the poor, *oppressed* vassal? Do we not know, on the contrary, that the *barbarity* of the *tyrannical* lord was the chief cause of that severity?—No. 82 was passed Aug. 8. 1788. Qu. Was it not one of JAMES II's laws. It is well known that he was an adventurer in the slave-trade.

and

and managers, and, in a word, effectually *secure the* COM-
FORT, *protect the* PERSONS *and the* LIVES, *and provide
for the* RELIGIOUS INSTRUCTION *of your* SLAVES.

You have frequently entrusted your slaves and free people of colour with arms. Have they ever abused your generous, unsuspicious confidence? If they have not, surely you will not, now that the eyes of the nation and of the other colonies are upon you, hesitate to impart to them such a participation of those rights, (of which you yourselves are so justly tenacious) as will secure them from the abuse of power, and effectually protect their lives—rights, for the preservation of which, and of your property, though *they* do not enjoy and are no way interested in either, you expect your *slaves* to expose *their* persons, if *your* country should be invaded—even by an enemy who are said to possess a *certain virtue* in a degree which is worthy of your imitation.

Civilization, science and religion, it has been remarked, have hitherto held their progress from *east* to *west*. They now flourish in the mild and enlightened region of Pennsylvania. They may, in time, reach even California. Let not future experience contradict an observation which already does credit to your little country; and from which Barbadoes, if you co-operate with the beneficent, and almost *apparent*, intentions of Providence, may be destined to derive so much honour—an honour yet greater than that of being one of the oldest and most loyal, if not *the* most loyal and dutiful colony, ever possessed by England.

I humbly and respectfully intreat you, to consider, for a moment, from what hand you yourselves, at your solemn anniversary,* acknowledge your late calamities proceeded, and for what purpose they were sent—the myriads of vermin and the destructive blast which laid waste your fields and frustrated the toil of the *slave*, and the hopes of the planter; your perpetual dread of invasion; your distress from an alarming scarcity; and, to sum up all in one tremendous word, your sufferings from the unutterably dreadful HURRICANE!! which seemed, at the time, to

* See Isaiah ch. lviii. and lix.

be no more than a prelude to the accumulated horrors of *pestilence* and *famine*.* 'Quæque [omnia] ipse miserrimus vidi.' When you consider these unparalleled visitations with the reference they too evidently have to the present subject, I trust you will pardon the plainness of this address, and acquit me of intemperate zeal and unmeaning enthusiasm (with which I will not be charged, by those who know me) if I conclude it in the mild and unadorned but sensible language which George Fox uttered to your forefathers, in the year 1671, and which was to this effect: 'Consider the condition of the blacks who came *strangers* unto you, and were sold unto you as *slaves*. If you should be in the like slavish condition, what hard bondage and cruelty would you think it? Consider seriously of this, I say, and do unto them, as you would they should do unto you, in the like condition. It is therefore my earnest desire, That you would cause your overseers to deal mildly with your slaves, and not to use cruelty towards them, as the manner of some is; and, after a certain time of servitude let them go out free.'

* Famine was to be apprehended from the total destruction of the provisions, and epidemical disease from the putrefaction of animal bodies. Happily neither took place. Between 4000 and 5000 people perished, and cattle and stock innumerable; and the sea coast was strewed with dead fish.—"Quis cladem illius Noctis, quis funera fando"—Explicet? Two fires happened in Bridgetown in 1766, by one of which about 400 families were burnt out, and most of the provision stores destroyed. All these calamities took place in the short space of 14 years. Let those who are fond of attributing every event *merely* to *second causes*, account for the quick succession of those calamities.

To

To the FREE NEGROES *and* MULATTOES, *and to the more enlightened and regular* SLAVES *in the Island of* BARBADOES.

———————

AS it is extremely probable that these sheets will fall into the hands of some of you, I think it highly proper they should be accompanied, with some cautions respecting your conduct, which is now become peculiarly interesting to the cause of humanity.

I shall not affect to make a secret of what most of you cannot but know, That the African slave-trade hath lately attracted the attention of all ranks of men in these kingdoms; and that it is very soon to be subjected to a parliamentary inquiry. What the result of that inquiry may be, it is impossible to predict: but it is foreseen that the West Indian planters, respectable from their property and numbers, joined by the slave-merchants in this country, will oppose, with all their power and influence, the abolition or the effectual regulation of a traffic which the majority of the nation detest.

Among other plans which have been devised to obstruct the wished for abolition, it hath been industriously reported, That nothing less is aimed at, than the immediate abolition of slavery in the sugar islands. But the friends of humanity never could entertain an idea of so mischievous a project. They very well know, That the possessors of West Indian property, who are far less to blame, in this business, than the English slave-mongers, would be ruined by the unqualified and sudden adoption of such a measure. Besides, your friends are fully convinced that the field-negroes are not prepared to enjoy, all at once,

the

the blessings of liberty; that liberty, instead of being a blessing, would be the greatest curse that could befal men totally ignorant of Christianity! and that such beings could and would make no other use of liberty than to run headlong into idleness and debauchery, and thus might involve themselves, the whites and you in one common scene of confusion, if not of destruction.

Another bug-bear which hath been conjured up to terrify the people of this kingdom, and to hinder the abolition of the slave-trade, is, That the bare mentioning of it, in the West Indies, will raise the expectations of the slaves so high, that unless they are immediately *freed* forsooth, commotions will take place in the islands.—You see, I have taken upon me to assure the public, that no such dreadful consequences are to be apprehended in Barbadoes: and I trust the event will prove that my prediction is founded on a competent knowledge of the general good dispositions of the slaves in your island. I hope too that the disorders in the other islands which have been foretold, will be found to exist only in the imaginations which invented them.

The object at present in view is, simply The abolition of the slave-trade, which will force the owners of slaves to treat them better, and to pay more attention to their natural increase than too many of them have hitherto done. Many gentlemen, I believe, do not dissemble that they look forward to the abolition of slavery itself, as the ultimate object of their wishes and views; but this, they are sensible, must be a work of time, and must be brought about by *slow* degrees; and this for very good reasons—because *the privileges granted to slaves must keep pace with their improvement in Christianity*, and because *the property of their owners must not be injured*.

Beware then, of entertaining the slightest expectation that immediate freedom is about to be granted to the slaves. Poor debased men! they must be contented to bear the yoke of bondage, which, however, is comparatively light and easy in Barbadoes, till it insensibly wear off, and till they be prepared for a higher rank in society,

by

by being converted to Christianity. That rank many of you now deservedly enjoy, and if you wish to render your enslaved countrymen worthy to enjoy it, you must be at some pains, as opportunity may offer, to teach them their duty to God and their neighbours, but particularly to their owners, the most humble submission to whom, *in all cases*, it is your duty strongly to inculcate on the slaves. Certainly you have no right to interfere between owner and slave : but if, at any time, you should be obliged to give your *opinion*, which indeed is not likely, let me beseech you to lean to the owner rather than to the slave ; even if the former, which, I am sorry to own is too often the case, should be in the wrong. In so doing, I leave you to judge, Whether you will not conform to the precept of the apostle : ' Servants be subject to your ' masters, with all fear, not only to the good and gentle, ' but also to the froward.'* If it be the duty of *servants* to obey even froward, *wicked masters*, with all *fear*, which, indeed, is the case, even in this free country, you may conclude, that it is much more the duty of *slaves*.† If submission, in all cases, to their owners, be the duty of slaves, a respectful deference to the whites is no less the indispensable duty of free persons of your description, and in your situation.

The wellbeing of every community depends, in a great measure, on the distinctions of rank. Hence it is, That the people of this country, the freest upon earth, pay so much respect to their nobility and gentry. Not that the Great are better Men or better Christians than their Inferiors ; but the good sense of Britons sees the propriety, if not the necessity, of those distinctions of rank, which wonderfully assist the laws, in preserving peace and good order. Your good sense, which I have witnessed, with pleasure, on many occasions, will, I trust, still prompt you to use the same means for promoting the same desirable end. Most of you may be said to hold a higher rank in society than the slaves. You justly consider yourselves, and they consider you, as their superiors ;

---

* St. Peter Epist. I. ch. 2. v. 18.
† Hic, ægrè, coactus sum, alienam, gerere personam—*ore Raymundi Harris*, Ex Societate Jesu.

but beware of grounding that superiority on riches, or on dress, or, in short, on any other foundation than the superior improvement of your minds; but even this by no means warrants self-conceit. Let me intreat you to avail yourselves of the respect with which your inferiors look up to you, only as an instrument to promote their instruction and their happiness, a duty which all men of superior rank, not excepting Monarchs themselves, owe to the communities to which they belong.—In a word, your complexion, your station, your leisure and the measure of your knowledge peculiarly fit you for promoting, both by precept and by example, the instruction of the field slaves in Christianity on which their future happiness and advancement in society will intirely depend.

' GOD, *who made the world, hath made of* ONE BLOOD *'* *all nations of men.'** Such is the doctrine of Christianity on the origin of mankind: and surely you cannot but revere a religion which teaches you that, in the eye of their Creator, the whole human race are on an equality. Yet your enemies, though some of them tell us they pay great regard to religion, have laboured, and vainly laboured, to prove that men of your complexion were created merely to administer to the avarice, the luxury, the pride and every vile passion of a race of men pretended to be naturally superior. Let this base and degrading insinuation urge you to press forward to that point of improvement which *men* only can reach, and at which monkeys and *orang outangs*† never will arrive. Nor need you despair of attaining to very high degrees of knowledge, virtue and religion. Those distinguished Africans Phillis Wheatley, Francis Williams, Ignatius Sancho, and your own JOSEPH RACHELL, would have looked down with just contempt on some late impotent

* Acts, ch. 17. ver. 26.
† The orang outang is a better kind of ape, such as some of you may have seen in Africa. *Some* travellers tell strange stories about this beast, and certain men, who will read any nonsensical book rather than their bibles, seriously believe those stories. In short it is part of their creed that this brute, which few if any of them ever *saw*, is almost as good and clever as most black men. When they catch one of this kind of Jockoo's, they mean to give it an University education—You laugh: but you must now prove your superiority to orang outang philosophers and ' shew yourselves men,' otherwise than by *merely laughing*.

and

and pitiful attempts to bereave Africans of their human nature as they have already been bereft of their liberty. I may venture to say, that no literary performance would be better received by the humane and liberal people of England, than a vindication of African capacity by the pen of an African.

But religion ought to be the grand object of men in your situation. To the christian religion, Europe, in general, and these happy kingdoms in particular, owe the superior advantages and privileges they enjoy. Christianity, whose very spirit and essence is peace and good will towards men, hath 'proclaimed liberty to the captives, and the opening of the prison-doors to them who were bound.'* To be christians is to be 'free indeed.' 'Ye shall know the truth,' said our SAVIOUR, 'and the TRUTH shall make you FREE.'† No man who knows the situation and circumstances of the West Indian slaves can hope for their becoming happy and free till they shall be taught and shall heartily embrace christianity. I know many of the white people, and in particular the clergy, would be happy to see you attend public worship more frequently than too many of you do. Should your numbers be inconvenient, which, were you all to go to church, might be the case, in Bridgetown especially, you may easily procure a large room or rooms for divine service. Some less wealthy descriptions of christians in Britain build places of worship, and maintain clergymen, by subscription. I see nothing to hinder you from doing the like; but, should you think of sending home young men, of your number, to be regularly educated for the church, in this country, it is to be feared that a mistaken generosity might induce you to allow them more money than is absolutely necessary for their support, and which, most probably, would effectually frustrate your end in sending them to England. In the mean time, the church ministers, I am sure, will not be backward in instructing you; and one of your most sensible and regular men might catechize your children, and even read prayers in the absence of a clergyman. Your first attempts of this kind may possibly be ridiculed; but, if you take no notice of

* Isaiah ch. 61. v. 1.   † St. John ch. 8. v. 32.

such

such indecent and profane behaviour, it will soon cease; especially as many of the white people will discountenance it. Be assured that no public reform was ever attempted, which was not, at first, more or less ridiculed and opposed.—Were the field-negroes to attend divine service (even though it were not particularly explained to them) a considerable change for the better would soon be wrought on them, by this means alone. Independent of other good effects, the decency they would be obliged to observe, would greatly conduce to form their manners. It cannot be doubted, that *if your Legislature, and the white people in general,* would, in good earnest promote, or even heartily favour the conversion of the field-negroes to christianity, they would soon see a change in their conduct which would more than compensate for their trouble. A general reform can be effected only by a *general plan* steadily pursued, and to the success of any such plan, your example will very much contribute.

Should any of the people called Quakers, from Philadelphia, visit you, as formerly, I need not tell you to be particularly respectful to them. By their disinterested conduct towards your countrymen, in Pennsylvania, they have given the world a proof of political wisdom and christian charity unequalled in the history of mankind. The enlightened and active zeal of their society, in promoting the cause of humanity, throughout these kingdoms, deserve your warmest acknowledgments.

Above all, *read your bibles,* with attention. There you will see the wonderful procedure of the Almighty, with his own chosen people; whom he appointed to serve the Egyptians for a long period. The same adorable Being who said 'I have seen—I have seen the affliction of my people which is in Egypt, and I have heard their groaning.'* He who 'doeth according to his will in the armies of Heaven and among the inhabitants of the earth,'† seeth the affliction, and heareth the groaning of

---

* Exod. ch. 3. v. 7, and Acts ch. 7. v. 34.

† Dan; ch. 4. v. 35.

your countrymen; and, doubtless will, in his own time and way, deliver them. The guilty nations of Europe ought to pray, that this deliverance may not be effected by his 'mighty hand' and his 'outstretched arm' but in the silent, unobserved course of his Providence!—What a great and exalted object is this! A whole nation led out of bondage, and reinstated in liberty by the Being who created them, and who 'made bare his holy arm,' for their redemption.—In your bibles, you will see that the Israelites, in Egypt, were, *like all other slaves*, an ignorant, stubborn race, and so very *stupid* that they ' hearkened not unto Moses, for anguish of spirit and ' for cruel bondage.'* Nay, like your countrymen, they were unable to make a right use of their freedom. They murmured and rebelled against their leaders; and, hence it was, that they wandered in the wilderness, till that whole generation of debased wretches had died. Of all that vast body of people who were led out of Egypt, only *two* entered, because they only were *fit* to enter, the promised land. Yet, in one respect, the conduct of the Israelites was highly worthy of your imitation: for, when Moses and Aaron had convinced them of the divine authority of their mission, the people did not express their joy, in a tumultuous manner; far less did they utter any unbecoming expressions against their oppressors; for ' *when they heard that the Lord had visited the children of* ' *Israel, and that he had looked upon their affliction, then* ' THEY BOWED THE HEAD AND WORSHIPPED.'† They afterwards received this express commandment, ' *Thou* ' *shalt not abhor an* EGYPTIAN, *because thou wast a stran-* ' *ger in his land.*'‡

You will not wonder at the earnestness of this address, when you consider, that, personally, I am much more interested in your conduct than any individual of you can be. In your cause, I have exposed myself to the fury, not of one tyrant, but of a legion of malicious, and powerful enemies, who, if they treat me in the unworthy manner in which they treated the respectable person who first dared to write in your behalf, will strive to effect my ruin. At my own hazard, I must repeat it, I have

* Exod. ch. 6, v. 9. † Exod. ch. 4, v. 31. ‡ Deut. ch. 23, v. 7.

assured

assured the public that, the field-slaves, in Barbadoes, (*at least*) by the comparatively mild treatment they are known to receive, are very sufficiently prepared for that improvement of their condition which will result from the abolition of the slave-trade. If you have in your nature a spark of generosity, or *feeling for the poor field-negroes*, you will strenuously endeavour by precept and example, to render them as worthy of some little advancement from their present disgraceful and debased condition, as many of you are of the superior happiness you enjoy. But if, you give a loose to that licentiousness which renders the want of police so apparent in your towns, and which, while it disgraces the conduct of too many of the domestic slaves, does honour to the good nature and lenity of many of the whites, I shall be under the disagreeable necessity of retracting the good opinion of the majority of the negroes in Barbadoes which I have hitherto entertained, and which I have published, with a view to promote their improvement and their happiness.

APPENDIX.

Containing Accounts of Negroes remarkable for their Virtues and Abilities.

'Feb. 23. 1788.'
'Extracted from the *private Journal** of ―――,'
See Introduction.

'JOSEPH RACHELL.'

'WHEN I resided in Barbadoes in the year 1769, I
' was very much struck with the accounts given
' me by my father and other inhabitants of the island
' concerning one Joseph Rachell, a negro. This J. R.
' was a free negro. I know not by what means he ob-
' tained his freedom. He was, however, a capital mer-
' chant, and kept what is called a dry-good-shop. He
' was, by all accounts, an ingenious, industrious, and up-
' right tradesman. Whenever the young tradesmen were
' at a loss how to proceed in any matter of commerce,
' they generally consulted J. R. and whenever any doubt
' arose about the value of the cargo of goods J. R.
' was often the man by whose opinion the price was
' fixed. Whenever the captains of vessels arrived with
' a cargo J. R. was one of the first persons waited upon,
' and one of the first to whom the cargo was offered.
' I have not heard that he traded much to England.
' His connexions seem to have been chiefly confined to
' the Leeward Islands, Demarara, Essequebo, &c. &c.
' He had some *white persons under him*,† such as his

---

* A private journal, to use the writer's own words, ' never was and
' never can be intended for the public eye;' and, 'it is hoped ' all proper
' allowances will be made on that account.'

† See Page 73.

book-

'book-keeper, his apprentices, &c. &c. and these always
'spoke of him in a very respectful manner,* and parti-
'cularly revered him for his humanity and tenderness.
'He was extremely kind in lending out money to poor,
'industrious men, in order to enable them to begin their
'trade, or to retrieve them from difficulties which their
'trade would unavoidably bring upon them. But there
'was one peculiar trait in his character. It is well
'known in our island that a planter or merchant is
'often obliged by some cogent or sudden distress to sell
'his property instantly for whatever he can procure, be
'it ever so small.† Now, such was the benevolence of
'this excellent negro, that he would go to the vendue,
'bid gravely for the property, give a fair market price
'for it, and tender it to the owner again, upon the
'very same terms, at which he himself bought it; and,
'if the price of the estate exceeded the value of the debt,
'J. R. always took care to pay off the debt himself be-
'fore the tender was made, and thus the planter might
're-enter upon his property, free from all incumbrances,
'excepting those owing to J. R. himself. By these hu-
'mane and judicious means, he has extricated many
'families from ruin.—J. R. was also very charitable.
'He kept a gang of fishing negroes, and, when his boats
'returned home, he set apart every day, a quantity of
'fish, for the use of the prisoners in the town gaol. *He
'visited the gaol regularly, enquired into the circumstances
'of the prisoners, and gave them relief, in proportion to their
'distresses and good behaviour.*‡ Nay, he used to give
'them good moral advice, and, for aught I know, reli-
'gious advice. His example stirred up a noble spirit
'of generosity in Bridge-town, insomuch that it was the
'custom, for some years before his death, for the better
'sort of people to send weekly, either money or pro-
'visions to the gaol.‖ He supported two or three old

* I have heard poor white persons talk of J. R. to this effect, 'Mr.
'Rachell was a blessed man, for no poor thing ever went away hungry
'from his house; and some, who had seen better days, were shewn
'into a back room, and had victuals set before them.' W. D.

† See p. 39. Thus it happens that 'a negro' to use a Barbadian
phrase 'is taken up and sold like a *bitt chicken*' (a sixpenny chicken.) W.D.

‡ This will point the readers reflections to the illustrious HOWARD.
W. D.

‖ It is still customary, in Bridgetown, to send the cold meat left at
'great entertainments to the prisoners in gaol. W. D.

'indigent

' indigent whites, and left them something at his death.
' It was remarkable too that he was extremely kind to
' his negroes. I have heard my father lament much
' that J. R's. generosity was much imposed upon, both
' by whites and blacks. He frequented St. Michael's
' church on the Sundays, and I have heard our worthy
' minister say, That he believed him to be a very at-
' tentive and devout hearer.——He died about 30 years
' ago' (i. e. about 1758) 'possessed of a good deal of pro-
' perty, and lies buried in the centre of the old church-
' yard in Bridgetown. His funeral was attended by
' thousands of whites (some of them very respectable
' people) and by a prodigious concourse of blacks, and I
' believe that his loss was very sensibly felt for many
' years. There is a tomb-stone over his grave, but no
' inscription or memorial.*

'J O H N.'

' My father, in the year 1760, had a very valuable
' negro called "John." He was master of one of our
' fishing-boats, and had five or six negroes under him.
' He understood his business thoroughly. He knew the
' art of catching the fish and selling them to advantage.
' The people in the market had a very high opinion of
' his honesty and his skill, and he bore the character of
' being a very fair dealer. My father placed unlimited
' confidence in him. He believed that J. always brought
' home every individual fish which had been caught, and
' every pistareen for which those fish had been sold. My
' father had so high an opinion of his accuracy, that J. never
' made up his accounts till Saturday night, and J. used
' very often on Saturday night to bring home 7 or 8
' moidores, being the joint produce of his own labour

* The tomb which was shewn to me, as that of J. R. is a handsome one of bluish marble. He left a widow, who, I think, is called *Betty Rachell*, of whom I heard nothing remarkable.——The above account of J. R. agrees very well with that given by Mr. Ramsay at p. 254. of his essay. To authorities so respectable I can add nothing but that, in Barbadoes, I have repeatedly heard similar accounts of that excellent negro. His innocent stratagem, in particular, to get rid of the tasting visits of a ——— avaricious colonel (whom I could name) I have more than once ——— related, with much glee. W. D.

' and

' and of the labour of the five or six negroes under him,
' in the course of the week. When my father came to
' England, in the year 1761, J. was extremely useful to
' my mother in managing all my father's affairs; and,
' so far was he from taking advantage of my father's ab-
' sence, that my mother found in him even more fidelity
' and industry than ever. My mother was extremely ill
' for a considerable part of my father's absence, and J.
' had the government of house, negroes, &c. and my mo-
' ther thought herself very much obliged to him for his
' great care and attention.

' J. was a *tolerable scholar*. He could read very well,
' and, at his leisure hours, used to be very *fond of reading
' the Bible*. He read also other books; but what they
' were I do not know. He was a constant attendant at
' church on Sundays. I myself have frequently read the
' Bible to him, and he took a deal of pains in teaching
' me how to read it. He gave me in my infancy a great
' deal of good advice, and particularly just before I was
' coming to England for education, in the year 1761.
' I have sat with him for whole hours by the sea-side,
' while he was mending his nets, and used to ask him
' many questions about England, about learning, &c.
' &c. He gave me a pretty good notion of the customs
' and manners of England, and of the things which
' would be taught me at school, and used to exhort
' me very much to be *submissive to my masters and supe-
' riors*. I feel to this day some impression of the excellent
' advice which has been given me by J. and I have a
' very great respect for his memory. I believe he had a
' very great affection and esteem for me.'

' He died of a consumption, in the year 1765. My
' mother has often told me, that, during his illness, mul-
' titudes of whites and blacks used to come frequently to
' our house and enquire anxiously after him. Some of
' the whites were people of rank and character. About
' two month's before J's death, my father was offered
' a thousand pounds (cur.) for him, but refused it, not
' only from policy; but, I believe, from gratitude and
' respect also. It is supposed that he caught his death by
' staying out whole nights at sea, in his fishing-boats.

ACCOUNTS of a *Negro Practitioner of Physic,** and a *self-taught Negro Calculator,* by BENJAMIN RUSH, M. D. Prof. of Chem. in the Univ. of Pennsylvania, Mem. of the American Phil. Soc.—of the Med. Soc. of London—of the Liter. and Phil. Soc. of Manchester—Hon. Mem. of the Roy. Med. Soc. of Edinburgh, &c. &c.

DOCTOR JAMES DERHAM.

' There is now in this city a black man, of the name
' of JAMES DERHAM, a practitioner of physic belonging
' to the Spanish settlement of N. Orleans, on the Missi-
' sippi. This man was born in a family in this city, in
' which he was taught to read and write, and instructed
' in the principles of christianity. When a boy, he was
' transferred by his master to the late Doctor John Kears-
' ley, jun. of this city, who employed him occasionally
' to compound medicines, and to perform some of the
' more humble acts of attention to his patients.

' Upon the death of Doctor Kearsley, he became (af-
' ter passing through several hands) the property of Doc-
' tor George West, surgeon to the sixteenth British re-
' giment, under whom, during the late war in America,
' he performed many of the menial duties of our profes-
' sion. At the close of the war, he was sold by Doctor
' West to Doctor Robert Dove of N. Orleans, who
' employed him as an assistant, in his business, in which
' capacity, he gained so much of his confidence and friend-
' ship, that he consented to liberate him, after two or
' three years, upon easy terms. From DOCTOR DER-
' HAM'S numerous opportunities of improving in medi-
' cine, he became so well acquainted with the healing
' art, as to commence practitioner at N. Orleans, under
' the patronage of his late master. He is now about 26
' years of age, has a wife, but no children, and does bu-
' siness to the amount of three thousand dollars a year.

' I have conversed with him, upon most of the acute
' and epidemic diseases of the country where he lives, and

* See p. 76.

' was

' was pleased to find him perfectly acquainted with the
' modern simple mode of practice in those diseases. I
' expected to have suggested some new medicines to him;
' but he suggested many more to me. He is very modest
' and engaging in his manners. He speaks French flu-
' ently, and has some knowledge of the Spanish language.
' By some accident, although born in a religious family,
' belonging to the church of England, he was not bap-
' tized in his infancy, in consequence of which, he ap-
' plied, a few days ago, to Bishop White, to be received
' by that ordinance, into the episcopal church. The
' Bishop found him qualified, both by knowledge and
' moral conduct, to be admitted to baptism, and, this
' day, performed the ceremony, in one of the churches
' in this city.

' Philadelphia, Nov.   BENJA. RUSH.
' 14. 1788.'

THOMAS FULLER.

' There is now living, about four miles from Alexan-
' dria, in the state of Virginia, a negro slave seventy
' years of age, of the name of THOMAS FULLER, the
' property of Mrs. Elizabeth Cox. This man possesses
' a talent for arithmetical calculations, the history of
' which, I conceive, merits a place in the records of the
' human mind. He is a native of Africa, and can nei-
' ther read or write. Two gentlemen, natives of Penn-
' sylvania, viz. William Hartshorn and Samuel Coates,
' men of probity and respectable characters, having heard,
' in travelling through the neighbourhood, in which this
' slave lived, of his extraordinary powers in arithmetic,
' sent for him, and had their curiosity sufficiently grati-
' fied, by the answers which he gave to the following
' questions:

' First, upon being asked how many seconds there are
' in a year and a half? he answered, in about two mi-
' nutes, 47,304,000.—Secondly, being asked how many
' seconds a man had lived who is seventy years, seventeen
' days and twelve hours old? he answered, in a minute
' and

' and a half, 2,210,500,800. One of the gentlemen
' who employed himself, with his pen, in making these
' calculations told him, That the sum was not so great
' as he had said, upon which the old man haftily replied,
' " 'Top Maſſa, you forget de leap year." On adding
' the ſeconds of the leap-years to the others, the amount
' of the whole, in both their ſums, agreed exactly.———
' Third. The following queſtion was then propoſed to
' him. Suppoſe a farmer has ſix ſows, and each ſow has
' ſix female pigs, the firſt year, and they all increaſe in the
' ſame proportion to the end of eight years, how many ſows
' will the farmer then have, if he loſes none? In ten mi-
' nutes, he anſwered 34,588,806. The difference of
' time between his anſwering this and the two former
' queſtions was occaſioned by a trifling miſtake he made
' from a miſapprehenſion of the queſtion.

' In the preſence of Thomas Wiſtar and Wm. B.
' Morris, two reſpectable citizens of Philadelphia, he gave
' the amount of nine figures multiplied by nine. He
' informed the firſt mentioned gentleman that he began
' his application to figures by counting ten, and that,
' when he was able to count a hundred (to uſe his own
' words) he thought himſelf a very clever fellow. His
' firſt attempt, after this, was to count the number of
' hairs in a cow's tail, which he found to be 2872. He
' next amuſed himſelf by counting grain by grain, a bu-
' ſhel of wheat, and a buſhel of flax-ſeed. From this
' he was led to calculate, with the moſt perfect accuracy,
' how many ſhingles a houſe, of certain dimenſions,
' would require to cover it; and how many poſts and
' rails were neceſſary to incloſe, and how many grains of
' corn were neceſſary to ſow, a certain quantity of ground.
' From this application of his talents, his miſtreſs often
' derived conſiderable benefit.

' At the time he gave this account of himſelf, he ſaid,
' his memory began to fail him. He was *grey-headed*,
' and exhibited ſeveral other marks of the weakneſs of
' old age. He had worked hard, upon a farm, during
' the whole of his life, but had never been intemperate
' in the uſe of ſpirituous liquors. He ſpoke with great
' reſpect of his miſtreſs, and mentioned, in a particular
' manner,

'manner, his obligations to her for refusing to sell him, which she had been tempted to, by offers of large sums of money from several curious persons.

'One of the gentlemen, Mr. Coates, having remarked in his presence, That it was a pity he had not an education, equal to his genius, he said "No Massa, it is best I got no learning, for many learned men be great fools.*

'I do hereby certify that the above account of Thomas Fuller is truly stated, as the facts were communicated to me.

'Philadelphia,   BENJA. RUSH.'
'Nov. 14. 1788.'

* The reader may compare the above account with that given of the famous self-taught calculator JEDIDIAH BUXTON, p. 251, of the Gent. Magazine for 1754. At p. 423, of the same very useful collection, is a Memoir of M. Swedenborg, concerning the mathematical talents of CHARLES XII. of Sweden, who frequently solved most difficult numerical problems, barely by thought and memory, in which operations others are obliged to take great pains and tedious labour.—He frequently used it as an adage, that "*He who is ignorant of numbers is* "*scarce half a man.*"' What would His Majesty have said of Thomas Fuller?——I have not room to add, as I intended, extracts from the poems of PHILLIS WHEATLEY, which are so many proofs of African capacity. They were printed in 1773, with an attestation that they were written by her, signed by His Exc. T. HUTCHINSON, Gov. and The Hon. A. OLIVER, Lieut. Gov. of N. England with nine other Gentlemen, and seven Clergymen. To these I might add a certain respectable gentleman in London, who tells me that he was acquainted with our poetess, while in England, that he corresponded with her after her return to Boston (where she was married to a Mr. Peters, a person of her own colour, who kept a shop) that she was uncommonly ingenious, and that she certainly wrote the poems ascribed to her.—In an epistle To W. EARL OF DARTMOUTH, &c. &c. she gives this account of herself:

'Should you MY LORD, while you peruse my song,
'Wonder from whence my love of FREEDOM sprung,
'Whence flow these *wishes for the common good*
'By *feeling hearts alone well understood*.
'I, young in life, by seeming cruel fate,
'Was snatch'd from AFRIC's fancy'd happy seat;
'*What pangs excruciating must molest,*
'*What sorrows labour in my parent's breast?*
'Steel'd was that soul and by no mis'ry mov'd
'*That from a father seiz'd his babe belov'd;*
'*Such—such my case;* and can I then but pray
'Others may never feel tyrannic sway?
&c. &c.

INDEX.

INDEX.

ADDRESS to the whites 167—to the the free negroes 172.
African negroes, simple and innocent 56 — their patriotism 75.
Agriculture, as practised in Barbadoes, 22 et seq.
Allowance of food, in Barbadoes, 13—in Jamaica 116.
Americans, their rapid increase 157. *N.*
Arguments, ridiculous ones, 80 et seq.
Attachment to the soil would be favourable to slaves 154.

Barbadoes, humanity of the inhabitants 18, 107, 113, 124, 132—their loyalty, INTROD.—Magistrates 17—Clergy 58—Militia 97—Cages and dungeons 137—Dispensary 138—General Assembly 139.
Britons, compared to W. Indian *slaves* 50, 121.
Burning alive 20, 131.

Cattle in Barbadoes 10—in Jamaica 120 and 158, *N.*
Charaibs (black) their increase 157 *N.*
Children (negro) their treatment 12.
Christianity, good effect of, 97. *N.*
Complexion not connected with mind 61—gradations of, 63—changes in, 65.
Coroner's inquests on negroes 127.
Cowskin described 14.
Crop, its effects 7—duration of, 118, *N.*
Cruelties 29 et seq.—' *extreme cruelties and inhumanity*' 129.

Decrease (causes of) of whites 40, *N.*—of negroes 153.
Domestic slaves, their treatment 6, 14, 52.
Drivers of negroes 42, 132.

INDEX.

ENGLISHMEN, their abhorrence of slavery 117, *N*.
Evidence of negroes not valid against whites 37, 142, 146.

Freedom should be gradually conferred, 90.

Gangs of slaves 12.
Gibbeting alive 19, 131.
Grounds, negroe, 119.

Hair, human and bestial, 71.
Hay, made in Jamaica, 9, *N*.
Hebrew nation, an instance of their charity 138—their bondage in Egypt comparatively easy, 139—their *increase* under it 158, *N*.
Human nature, mark of, 68.

Interest, a sense of, protects not slaves, 37, 55, 113.
Insurrection unreasonably dreaded 93—causes of, 130.

Jamaica, workhouses 137—General Assembly 141, 142. and INTROD. vii.—Marons 157. *N*.
Jumper, his office 16.

Ladies, British, 18—of Barbadoes 18, 38, 107.
Laws (the colonial) harsh 77.
—— of Barbadoes, 4, 16, 19, 37, 38, 56, 144.
—— of Jamaica 114, 129, 132, 133, 140, 143.
Lock'd jaw 155.

Managers 39, 43, 125.
Men with tails 67.
Militia of Barbadoes 97.
Multiplication of men, &c. 157.
Mutilation of slaves 136.

Negroes, their capacity and equality to the whites vindicated 59 et seq.—their music and dancing 77, 93.
—— (free) sober and industrious 92.
—— of extraordinary virtue and talents 180.
—— (new) their treatment, INTROD.

Orang outang, the opinion of *Linnæus* concerning it 69,

Plantation-bell 8.

Plough, 'answers extremely well' in Jamaica 27, 115. *N.*
Ploughman, letter of an English one, 115.
Population, great in the West Indies, 40, 88.
Power, absolute, generally abused 55.
Principles, general ones, 43.
Provisions, ground, 13, 124. *might* abound in Jamaica 158.—*N.* putrid and rotten 114.
Punishments ordinary 15, 115.—capital 18, 131.

Quakers, their humanity and disinterestedness 100, 177.

Religion 58, 176.
Robbery committed on the slaves 41.
Runaways, their treatment, 16, 122.

SCOTLAND, resolution of the church of, 101.
Scramble, descriptions of, 111.
Seamen, sick, left on shore by Guinea captains 86.
Servants, white, 42, 117—Bond 43, 44.
Slaves, their treatment, 6 et seq. 103, 110, 115—Worn out and diseased, 34, 126, 140, 152—majority of them creoles, 88, 159. *N*—increase of, 89—intrusted with arms, 94—their loyalty, ib.——" overworked and " under-fed" 104—" *branded,*" 122—frequently" " *killed,* 129—causes assigned for their decrease examined 153—aged 156—their unparalleled decrease, 159—not protected 37, 147, 153, &c.
Sunday, how spent by the slaves, 11, 116.

Tortures 19, 32, 131.

West Indians not more cruel than Europeans 54.
Whites, sketch of their character 38 et seq.—work in the fields 41—their prejudices 57—not superior to negroes 61—their loyalty 95, and INTROD.
Women pregnant, their treatment 12.
———— indecently exposed and whipt 18.

Yaws 153 and 154, *N.*

ERRATA.

Page 3. line 39, *from the top*, for *or* read *nor*.
—— 4. —— 19. note, for *ch* read *cl*.
—— 9. —— 24. dele *for that use*.
—— 33. —— 11. after the word "explained" *insert* by a jumper who either had put it, or had seen it put, in practice.
—— 39. —— 25. for arguments powerful *read* powerful arguments.
—— 64. note, for *irradiation* read *irradiations*.
—— 81. —— 22. read "the harmless doctrine that the Africans are true and *bona fide* men."
—— 88. —— 9. for affects *read* effects.
—— 99. note, l. 5. for *pitie* read *pitié*.
—— 121. line 16. for says *read* say.
—— 128. —— 2. for " many *read* some."

There are also some errors in the spelling and pointing, which the Reader is requested to correct.

www.ingramcontent.com/pod-product-compliance
Lightning Source LLC
Chambersburg PA
CBHW020920230426
43666CB00008B/1510